Contested Territory

STUDIES OF COMMUNISM IN TRANSITION

General Editor: Ronald J. Hill
*Professor of Comparative Government
and Fellow of Trinity College,
Dublin, Ireland*

Studies of Communism in Transition is an important series which applies academic analysis and clarity of thought to the recent traumatic events in Eastern and Central Europe. As many of the preconceptions of the past half century are cast aside, newly independent and autonomous sovereign states are being forced to address long-term, organic problems which had been suppressed by, or appeased within, the Communist system of rule.

The series is edited under the sponsorship of Lorton House, an independent charitable association which exists to promote the academic study of communism and related concepts.

Contested Territory

Border Disputes at the Edge of the
Former Soviet Empire

Edited by

Tuomas Forsberg
The Finnish Institute for International Affairs,
Helsinki

STUDIES OF COMMUNISM IN TRANSITION

Edward Elgar

© Tuomas Forsberg 1995

Published by
Edward Elgar Publishing Limited
Gower House
Croft Road
Aldershot
Hants GU11 3HR
England

Edward Elgar Publishing Company
Old Post Road
Brookfield
Vermont 05036
USA

British Library Cataloguing in Publication Data

Contested Territory: Border Disputes at the Edge of the
Former Soviet Empire.- (Studies of Communism in Transition)
  I. Forsberg, Tuomas II. Series
  327.47

Library of Congress Cataloguing in Publication Data

Contested territory : border disputes at the edge of the former
  Soviet empire / edited by Tuomas Forsberg.
      p.   cm. — (Studies of communism in transition)
    Includes index.
    1. Former Soviet republics—Boundaries. 2. Former Soviet
  republics—Foreign relations. I. Forsberg, Tuomas, 1967-
  II. Series.
  DK293.C66   1995
  911'.47—dc20
                                         94-45908
                                            CIP

ISBN 1 85278 949 2

Printed and bound in Great Britain by
Ipswich Book Co. Ltd., Ipswich, Suffolk

Contents

Foreword

The idea to study historical border disputes around the borders of the former Soviet Empire sprang from the unanticipated geographical tumults after the end of the Cold War. The changes in Moscow and the collapse of the Soviet Union coincided with the public debate in Finland on the status of the territories that Finland lost to the Soviet Union as a result of World War II. In particular, the issue of Karelia became salient.

The official policy of the Finnish Government is that it has no territorial demands. As long as Moscow is not willing to discuss the borders, Finland will not raise the matter. However, Karelia is an issue in Finland. Despite the official policy, every fourth Finn would like the government to initiate negotiations with Russia for the return of Karelia.

The debate in Finland has concentrated mainly on the former Finnish territories, but there are seven other countries whose territories were annexed by the Soviet Union. Therefore, the Finnish Institute of International Affairs decided to launch an international research project to compare these eight cases. The purpose is both to produce information about these cases and to improve our knowledge of the border issue in general. I hope that this book performs the tasks.

Eleven experts from nine countries took part in the project. The role of Tuomas Forsberg, a visiting research fellow at the Finnish Institute of International Affairs, was crucial to the success of the project. Besides contributing to the book, he has been responsible for managing the research team and getting the book published. I want to thank all the experts who took part in the project. In particular, I thank the Sasakawa Peace Foundation, which financed the international part of the project. Finally, I thank Edward Elgar who kindly published this book.

Helsinki
Tapani Vaahtoranta
Director

Preface

The dissolution of the Soviet Union at the end of 1991 was a huge metamorphosis in terms of political geography. As a consequence, the landmass of the Eurasian superpower has shrunk to a size comparable to 17th century Russia and a state that had been expanding almost continuously in the modern era had to face unexpected territorial challenges, similar to those after the October Revolution. Although the process of territorial withdrawal was mainly determined by separatist forces from inside, the collapse of the Soviet Union, both in terms of perceived power and in terms of communist ideology, also awoke territorial claims from outside: in the first place it raised the question of the legitimacy of the Soviet annexations in World War II. These issues had not been on the agenda during the Cold War.

The sudden emergence of these territorial questions in the media and public debates at least, if not always at the level of interstate relations, led to the examination of when historical border changes become disputed. Given both the small amount of existing research on territorial disputes, and the current challenges set by territorial problems not only in the former Soviet Union but also in the former Yugoslavia and in Eastern Europe in general, it seemed to be a momentous task to shed more light on the issue of historical border disputes. The comparative perspective was needed because in most cases the discussion over boundaries had been predominantly national and lacked an international context. Right from the start the comparison revealed that there were substantial differences in the attitudes of the pre-war possessors to their territories that were annexed by the Soviet Union in World War II. Moreover, there was a considerable lack of knowledge of the history and current situation of the annexed territories. The question as to how the background of having been a part of some other country before World War II affects the territories today seemed to have many answers, since the territorial identities of these once annexed areas appeared to be developing at different speeds and with several orientations.

The former Japanese Kurile Islands (the Northern Territories), former Finnish Karelia and the former German Kaliningrad (Königsberg) regions are typical cases of such historical border questions in post-Soviet Russia. Along with these three, five other areas were included in the study to cover roughly similar border questions that have their origin in World War II. Two of these areas were incorporated into the Russian Federation from the Baltic states: Pechory (Petseri) and Ivangorod (Jaanilinn) from Estonia and Pytalovo (Abrene) from Latvia. Furthermore, three areas that were annexed by the Soviet Union in World War II but did not remain part of Russia after the dissolution of the Soviet Union were included. Inter-war Eastern Poland now belongs to Lithuania, Belarus and the Ukraine, Transcarpathia (Carpatho-Ukraine), which before World War II was at first part of Czechoslovakia and then, from 1939, part of Hungary, is now part of the Ukraine, and areas annexed from Romania are now either independent (Moldova) or belong to the Ukraine.

The study is based on theoretical articles and expert analyses of the chosen cases. One researcher from each of the former possessor states was asked to report on their respective areas (on Transcarpathia this has been done by a Hungarian). Moreover, articles dealing with the nature of territorial disputes, Russian policies of territorial expansionism and contraction, regional identity formation in border areas as well as an article on the historic territorial questions, written from the Russian point of view, were included. Most of the articles were presented at a seminar held in Kerimäki in Finland on 13–15 August 1993, and they have been influenced by the discussion at the seminar and by a further exchange of letters. In a way, the project as a whole and the seminar in particular was an extraordinary attempt to discuss politically sensitive issues by diverse scholars with a common scientific goal.

The composition and the national backgrounds of contributors to this project may naturally raise the question of the objectivity of the analyses. Because it is a relevant and legitimate question, it should be answered. First, even if the postmodernist view that any interpretation is similarly 'true' were not subscribed to, the need to understand the subjective lenses through which people view the disputed territories should be emphasized. It can be argued that a resolution of territorial disputes is not possible by purely objectivist analysis. Yet, the articles are not supposed to be political pamphlets but scientific essays. Even if scientific treatises are never fully neutral, the contributors were asked to pay attention to scientific standards, and each of the articles can be judged by them. None of the articles represents the final 'truth', but the least they can do is to bring these neglected themes into a forum of scientific discussion. My personal conviction is that especially in scientific forums we ultimately need more discussion, even on sensitive historical matters, which aims at intersubjective understanding of the issues rather than ban the whole disputed history and its contemporary traces.

Finally, I would like to stress that all the articles represent the views of the individual contributors, not those of their institutes or nation-states. As a whole, this book tries to be empirically oriented and to avoid the normative dimension about who rightfully owns these, possibly disputed, territories. By the same token, the selection of cases reflects more theoretical than political purposes as it tries to focus on history instead of ethnicism in the discussion of territorial disputes. In any case, history might offer fallible arguments for determining today's policies. Because all the cases have their pre-histories, the territorial questions are not mere products of the events of World War II. Furthermore, it should be clear that historic ownership does not by itself imply a moral right for territorial changes now.

Many people have contributed to the successful fulfilment of this project. I would like to express thanks to all of them, personally as well as on behalf of the Finnish Institute of International Affairs. I am grateful to those people who have read parts of the text and helped with their valuable insights. Special acknowledgements are directed to Godfrey Weldhen, who reviewed the linguistic correctness of the text, to Pirkko Numminen, who drew the maps for the volume, and to Krista Berglund and Jaana Keho-Kosonen, who worked as editorial assistants and compiled the typescript.

Helsinki
Tuomas Forsberg

List of Contributors

Pavel K. Baev, Head of Section for Military–Political Studies, Institute of Europe, Russian Academy of Sciences, Moscow, Russia (1993–94 on sabbatical leave); Researcher, International Peace Research Institute, Oslo, Norway.

Ioan Chiper, Chief of Department at the Institute of History 'Nikolae Iorga', Bucharest, Romania; Associated Professor at the University of Bucharest, Romania.

Bonifacijs Dauksts, Centre of Baltic–Nordic History and Political Studies, Riga, Latvia.

Tuomas Forsberg, Visiting Researcher, Finnish Institute of International Affairs, Helsinki, Finland; Research Associate, Academy of Finland, Helsinki, Finland.

Jyrki Iivonen, Senior Research Fellow, Finnish Institute of International Affairs, Helsinki, Finland; from September 1994 Special Adviser, Ministry of Defence, Helsinki, Finland.

Toshiyasu Ishiwatari, Professor, Nihon University, Mishima-Shi, Japan.

Indrek Jääts, University of Tartu, Estonia.

Istvan Madi, Senior Research Fellow, Institute for World Economics of the Hungarian Academy of Sciences, Budapest, Hungary.

Wojciech Materski, Institute of Political Studies, Polish Academy of Sciences, Warsaw, Poland.

Anssi Paasi, Professor, University of Oulu, Finland.

Arturs Puga, University of Latvia, Riga, Latvia.

Peter Wörster, Herder Institute, Marburg, Germany.

PART I

Introduction

1. The Collapse of the Soviet Union and Historical Border Questions

Tuomas Forsberg

1. BORDER QUESTIONS AND SOVIET STUDIES

Since the failed *coup d'état* of Moscow in August 1991, the changes in the political landscape of the former Soviet Union have been radical and manifold. The breakup of the Soviet Union has produced several new states to displace the old state structure, the fading of communist ideology has resulted in a very diffuse ideological mobilization, and the collapse of the Soviet hegemony has generated growing controversies between the new political entities.[1] These developments signify that issues and questions on the agenda of what used to be Soviet studies have not only changed but also multiplied.

It is now often acknowledged that the future course of events in Russia is anything but predictable.[2] The emergence of new potential issues of conflict and the high instability in the area of the former Soviet Union contains both many dangers and opportunities for the peoples living there, for her neighbours as well as for other states and peoples of the international community. Given the speed and the breadth of the changes, the need to know about such topics has grown enormously. In comparison to the earlier period one thing, however, facilitates the task of research. It is now easier to get and collect information which is nevertheless often dispersed and distorted. At the same time the gap between Sovietological and other disciplinary studies, in particular those of political science, seems to be narrowing. Although the former Soviet Union can still be regarded as an area of *sui generis*, the application of theories and concepts from other disciplines can certainly bring new insights to both sides.[3]

Border questions are widely regarded as lying at the core of the political challenges that have emerged in the former Soviet Union.[4] In fact, because of the nature of empire building, the fall of empires anywhere is likely to be fraught with territorial and related conflicts. In this sense, the Soviet case is no exception. The breakup of the Soviet state as such created new interstate borders that lack legitimacy in comparison to areas where stable borders have existed for several generations. Furthermore, many of the outer borders of the Soviet Union were achieved by force and without the consent of the neighbour states. Finally, the doctrines of the nationalist and other separatist movements that have comprised the old communist ideology put considerable emphasis on territorial questions. It is no wonder if these facts are regarded as troublesome since, in general, it is exactly territorial disputes that are often assumed to be the most dangerous kind of political dispute – they are both difficult to settle and may easily lead to violent clashes.

This book aims at enhancing our knowledge of three overlapping themes related to borders that are, as the result of the collapse of the Soviet Union, both absorbing and not yet sufficiently studied.[5] First, this study addresses the question of the Soviet and Russian policies towards the borders and border areas in general and towards historical border disputes in particular. Second, this study discusses the changing status and identity of possible contested borderland territories of the former Soviet Union. Third, the focus is laid on border disputes, or the consequences of historic changes of borders, in relations between the former Soviet Union and her neighbouring states. Concretely, eight cases of territories around the borders of the former Soviet Empire, from Moldova in the south, to Karelia in the north and the Kurile Islands in the east, that were annexed by the Soviet Union as a result of World War II, will be examined. Finally, these eight cases will be compared with regard to the aforementioned research themes.

2. SOVIET/RUSSIAN POLICY TOWARDS BORDERS

The first research theme deals with the attitudes and policies of the Soviet Union/Russia towards her borderlands, including ideas and measures that concern both the location and functions of borders. These attitudes and policies can best be understood in the context of a Russian and Soviet imperialist tradition, since Russian conceptions of borders and territory are strongly rooted in the past.[6] This tradition bears a tendency to view borders as sacrosanct but at the same time as something expandable. Stalin's policy towards borders has often been seen as a part of this tradition but also the current attitudes have much to do with the historical, in a way deep-cultural, conceptions of territory and borders, which are still alive in Russia.

Territorial expansion and the administration of borderlands has often been carried out by brutal and forceful methods and this was also the case in the Soviet Union. Even if the territorial expansion of the Soviet Union in World War II is generally known, the varieties of the processes of the annexation and incorporation of border areas and legitimation of the territorial changes are less well known or they are regarded as being very similar. In reality, these processes have had manifold aspects and there is a need to highlight the reasons as well as methods and consequences of the annexation in a more systematic manner. For example, it is frequently studied how Stalin wanted to build a security zone around the Soviet Union in World War II, and how he tried to promote the 'victory of socialism' by territorial expansion, but it is seldom asked why he wanted to incorporate certain territories directly into the Soviet Union or into the Russian Federative Republic. What were his motives, how did the motives differ? What principles did he rely on in the drawing of borders? Separate historical studies on the Soviet annexation policy exist, but the comparative approach has not been commonly used.[7] Although this study does not draw on any new archive sources, the comparison points out that the reasons for the Soviet annexations are too often seen narrowly as strategic needs or only as attempts to expand the influence of communist ideology.

The examination of the history of annexed border territories may lead to questions that deal with the modes of annexation, incorporation and legitimation of territorial changes more generally. Theoretically informed research on such techniques has been rare, perhaps partly because interest in such knowledge might be regarded as of doubtful value.[8] Despite the growing tendency of seeing territorial enlargement as useless, the theme does not seem to have become obsolete since it is pivotal for the political leaders, for example in the former Yugoslavia.[9] It is, however, certainly difficult to transfer the 'lessons' that can be drawn from the Soviet policies on the annexed territories to any of the present contexts in a meaningful way. Anyway, retrospectively it seems to be the case that despite his ethnic, political and historical manipulation, Stalin succeeded only partially in making his territorial annexations indisputable.

The study will also discuss how the changes in the era of *perestroika* and thereafter have affected Russian policies towards its borders and potentially contested borderlands. After the collapse of the Soviet Union, the discussion of borders is closely related to ideas of Russian identity not only because geopolitical space constitutes national identity but also because historical border questions inevitably deal with the relationship with the past.[10] So far President Yeltsin and many other leading politicians in Russia have relied on the principle of 'inviolability of borders',[11] but recently, the nationalist and expansionist conceptions of Russian state territory, which have been put forward especially by Vladimir Zhirinovsky, but not only by him, have been gaining political ground.[12] Both of these approaches omit the challenges put by the historical border questions that stem from the Stalinist era. The former would like to abolish the Soviet past as whole, while the latter would like to preserve the glorious past of Soviet history.[13] The adoption of the latter stand is, however, often based on a qualified reading of the past.[14] Indeed, many of the present attitudes towards borders in Russia reflect the uneasy historical consciousness burdened by the imperial past and coloured by nationalist and socialist writing and teaching of history. The attitudes and adopted policies towards the territorial issues that stem from the Soviet expansion in World War II indicate Russia's difficulties in coming to terms with her Soviet legacy. Although orthodox Soviet interpretations of history have been abandoned, and the need to tell the 'truth' to the people is recognized, and although the wrongdoings of the Soviet state, and Stalin especially, are condemned in current Russian foreign policy, only a few people are ready to accommodate to the past borders, if it means territorial cession.

Yet, the attitudes towards potentially contested border areas depend largely on the conceptions of the outside world in general. In stereotypical terms, Westernizers are more eager to develop transboundary cooperation, while conservatives want to preserve the border as a shield.[15] Also this study points out how Russian politics oscillates between poles of openness and closedness, economy and strategy, cooperation and confrontation in her attitudes towards the role of boundaries and borderlands. Some of the border territories are regarded as potential experimental areas for economic reforms in Russia as whole, while some of them have been the subject of heated political debates that concern issues of military security and Russian identity. In sum, although most of the once contested border areas in Western Europe have become zones of cooperation and harmony, it is still unclear if a similar development is going to take place in the former Soviet Union as well.

3. REGIONAL POLITICS AND IDENTITIES OF CONTESTED BORDER AREAS

The second of the three research themes focuses on the history of the borderland regions and especially on their changing position in the midst of and after the breakup of the Soviet state. It is generally recognized that as a result of the Soviet disintegration, regional politics in the former Soviet Union need to receive more attention than has been the case before.[16] When the Soviet Union was considered as a monolithic state, it was natural to disregard the local and regional identities and acts of respective units there. The failure of the top-down approach was, however, evident, when the transformation process started. After the collapse of the Soviet state many regions have defined their status anew and various forms of centre–periphery relations have been emerging, besides the relations between Russia and other former Soviet republics. Regional and local governments are now actively increasing their political autonomy, seeking direct foreign investments and concluding contracts with the outside world. In particular, many contested border areas of the former Soviet Union that were isolated as a part of the Soviet Union, but can now benefit thanks to their more international location, have been changing rapidly. As it has been noted, 'where an area has been part of the Soviet Union since the beginning, conditions and memories differ from those common in regions incorporated more recently, in the 1940s.'[17]

The striving towards more political autonomy and increasing cooperation with regions on the other side of the border, which characterizes many of the borderland regions of the former Soviet Union, is a part of the increasing regionalization of the European political space.[18] This regionalization usually requires that distinct identity will be created. As 'identity' has become one of the central concepts when discussing and explaining changes in Europe since the Cold War,[19] there are also good reasons to try to achieve a better understanding of the dynamics of local and regional identity formation of the former Soviet borderlands. These areas are crucial from the point of view of Europe as a whole since borderlands seem to play a central role in the dynamics of the new Europe. In general, border territories can be assumed to have a separate identity from the centre, because they have not only threats but also opportunities that are unavailable to people from the heartland area. Moreover, border territories where borderlines have varied and from where peoples have fled, been deported or immigrated, offer a rich field for investigations of identity formation.[20] At the same time the question can be directed to explore the changing identity of those residents who either voluntarily or by force left their former home territories.

Although the study can only scratch the surface of these questions, it clearly supports the view according to which it is important to pinpoint the meaning of history for regional politics and in the development of regional identities. Traditionally, it has been more commonplace to discuss local and regional identities mainly from the perspective of ethnicity and geographical location. Although these two factors are important elements in the development of territorial identities in many places, they do not explain different identities as a whole and the meaning of history cannot be subsumed under the concept of culture, if culture is defined ethnically. History, it seems, may strongly shape the ideas of regional identities in the former Soviet Union and it is often treated rather as a resource than a burden. In other words, regions are constituted not only in history but also with the help of it.

4. THE SALIENCY OF HISTORICAL BORDER DISPUTES

The third theme, the saliency of historical border disputes or, more generally, the consequences of territorial change in the politics of the former possessor state, is an important issue in the relations between the states of the former Soviet Union and many of their neighbours. The legitimation of the pre-communist history, which is often loaded with national interpretations, has had a very powerful influence on the behaviour of Eastern European states. Since border questions are typically sensitive and long-standing themes, they often dominate the overall view of the common history between neighbouring countries. They may hence easily determine the basic nature of the relationship when located on the cordiality–animosity axis. Yet, to understand the saliency of a historical territorial change only as a conflict in the relations between states may be severely misleading, since much of the saliency is often manifest in cooperative terms.

From the point of view of Sovietological research especially, border and territorial questions have been a neglected theme. In the 1980s, one of the few observers who gave attention to the border disputes in the former Soviet Union complained that it seemed to be legitimate to accord the borders little importance since it was generally assumed that they had proved to be irrelevant.[21] The same can be said about border disputes between socialist states. According to the communist leaders, the question of boundaries was not of major importance, since they were regarded as temporary. Moreover, it was asserted that there could be no conflicts over territory between socialist states. Given the hard availability of information and the communist ideology which categorically denied the existence of territorial disputes, the neglect was at that time understandable. But now, even if issues connected with territorial disputes are still sensitive, the task of research has to be carried out. Some surveys have already been published, but the research done in recent years on territorial disputes in the former Soviet Union and Eastern Europe has still to be enlarged and deepened.[22]

The relevance of studying the saliency of historical border disputes can also be stressed by pointing to the large number of such conflicts, both actual and potential, generally in the former Soviet Union and in Eastern Europe. Clearly, the sudden emergence of territorial disputes was one of the unanticipated consequences of the end of the Cold War and it has remained poorly understood. Although territorial disputes are regarded as dangerous problems in world politics, we lack a general knowledge of how border disputes evolve and how they can be resolved, since relatively little has been written about these issues.[23] We surely need more sophisticated theories about boundary disputes than simple power-political explanations that have been commonplace in geopolitical thinking. In contrast to the power-political theories, it seems, on the basis of this study, that moral conceptions and attached sentiments of being able to govern a territory that is regarded as one's 'own' clearly affect the saliency of border disputes.

Many questions arise now, after the end of the Cold War and communist rule, from the tendency to deny the legitimacy of all remaining arrangements and especially territorial regulations that have resulted from World War II in general and from Stalin's policies in particular. The Soviet expansion in World War II is still fresh in the memory of older generations who have experienced the change of border themselves. Although territorial issues were publicly taboo in all countries under the Soviet hegemony, the conceptions of territorial injustice perpetrated in the past survived amazingly well, because such conceptions are deeply rooted in both national and family narratives and belong to the consciousness of younger generations, as well. Today, the former possessors can have a variety of attitudes towards the issue. Some people are still bitter about what they have experienced, especially when they have been forced to leave their homes, and are not content if the territory is not returned. Some are satisfied when they are able to visit their former homelands, restore culturally and emotionally important monuments and develop contacts with the new settlers or ethnic relatives who have remained in the territory. Some people, who belong mostly to the younger generations, are indifferent and see the question primarily in terms of strategic and economic state interests.

Most states that have lost territory see a cooperative stand with regard to their former territories as sufficient, especially when assumed rational state interests and international norms do not sustain the idea of the return of the territory. In many cases novel cooperation has indeed emerged, although it is not very intensive. But some states, organizations and individuals are also presenting wishes and demands of measures that would return the annexed territories. They feel that the historical injustice connected with the annexation of the territory is still unresolved. In these cases disputes arise, since the implications of the history of the border changes that resulted from World War II are often very differently understood in Russia and in some of its neighbour states. People who live in the countries that suffered because of the Soviet Union rarely regard Soviet history in World War II as anything to be proud of, whereas Russians still value the Great Patriotic War in moral terms as a victory over fascism. Even if there were no strong tendencies to view Russia now as a defeated power, many people in the West may still think that Russia must go through a long period of reflection and redemption akin to that of post-war Germany and Japan and rectify the wrongdoings of the Soviet Union in order to be accepted as a 'normal' state. Most Russians, however, do not perceive Russia in this manner but rather as both victim and victor over the Soviet Empire.[24] This means that the Russians do not share such a concept of historical responsibility as some of their neighbours might expect, but stress the need to accept the current state of affairs, when territorial claims to Russia are being presented.

5. THE RESEARCH DESIGN: CASES AND THEIR COMPARISON

Eight territories that were annexed by the Soviet Union as a result of World War II were chosen as subjects of this study.[25] The territories under examination (and their former possessors) are:

1) Bessarabia and Northern Bukovina/Moldavia (Romania);
2) Transcarpathia/Carpatho-Ukraine/Subcarpathia/Ruthenia (Czechoslovakia and Hungary);
3) Eastern Poland/the western parts of Belarus and Ukraine and the area of Vilnius (Poland);
4) the northern part of East Prussia/Königsberg/Kaliningrad area (Germany);
5) Abrene/Pytalovo (Latvia);
6) Petseri/Pechory and East of Narva/Ivangorod/Jaanilinn (Estonia);
7) Karelia (Finland);
8) the Northern Territories/ the Kurile Islands (Japan).

(The location of the territories can be seen in Map 1.1.)

With regard to the cases above, two aspects in the composition of this study are problematic. Firstly, most of the regions chosen for this study are, in a longer historical perspective, fairly artificial: in their present form they exist only as a result of fairly recent border changes, or have been constructed only for the purposes of this research. For the same reason, the historical background has a very dissimilar impact for their regional identity today. As a consequence, the study has to oscillate between geographically defined historical territories and present politico-administrative territories.

Secondly, although the study deals with territories which have been transferred in history, most of the chosen cases are currently not the subject of interstate disputes at all and in some cases not all the territories that were ceded are contested. Almost none of the disputes looks very war-prone or likely to evolve violently at the moment. Most of the questions are, indeed, legally settled, and although some of them can be regarded as legally open, the focus of the study is not on questions of international law or normative theory. Nevertheless, the cases have been tied together by the historical background and political arguments. Because the territories have been transferred in the past, we may in any case hypothesize a conflict,[26] and at least most of the border changes still evoke sentiments and are often popular, although sometimes publicly avoided, subjects of discussion. More important, however, is that by choosing these eight territories we can better compare questions concerning the saliency of historical border disputes.[27]

Yet, these eight cases, as far as they are regarded as territorial disputes, cannot be treated in the real world as phenomena isolated from other

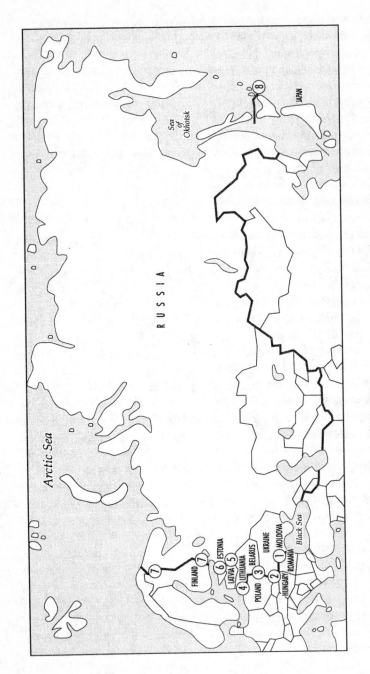

Map 1.1. Border questions from World War II.

territorial disputes in the former Soviet Union. For the sake of a solid overall picture, it has to be stressed that historical border disputes are not the most typical kind among border disputes in the former Soviet Union and that the direction of most of the potential territorial claims in the former Soviet Union is actually the reverse. In other words, the trend of possible border changes seems to oscillate between shrinking and enlarging Russia: currently there is no clear one-way direction. Furthermore, most of the territorial and border disputes in the former Soviet Union stem rather from various ethnically-based attempts to achieve territorial autonomy. One of the greatest problems associated with the current borders derives from the Russian population of 25 million living outside the present Russian state. Also some of the potential Russian claims are based on history, as in the dispute over Crimea. Neither are the eight countries that lost land to the Soviet Union as a result of World War II the only states that may raise territorial claims against Russia on historic grounds. Many historic claims on the territory of the former Soviet Union may have more ancient origins. Some of these questions can be much more alarming, especially potential claims that can be put forth by China.

Although we try to focus on 'historic' territorial disputes, we are of course not able to deal with purely historical border questions in practice. Typically, ethnic, historic and other claims often coincide in territorial struggles, but still, historic border disputes do not necessarily have any ethnic dimension. Although ethnically-based territorial demands often dominate the picture of a typical territorial dispute, purely historic border disputes also have enough potential to influence state policies and to my mind there has been an unfortunate tendency to treat border disputes as a subcategory of ethnic disputes. This might have prevented us from seeing territorial disputes in their own terms.

The case studies on the annexed territories include answers to a broad set of questions:

- how did the status of the territories vary before the Soviet annexation?
- how did the Soviet Union get the territories and what was their legal and administrative status after World War II?
- what are the basic characteristics of the territories – the ethnic composition of the population as well as the military and economic significance?

- what kind of policy did the Soviet Union practise in the annexed territories?
- what kind of an attitude do the former possessor states and inhabitants have towards the annexed territories?
- how have the changes in the international system and the Soviet Union affected the position of the territories, what is the current Russian policy and the policy of the former possessor state with regard to the territory, how have the territories been discussed in the Soviet Union and in the former possessor states and what is the significance of the issue now?
- what kind of prospects are there for the future development of the territory and what would be the impact of the changing international status of the territory?

The presentation of the eight cases is considered to be important because, with the exception of the Kurile Islands and Moldova perhaps, very little has been written on the current status of the territories and on the related disputes and attitudes.[28] Moreover, the theoretical issues that arise in this context are much more generally neglected. Consequently, in addition to a mere presentation of the Soviet policies towards the annexed territories, their internal development and their saliency as disputed territories, the study also has some theoretical goals that can be approached by putting the cases together.

To enrich both the empirical and theoretical analysis the study aims at comparing the cases.[29] Comparison helps us to give some proportion to the cases but it is not merely an end in itself. Comparison is also a method to invent and test theories. The comparative method has sometimes been regarded as an intermediate between qualitative and quantitative analysis and as such it has both advantages and disadvantages. Usually it is thought that a comparative method gives a weaker basis for generalizations than statistical studies but that it gives more general information than single case studies. Because the representativeness of the cases is limited, universal generalizations or strict laws, if there are any, cannot be the object of the comparative study. However, comparison is used not only because the number of relevant cases is too small to allow the investigator to establish statistical control, but also because it can be regarded as superior to the statistical in several important respects. The comparison of a limited number of cases allows an elastic treatment of the questions, and it offers better opportunities for identifying causal relations.[30]

In this study the comparative method will be used loosely as a tool of analysis. The approach of the study represents a kind of soft methodology where the data will not be forced into rigid variables and no single theory will be chosen as a framework. Because all attempts to produce general substantial theories about annexation of borderlands, regional identity formation and international boundary disputes are likely to fail, the cases will be reflected against a range of partial theories. Behind this approach is the idea that the science of international relations has at best 'weak' theories that are always context bound, provide only tentative and partial explanations of international events, and necessitate the use of very fallible human judgement in application.[31]

6. TERMINOLOGICAL CHOICES

The text that follows is burdened with many terminological and conceptual choices. Uppermost is the choice of the term and concept for the unit of study. We have spoken of 'territorial disputes' and 'territorial conflicts' as if they were synonyms. Even if some scholars have distinguished between disputes and conflicts, we have consciously not followed that practice simply because there is no commonly accepted way to do it. Similarly, it can be pointed out that there are differences between a 'border dispute' and a 'territorial dispute' but in this study the two terms are interchangeable.[32]

There is also a difference that can be drawn between concepts of 'frontier' and 'boundary'. The main difference between them is that frontier is understood to be outer-oriented and zonal and 'boundary' inner-oriented and linear. According to this distinction 'frontier' represents an idea of an expansive border, whereas 'boundary' is a border which is tied to mutual respect.[33] This difference notwithstanding, the distinction has remained ambiguous in ordinary usage. In this book the two terms are mostly used interchangeably although the distinction becomes relevant in some of the chapters.

The histories of territorial changes are impossible to write without politically loaded vocabulary. Often it makes a huge difference whether one speaks of liberation, seizure or conquest of a piece of territory; expulsion, migration or movement of peoples; or ceded, annexed, transferred or lost lands. Also the names of many territories under examination are contested. In many cases the dispute over the proper name of a territory can be almost as hard as the dispute over the territory itself. The most illuminating example of these problems currently is the question whether one republic of the former Yugoslavia has the right to use the name of Macedonia. Similarly, whether we talk of the Kurile Islands or the Northern Territories, for instance, can already be interpreted as a stand in the dispute. Yet, some choice of names has to be made for reasons of simplicity. The choice was left to individual writers, but in the concluding chapter the most commonly used forms of the names have been preferred. Therefore it is hoped that the reader understands that because a certain name is used, a conscious stand in the dispute has not necessarily been taken.

7. THE ORGANIZATION OF THE BOOK

The study consists of both theoretical, conceptual and general historical chapters that build up the framework and of eight special case studies. The second part of the book consists of chapters that deal with general aspects of the research themes. The discussion starts with the third research theme, border disputes, followed by the question of regional identities, and then two chapters on the Russian policy towards borders and border areas. The eight chapters that form the third part of the book will deal in turn with each of the historical border questions. These are written by specialists from each of the former possessor states. We will start our journey from Romania, then go further north to Finland and finally end in Japan. The last chapter of the book, the fourteenth, will be a comparative analysis.

NOTES

1. See e.g. David Lane (ed.), *Russia in Flux. The Political and Social Consequences of Reform* (Aldershot: Edward Elgar 1992) and Stephen White, Graeme Gill and Darrell Slider, *The Politics of Transition. Shaping a Post-Soviet Future* (Cambridge: Cambridge University Press 1993).
2. See e.g. Elizabeth Teague, 'The CIS: An Unpredictable Future', *RFE/RL Research Report*, vol. 3, no. 1, 1994, pp. 9–12 and Douglas W. Blum (ed.), *Russia's Future. Consolidation or Disintegration* (Boulder: Westview Press 1994).
3. For the discussion, see Jack Snyder, 'Science and Sovietology: Bridging the Gap in Soviet Foreign Policy Studies', *World Politics*, vol. 40, no. 2, 1988, pp. 169–93; Robert Tucker, 'Sovietology and Russian History', *Post-Soviet Affairs*, vol. 8, no. 3, 1992, pp. 175–96; Alexander Motyl, 'The End of Sovietology: From Soviet Studies to Post-Soviet Studies', in Alexander Motyl (ed.), *The Post-Soviet Nations. Perspectives on the Demise of the USSR* (New York: Columbia University Press 1992); Frederick J. Fleron Jr. and Erik P. Hoffmann, 'Communist Studies and Political Science: Cold War and Peaceful Coexistence', in Frederick J. Fleron Jr. and Erik P. Hoffmann (eds), *Post-Communist Studies & Political Science. Methodology and Empirical Theory in Sovietology* (Boulder: Westview Press

1993); Susan Gross Solomon, 'Beyond Sovietology: Thoughts on Studying Russian Politics After Perestroika', in Susan Gross Solomon (ed.), *Beyond Sovietology. Essays in Politics and History* (Armonk: M.E. Sharpe 1993) and Andrea Chandler, 'The Interaction of Post-Sovietology and Comparative Politics', *Communist and Post-Communist Studies*, vol. 27, no. 1, 1994, pp. 3–17. See also Charles King, 'Post-Sovietology: Area Studies or Social Science', *International Affairs*, vol. 70, no. 2, 1994, pp. 291–7.

4. See e.g. 'The Panel on Patterns of Disintegration in the Former Soviet Union', *Post-Soviet Geography*, vol. 33, no. 6, 1992, pp. 347–404; Stephen Van Evera, 'Managing the Eastern Crisis: Preventing War in the Former Soviet Empire', *Security Studies*, vol. 1, no. 3, 1992, pp. 361–81; Victor Zaslavsky, 'Nationalism and Democratic Transition in Postcommunist Societies', *Dædalus*, vol. 121, no. 2, 1992, pp. 97–121; Charles J. Dick , John F. Dunn and John B.K. Lough, 'Pandora's Box. Potential Conflicts in Post-Communist Europe', *International Defence Review*, no. 3, 1993, pp. 203–8 and Jessica Eve Stern, 'Moscow Meltdown. Can Russia Survive?', *International Security*, vol. 18, no. 4, 1994, pp. 40–65.

5. The aim of the book may fit the following conclusions that were set out in 'The Panel on Patterns of Disintegration in the Former Soviet Union', *Post-Soviet Geography* (1992), p. 351: 'The current troubling spatial conflicts do present an important set of opportunities for scholars concerned with the entire range of geographic, political and other social processes related to conflict. We are provided with a remarkable opportunity to learn much about the etiology of conflict and the complexity that surrounds such events. Careful collection and analysis of data for the wide range of types of conflict may even provide some insights into the manner and method of monitoring such phenomena and even to attempt prediction, at however crude level of accuracy. Finally, we are in an excellent position to learn a great deal about human actions and reactions in a wide variety of conflict contexts, a source of information which may lead us to develop more effective and acceptable means of not solving, but managing conflict. Such policy information certainly would serve us well, not only in the former USSR, but in many other parts of the globe where analogous problems exist.'

6. See e.g. Ladis Kristof, 'The Russian Image of Russia. An Applied Study in Geopolitical Methodology', in Charles Fisher (ed.), *Essays in Political Geography* (London: Methuen & Co 1968).

7. On Russian and Soviet expansion, see e.g. Walter Kolarz, *Russia and Her Colonies* (Handen: Archon Books 1967); Joseph L. Wieczynski; *The Russian Frontier. The Impact of Borderlands upon the Course of Early Russian History* (Charlottesville: University Press of Virginia 1976); Marvin Sicker, *The Strategy of Soviet Imperialism* (New York: Praeger 1988); Hugh Ragsdale, *Imperial Russian Foreign Policy* (Cambridge: Cambridge University Press 1994) and Adam Ulam, *Expansion and Coexistence. Soviet Foreign Policy 1917–1970* (New York: Praeger 1974). The seminal study on Soviet expansion after the October Revolution from a comparative perspective is Richard Pipes, *The Formation of the Soviet Union. Communism and Nationalism* (Cambridge: Harvard University Press 1964). For Stalin, see e.g. Milovan Djilas, *Conversations with Stalin* (New York: Harcourt & World 1962); Isaac Deutscher, *Stalin. A Political Biography* (Harmondsworth: Penguin 1970); Robert C. Tucker, *Stalin in Power. The Revolution from Above 1928–41* (New York: Norton & Company 1990) and Dmitri Volkogonov, *Stalin. Triumph and Tragedy* (London: Weidenfeld Nicholson 1991). For specific studies on Soviet annexations in World War II, see F. Nenec and V. Moudry, *The Soviet Seizure of Subcarpathian Ruthenia* (Toronto: William B. Andersson 1955); David Rees, *The Soviet Seizure of Kuriles* (New York: 1985); Edgar Anderson, 'How Narva, Petseri and Abrene Came to Be in the RSFR', in Dietrich André Loeber (ed.), *Regional Identity Under Soviet Rule: The Case of the Baltic States* (Hackettstown: University of Kiel 1990); George Cioranescu, *Bessarabia. Disputed Land Between East and West* (München: Jon Dimitru 1985) and Osmo Jussila, *Venäläinen Suomi* (Helsinki: WSOY 1983), which includes also a comparative perspective.

8. The classic study on these questions is Niccolò Machiavelli, *The Prince* (Cambridge: Cambridge University Press 1988 [1512]). For a recent study, see Eric Carlton, *Occupation. The Policies and Practices of Military Conquerors* (London: Routledge 1992).

9. See e.g. Stan Markotich, 'Serbian President Focuses on Creating a Greater Serbia', *RFE/ RL Research Report*, vol. 3, no. 30, 1994, pp. 11–16.
10. See e.g. Igor Torbakov, 'The Statists and the Ideology of Russian Imperial Nationalism', *RFE/RL Research Report*, vol. 1, no. 49, 1992, pp. 10–16 and Stephen Shenfield, 'Post-Soviet Russia in Search of Identity', in Douglas W. Blum (ed.), *Russia's Future. Consolidation or Disintegration* (Boulder: Westview Press 1994).
11. See e.g. Ruslan Ignatyev, 'We Do not Want Others' Land But Shall not Give an Inch of Ours', *Rossijskaya Gazeta*, 14 April 1994.
12. See e.g. Jacob Kipp, 'Zhirinovsky Threa', *Foreign Affairs*, vol. 73, no. 3, 1994, pp. 72–86. For the debate see e.g. Lena Jonson, 'In Search of National Interest: The Foreign Policy Debate in Russia', *Nationalities Paper*, vol. 22, no.1, Spring, 1994, pp. 175–94.
13. See e.g. Thomas Sanders, 'Historical Consciousness and the Incorporation of the Soviet Past', *Problems of Communism*, vol. 40, no. 6, 1991, pp. 115–23; Dimitri Simes, 'The Return of Russian History', *Foreign Affairs*, vol. 73, no. 1, 1994, pp. 67–82; John W.R. Lepingwell, 'The Soviet Legacy and Russian Foreign Policy', *RFE/RL Research Report*, vol. 3, no. 23, 1994, pp. 1–8, and Gerard Holden, *Russia After the Cold War. History and the Nation in Post-Soviet Security Politics* (Franfurt am Main: Campus 1994), chapter 3.
14. For a standard Soviet interpretation of the annexations that resulted out of necessity, because of provocation, on the popular consent or on the basis of historical belonging to Russia, see e.g. B. Ponomaryov, A. Gromyko and V. Khvostov (eds), *History of Soviet Foreign Policy 1917–1945* (Moscow: Progress 1969), pp. 391–406.
15. See e.g. Vera Tolz, 'Russia: Westernizers Continue to Challenge National Patriots', *RFE/ RL Research Reports*, vol. 1, no. 49, 1992, pp. 1–9.
16. For studies on regional politics in the Soviet Union and Russia, see e.g. V. V. Alekseev, 'Soviet Regional Problems: Causes and Effects', *Russian History*, vol. 18, no. 1, 1991, pp. 77–83; Jeffrey W. Hahn, 'Local Politics and Political Power in Russia', *Soviet Economy*, vol. 7, no. 4, 1991, pp. 322–41; Irina Busygina, 'Regional Separatism and Its Consequences for the Future of Russia', in Hans-Georg Ehrhart, Anna Kreikemeyer and Andrei V. Zagorski, *The Former Soviet Union and European Security: Between Integration and Re-Nationalization* (Baden-Baden: Nomos 1993), Frank Evers, 'Reformen und Soziales in der russländischen Provinz am Beispiel von Uljanowsk', *Osteuropa*, vol. 44, no. 3, 1994, pp. 256–66 and Klaud Segbers (ed.), *Russlands Zukunft: Räume und Regionen* (Nomos: Baden-Baden 1994).
17. Ernest Gellner, 'Ethnicity and Faith in Eastern Europe', *Dædalus*, vol. 119, no. 1, 1990, p. 279.
18. See e.g. Peter J. Taylor, 'A Theory and Practice of Regions: the Case of Europe', *Environment and Planning D. Society & Space*, vol. 9, no. 2, 1993, pp. 183–96; Iver B. Neumann, 'A Region-Building Approach to Northern Europe', *Review of International Studies*, vol. 20, no. 1, 1994, pp. 53–74 and Pertti Joenniemi, 'Regionality and the Modernist Script: Tuning into the Unexpected in International Politics', *Occasional Papers*, no. 57, 1994 (Tampere: Tampere Peace Research Institute 1994).
19. See e.g. Ole Waever et al., *Identity, Migration, and the New Security Agenda in Europe* (London: Pinter 1993) and Michael Keith and Steve Pile (eds), *Place and the Politics of Identity* (London: Routledge 1993).
20. See especially, Julian Minghi, 'European Borderlands. International Harmony, Landscape Change and New Conflict', in Carl Grundy-Warr (ed.), *Eurasia. World Boundaries*, vol. 3 (London: Routledge 1994), p. 97. For studies on the role of boundaries and identity of borderlands see Eric Fischer, 'On Boundaries', *World Politics*, vol. 1, no. 2, 1949, pp. 196–222; Feliks Gross, *Ethnics in a Borderland. An Inquiry into the Nature of Ethnicity and Reduction of Ethnic Tensions in a One-Time Genocide Area* (Westport: Greenwood Press 1978); Jean Gottmann (ed.), *Centre and Periphery. Spatial Variation in Politics* (Beverly Hills: Sage 1980); Malcolm Anderson, 'The Political Problems of Frontier Regions', in Malcolm Anderson (ed.), *Frontier Regions in Western Europe* (London: Frank Cass 1983); Anssi Paasi, 'The Institutionalization of Regions: a Theoretical Framework for Understanding the Emergence of Regions and the Constitutions of Territorial Identity',

Fennia, no. 164, 1986, pp. 105–46 and Oscar Martinez, *Life and Society in the US–Mexico Borderlands* (Tucson: University of Arizona Press 1994).

21. See Julian Birch, 'Border Disputes and Disputed Borders', *Nationalities Paper*, vol. 16, no. 1, 1987, pp. 43–70.

22. For basic studies on territorial conflicts in the former Soviet Union, see *Moscow News*, no. 11, 1991; Uwe Halbach, 'Ethno-territoriale Konflikte in der GUS', *Berichte des Bundesinstituts für ostwissenschaftliche Studien*, no. 31, 1992 and Valeri Kolossov, 'Ethno-Territorial Conflicts and Boundaries', in The Former Soviet Union. *Territory Briefing*, no. 2 (Durham: International Boundaries Research Unit 1992). For more general surveys, see Allcock et al., *Border and Territorial Disputes* (Harlow: Longman 1992) and Ewan Anderson, *An Atlas of World Political Flashpoints. A Sourcebook of Geopolitical Crisis* (London: Pinter 1993).

23. Some exceptions are Saadia Touval, *The Boundary Politics of Independent Africa* (Cambridge: Harvard University Press 1972); Sven Tägil (coord.), 'Studying Boundary Conflicts. A Theoretical Framework', *Lund Studies in International History*, no. 9 (Lund: Esselte Studium 1977); Friedrich Kratochwil et al., *Peace and Disputed Sovereignty. Reflections on Conflict over Territory* (Lanham: University Press of America 1985) and Gary Goertz and Paul Diehl, *Territorial Changes and International Conflict* (London: Routledge 1992).

24. See Simes (1994), p. 77.

25. These eight cases do not include all the areas the Soviet Union annexed in World War II. The Soviet Union swallowed the Baltic states as a whole, but because these states have now regained their independence, we will rather examine the boundary questions which remained in the relations between the Baltic states and Russia. The Soviet Union also annexed Tuva, a small semi-independent state in Asia between her and China, and she regulated borders also with Afganistan. On Tuva see e.g. Toomas Alatalu, 'Tuva – a State Reawakens', *Soviet Studies*, vol. 44, no. 5, 1992, pp. 881–96 and Mergen Mongush, 'The Annexation of Tannu-Tuva and the Formation of the Tuva ASSR', *Central Asian Survey*, vol. 12, no. 1, 1993, pp. 81–6; on Afganistan–USSR boundary, see 'Afganistan–U.S.S.R. Boundary', *International Boundary Study*, no. 26, 1963.

26. For example Erich Weede, 'Nation–Environment Relations as Determinants of Hostilities Among Nations', *Peace Science Society (International) Papers*, vol. 20, 1973, pp. 67–90, p.79 assumes that a territorial problem exists 'if the frontier has been changed in or after war during the last sixty years'.

27. An analogous research question, but at the individual level, has been put also by Neil Vidmar, 'Justice Motives and Other Psychological Factors in the Development and Resolution of Disputes', in Melvin Lerner and Sally Lerner (eds), *Justice Motive in Social Behaviour. Adapting to Times of Scarcity and Change* (New York: Plenum Press 1981), p. 408: 'We ... need to address a comparative question: Why do some potential disputes escalate and others fail to develop into disputes?'

28. For parallel descriptions of these cases one might consult e.g. Allcock et al. (1992); Anderson (1990) and moreover, William Crowther, 'Romania and Moldavian Political Dynamics', in Daniel Nelson (ed.) *Romania After Tyranny* (Boulder: Westview Press 1992); Charles King, 'Moldova and the New Bessarabian Questions', *The World Today*, vol. 49, no. 7, 1993, pp. 135–9; Anneli Ute Gabanyi, 'Moldova Between Russia, Romania and the Ukraine', *Aussenpolitik*, vol. 44, no. 1, 1993, pp. 98–107; Alfred Reisch, 'Transcarpathia's Hungarian Minority and the Autonomy Issue', *RFE/RL Research Report*, vol. 1, no. 6–7, 1992, pp. 17–23; Mark Galeotti, 'Kaliningrad: a Fortress Without a State', *Boundary and Security Bulletin*, vol. 1, no. 3, 1993, pp. 56–9; Alan Day, 'Back to the Finland Station', *Boundary and Security Bulletin*, vol. 1, no. 3, 1993, pp. 60–65; Leszek Buszynski, 'Russia and Japan: the Unmaking of a Territorial Settlement', The *World Today*, vol. 498, no. 3, 1993, pp. 50–54 and Richard de Villafranca, 'Japan and the Northern Territories Dispute. Past, Present and Future', *Asian Survey*, vol. 33, no. 6, 1993, pp. 610–24.

29. For comparative studies on territorial disputes, see Tägil (1977) and Kratochwil et al. (1985). For a study in comparative frontier history, see Howard Lamar and Leonard

Thompson, *The Frontier History. North America and Southern Africa Compared* (New Haven: Yale University Press 1981). For a comparative study on borderlands, see Anthony Asiwaju, 'Borderlands in Africa: A Comparative Research', *Journal of Borderland Studies* vol. 8, no. 2, 1993, pp. 1–12. For a wish to develop studies on borderlands and borderland people from a comparative perspective, see Minghi (1994), p. 97 and Oscar Martinez, 'The Dynamics of Border Interaction. New Approaches to Border Analysis', in Clive Scofield (ed.), *World Boundaries,* vol. 1 (London: Routledge 1994), p. 8.

30. See Alexander George, 'Case Studies and Theory Development: The Method of Structured, Focused Comparison', in Paul Gordon Lauren (ed.), *Diplomacy: New Approaches in History, Theory and Policy* (New York: Free Press 1979) and Charles Ragin, *The Comparative Method. Moving Beyond Qualitative and Quantitative Strategies* (Berkeley: University of California Press 1987).

31. For definitions and defense of a 'weak theory' in international relations, see Kjell Goldmann, *Change and Stability in Foreign Policy. The Problems and Possibilities of Détente* (Princeton: Princeton University Press 1988), pp. 223–8 and Robert Rothstein, 'Limits and Possibilities of Weak Theory: Interpreting North–South', *Journal of International Affairs,* vol. 43, no. 1, 1990, pp. 159–81.

32. See e.g. J.V.R. Prescott, *Political Frontiers and Boundaries* (London: Allen & Unwin 1987), p. 98, and Surya P. Sharma, *International Boundary Disputes and International Law* (Bombay: Tripathi 1976), pp. 4–7.

33. See Ladis Kristof, 'Frontiers and Boundaries', *Annals of the Association of American Geographers,* vol. 49, no. 3, 1959, p. 278 and Ellwyn Stoddard, 'Frontiers, Borders and Border Segmentation: Toward a Conceptual Clarification', *Journal of Borderland Studies* vol. 6, no. 1, 1991, pp. 1–22. This has become a standard distinction in the political geography, see e.g. Peter J. Taylor, *Political Geography. World-Economy, Nation-State and Locality* (London: Longman 1985), pp. 104–5.

PART II

Borders and Russia

2. Theories on Territorial Disputes

Tuomas Forsberg

---

1. THE RISE OF TERRITORIAL DISPUTES

The sudden emergence of territorial disputes in Europe after the end of the Cold War raises a number of questions. Where overall do they exist? Why do they exist? How severe are the disputes? What are the consequences of the disputes? Are they likely to result in wars? How can they be solved? On what principles should a resolution be based?

These and similar questions have facsinated international policy-makers and scholars alike in recent years. During the Cold War territorial disputes received little attention, simply because, notwithstanding a few exceptions, they did not exist in the Northern hemisphere. The struggle between the leading states, which had no common land border, had moved from territory to other issues. The tight international system of the Cold War which was based on the rigid structure of clearly defined blocs was territorially stable. The threat of nuclear weapons effectively froze territorial disputes between the blocs whilst Soviet hegemony in the East and integration in the West dampened the disputes inside the blocs themselves. Moreover, we might suppose that international norms which protected the territorial integrity of states and the decreasing value of territory also helped to keep the number of territorial disputes at a low level.

Territorial disputes were even supposed to have vanished into history. 'Whether we like it or not', wrote Ladis Kristof, 'boundary disputes, so dominant in international politics a generation ago, are fading away from the diplomatic agenda'.[1] Similarly, in the 1980s J.R.V. Prescott concluded that 'for the present the cycle of territorial dispute, war, boundary adjustment and new territorial dispute appears to have been broken'.[2] As

23

Prescott's motivation indicates, there was a belief that historical territorial disputes had been settled. However, it has often been acknowledged that changing power relations might raise historical border problems anew. As Quincy Wright, for instance, noted, historical claims long dormant may rapidly arise if political conditions seem favourable.[3] In a similar manner, although the reference publication to border and territorial disputes in the 1980s contended that Europe today probably has the lowest incidence of intergovernmental dispute over territory, it nevertheless noted that 'it remains an open question – whether a transformation of existing power relationships in Eastern Europe would leave post-war territorial arrangements unchallenged'.[4]

Indeed, since the end of the Cold War territorial disputes have become salient problems of Eastern European politics. Usually, territorial disputes are regarded as dangerous and their emergence as a sign of the return of a warlike past. It is widely supposed that the absence of territorial disputes in Western Europe is one of the best guarantees of peace and that the main threat to European security comes from the post-communist ethnic and territorial conflicts.[5] In general, however, their violent potential might be exaggerated. In the former Yugoslavia and in the former Soviet Union, burning territorial conflicts are numerous, but elsewhere in Europe interstate territorial disputes have so far not evolved into militarized conflicts.

Although territorial disputes are regarded as major diplomatic challenges, knowledge about their nature, occurrence, causes and resolution is weak. In a recent book, for example, Gary Goertz and Paul Diehl argue that 'at present, the theoretical understanding of territorial conflict is primarily anecdotal'.[6] Similarly, Alexander Murphy contends that 'comparatively little has been written that treats territory as a basic cause of conflict'.[7] In short, scientific analysis about territorial conflicts is clearly needed and sought after more than in previous decades.

It would have been highly improbable if the scholarly neglect of territorial disputes had not resulted in an incapability of dealing with them. Indeed, it seems that both policy-makers and scholars have had difficulties in grasping the nature of territorial disputes, and the responses of the international community to territorial disputes are often retrospective, inconsistent and confusing.[8] Before territorial questions blow up, there is a tendency to deny the very existence of these disputes, to convert them into other kinds of disputes or to think that such disputes are impossible to solve in any satisfactory manner. Independently of the reasons that lie behind such attitudes, the rise of territorial questions is widely regarded as negative.

In our era, emerging territorial claims are not well understood because they do not correspond with the view of rational policy-making. In Western Europe there seems to be a trend towards reducing the significance of borders and decreasing the sovereignty of nation-states. On this basis, it is easy to wonder why this does not occur in the East as well. The move in a contrary direction in Eastern Europe is often regarded as an atavistic and frightening course of affairs.[9] Although we have a right to be worried over the potential riskiness of emerging territorial disputes, these reactions are often burdened by the tendency of seeing territorial questions simply as a return to history.

Territorial disputes are more common in the East than in the West because of the specific nature of East European history. Neither democracy nor a high level of technology are sufficient factors to restrain territorial claims from arising as the Japanese claims on the Kurile Islands/Northern Territories demonstrate. Of course, to raise and discuss historical problems after the collapse of the communist system is a natural corollary of attempts to rebuild the national identity and rewrite the national past. Yet, the reemergence of historical border questions as such does not indicate a return of warlike history since territorial disputes after the Cold War are not necessarily dangerous. In many cases, the discussion can also be conceived as a means of learning from history in order to overcome it and not as a means of returning to it.

2. THE NATURE OF TERRITORIAL DISPUTES

Territorial disputes have most often been studied as individual cases. On the basis of historical and legal studies a range of diverse causes and characteristics, and numerous ways to resolve territorial conflicts, have been identified. On the level of clashing territorial claims it also seems very easy to infer what is the cause of dispute. In other words, the cause of historic border disputes lies naturally in history. But is there any general knowledge which could be offered to policy-makers and which could help us to understand territorial disputes better than the disputants do themselves?

There is certainly no single theory of territorial disputes, which would be exhaustive. On the contrary, there is a tendency to argue that because boundaries and territorial disputes are unique, no such theory can be possible. As Lord Curzon taught in his lectures at the beginning of this century, the drawing of frontiers is more like art than science.[10] Such an argument would however be too easy a way to escape the quest for theorizing about borders. Yet, generalized knowledge on territorial disputes has been difficult to achieve and no generally accepted pattern of explanation exists. From the positivist point of view the failure is that only a few statistical studies on territorial disputes have been conducted. However, it is probable that correlative studies will not help us much, if we have no proper theory of territorial disputes. In fact, the quest to identify different issue types and base theories on them is tempting in a more general sense. For example Paul Diehl has suggested, that a better understanding of issues could be a way to extend current approaches to international behaviour in conflict research.[11]

When trying to build a theory on territorial disputes, the interesting question is, how can we distinguish explanations of territorial conflict from general explanations of conflict? Do we need a distinct theory of territorial disputes? Territorial conflict can of course be merely a symptom of some other conflict between states, as realist theory suggests. In other words, territorial dispute can be seen as an epiphenomenon of the struggle over power. Or, as is often the case, territorial dispute can be seen as a corollary of ethnic dispute. It is, however, important also to regard territory as an independent source of conflict, but without a theoretical base – separating territorial disputes from other conflicts can be misleading. At present it is still unclear on what basis territorial dispute is such a distinct phenomenon that 'quite refined theories about their occurrence can be made'.[12] More generally, the attempts to constitute the political inquiry on an issue paradigm have so far not fulfilled expectations. It seems that issue theories unfortunately do not help us to understand territorial disputes any better than general theories of conflict.[13]

Typically, two characteristics of territorial disputes are often mentioned. First, it is assumed that territorial issues are tangible, concrete objects. Because of their tangibility, territorial disputes should be easier to bargain over than abstract issues.[14] Second, territorial disputes are regarded as zero-sum games, which means, in turn, that they are less likely to lead to a negotiated solution.[15] However, both of these propositions are problematic: tangibility because territorial disputes have a lot of symbolic value and zero-sumness because several other values can be attached to territory that can convert the dispute into a positive-sum play. As Friedrich

Kratochwil et al. have argued, boundary disputes show in the real world features of mixed motive games and it is best to conceive them not as static bargaining games but as processes.[16]

The permanence of territory may, however, explain why territorial disputes are so persistent, since territorial disputes seem to be more long-standing than other kinds of disputes.[17] Territorial disputes often survive not only over decades but also over generations. Among all injustices that have been done in the past, territorial questions are those that are easy to remember and that can be claimed for return for the simple reason that lost territories still exist, although the landscape might have changed drastically.

Their objective characteristics notwithstanding, territorial disputes cannot be understood without recognizing the human tendency to organize power territorially. Indeed, one obvious fallacy in much of the discussion about territorial disputes has been the neglect of the role of territoriality. According to Robert Sack, territoriality is not any relationship between man and his environment but an attempt to affect, influence or control actions by enforcing control over a specific geographical area.[18] But the role of territoriality in international politics has not been recognized, not to mention analysed, sufficiently. Territoriality is not an easy concept and in spite of its central role in international politics we do not know much about its dimensions. It is, perhaps, too much a part of us: as John Ruggie has put it, 'its neglect is akin to never looking at the ground that one is walking on'.[19]

The central features of human territoriality are sometimes traced back to sociobiological genealogical facts. Man is said to follow a 'territorial imperative' and the struggle over territory is assumed to be on a par with other animals who defend their territories against intruders.[20] It is, however, debatable how inherent a feature of human life territoriality, and especially certain forms of it, is. There certainly exist very deep psychological links between man and his environment, but it is better to conceive state territoriality as a product of cultural, societal and political development than as a necessary corollary of sociobiological evolution.[21] It is therefore much more interesting to investigate why territoriality is chosen as a means to use and limit power. When thinking about state territoriality, and especially the tendency of states to aim at acquiring more territory, we have to ask why human communities need territory if it is not a genetic must. These questions lead us to scrutinize the value of territory.

3. THE VALUE OF TERRITORY

The value of territory is clearly a factor that affects the emergence of territorial disputes and their nature. However, it is much more difficult to say on what kind of factors the value of the territory depends.

The value of territory is usually rationalized in two ways. First, control over territory is needed because of security issues. Because physical force is used spatially, nations can defend themselves by controlling their living area. Second, territory is needed for economic opportunities. Not only is land in itself, both for food and for industrial production, seen as an economic asset, but other forms of state economy like taxation and customs have also been based on territorial control.[22]

The linkage between basic human goals, such as security and economy, and territory explains partially why territory has been so often the issue of pointed disputes and war between states. Moreover, security and economy are not the only human goals that can be achieved by territorial control since many other values have also been attached to territory. The notion of territorially-based sovereignty allows for the possibility of making decisions about various ideological values of the territory and about its population. Thus, control over territory can also be seen as a means to promote religion, national culture and political system in a given area.

Yet, ahistorical theories about territorial disputes that are based on objective values remain weak since the value of territory clearly depends on the context. Indeed, the history of the international system suggests that the value of territory is not constant or independent of the international environment. As many analysts have pointed out, the value of territory has undergone substantial changes during the history of the nation-state system. The changes have been understood to be taking place with a particular speed and depth in the last years and decades.

For a long time in international relations power was synonymous with territory and territory became a kind of dominant good through which a range of other goods could be commanded. Territorial expansion was regarded as necessary for a powerful state and a secession of territory as a weakening of its power position. But since World War II, it has been assumed that the value of territorial expansion has diminished, borders have become more open and territorial sovereignty more vulnerable. According to these ideas, the significance of the territorial borders will constantly diminish, and at the end they will mark only the limits of some less significant administrative units.[23]

The erosion of the value of territory has been noted on many levels, and it may suffice merely to recall the main trends which have been assumed to have affected the evolution. First of all, it can be argued that the value of territory has lost its significance in terms of defence. According to the thesis posed by John Herz (although he later revised it) state boundaries cannot guarantee the military security of nations in an era of nuclear weapons and air warfare as effectively as before.[24] The strategic value of territory has decreased because states do not necessarily need strategic buffer-zones for defence to the extent that they did earlier. Secondly, economic trends have resulted in many important changes in the value of territory. Already, at least since Sir Norman Angell's 'The Great Illusion',[25] it has been claimed that territory is overvalued and that the assumed utility of expansion is based on a distortion of rational thinking. After World War II, the idea that territorial expansion is of little or no use and attempts to conquer new territories are anyway too dangerous, has become fairly common. Because international interdependence has grown and trade is based increasingly on free markets, the value of the possession of territory as a means to autarky has been reduced. Territorially unbounded knowledge and capital, rather than territorially bounded land and raw materials, determine the wealth of nations. This has led analysts to feel that states no longer compete for new territories[26] or that states are now competing more for the means to create wealth within their territory than for power over more territory.[27] In Richard Rosecrance's words, there will be a shift from a territorial military–political world to a non-territorial trading world.[28]

Thirdly, there are cultural and normative tendencies which have eroded the functions of boundaries and thereby decreased the need for and the possibilities of maintaining territorial sovereignty. First, the position of minorities and human rights in general has improved. Hence, states do not usually see territorial intervention or annexation as a means of protecting important national or human values. Second, cultural transactions cross borders almost everywhere, and states cannot totally close the borders of a given territory even if they wanted to. Growing opportunities for spatial mobility and tourism may replace the wish for annexation. Third, the identity of peoples has been dispersed away from its national basis. The post-nationalist nature of Western societies, which has been assumed to have developed along with global and European integration and growing individualism, should no longer be based on territorial principles but on abstract ideological elements. According to some, the whole mode of territorial integration is fading away.[29]

Significant as these trends are, they are, however, spatially and tempo-
rally bounded and we have no firm ground for expecting an increasing
erosion of borders and a decrease in the value of territory. Some people
argue that conquest of territory still pays economically.[30] Moreover,
environmental problems and resource scarcity may well increase territorial problems in the future. At least in the former Soviet Union and in
several places in Eastern Europe many of these trends that should affect
the value of territory by decreasing its importance do not hold. If the threat
of conventional warfare is present, territory can still be seen as strategically important. If agriculture and heavy industry dominate the economy,
territory may offer major economic benefits. Furthermore, territorially-
based nationalism still serves as a central basis of peoples' identity.
Finally, in the former Soviet Union and Eastern Europe, changes of
borders are also frequently seen as a means to create or maintain an ethnic
or historical state unity or to avoid discrimination of ethnic relatives.

Despite various important values that have been attached to territory, it
is evident that the rational objectivist value of territory alone does not
suffice to explain the wish to raise territorial issues in our time. It should
be clear that the value of territory is subjectively conceived. Moreover,
much of the assumed rational value of territory is intersubjective rather
than purely objective. Although security and economy are quite easily
seen as rational values, their relationship to territory is to a great extent
socially constructed, which means that territory has a lot of symbolic
value. Most important is that, since the emergence of the Westphalian
state-system, territory and statehood have been linked essentially together. Because much of the value of a territory can be seen as a relic of earlier
centuries, it seems that the symbolic value of territory for a state often
extends its 'rational' instrumental value. In the current state-system, a
state is still fundamentally a place and territorial sovereignty its essence.
From this point of view we might be able to understand better why moral
values and rights are so often coupled with territorial problems and why
territorial disputes are as sensitive as they are. Indeed, subjectively
perceived justice rather than typical 'rational' state interests might
provide an alternative basis for explaining the emergence of historic
border disputes.[31]

Unless we believe in a sudden abolition of the state system, territoriality
will remain with us. Even if the desire for territorial expansion has
diminished, which those who have their eyes targeted towards the former
Yugoslavia and some corners of the former Soviet Union naturally doubt,

the existing state territory is still much valued. An attack upon a state's territory is readily regarded not only as an attack upon the state but against the state identity as well. In short, even if the wish to acquire more territory can be based on several important values, it can not be understood without reference to the complex web of symbols created by international law and political practices that underpin most historical border disputes.

4. EXPLANATIONS OF TERRITORIAL DISPUTES

In order to present various possible explanations of territorial disputes, let us distinguish between three broad variables and four levels of explanation. It can be suggested that by and large, three factors – power relations, interests and norms – affect the likelihood of territorial conflict.[32] Correspondingly, at least four levels of explanation can be distinguished: the international system, the dyad of states, the state and the individual.[33] Although both the explaining factors and the levels of explanation can be seen as conceptually distinct, they are not unrelated and it is not always easy to interpret how various theories are related to them. On this basis, however, various hypotheses can be formed and the existing, albeit few, empirical results can be systematized.

First of all, the international power structure can be regarded as having some impact on the occurrence of territorial disputes on the systemic level. Here I will only point out that there are theories which explain international stability (and implicitly also the stability of borders) by the number of power centres, but my intention is not to suggest which of these theories is right, if any. More directly, territorial disputes have been connected with major power shifts in the international system. According to the theory of Robert Gilpin, for example, changing power relations in the international system usually result in territorial redistribution.[34] We can also try to identify systemic conditions that affect state interests in territory. As was pointed out, it is believed that the value of territory has decreased, because of systemic changes caused by technological evolution and growing interdependence. Finally, we can distinguish international norms in terms of border regimes. As Evan Luard has pointed out, international norms might both constrain and launch territorial demands.[35] However, when there are international regimes and institutions enforcing the status quo, it can be supposed that territorial disputes are less likely to emerge.

On the dyadic level similar patterns of explanations can be distinguished. Perhaps the most tempting explanation is to refer to the changing power relations between states as a cause of territorial disputes. From this point of view boundary changes may be regarded as mere indications of the shift in the balance of forces.[36] A suggested explanation of territorial disputes is also the idea that power disparity is more likely to cause territorial disputes than is inequality of states.[37] The dyadic relationship can also affect state interests and it can be hypothesized that border disputes occur with greater scope between states that are members of opposing blocs than between states that are members of the same bloc.[38] A particular hypothesis belonging to this level is that border disputes occur with greater severity between pairs of states in two-nation sets than between states in three-nation sets – in other words in contexts where three states share mutual borders.[39] As far as norms in dyads are concerned, it can be suggested that democratic states have special norms in regard to their disputes. It is, however, very unclear if there are fewer territorial disputes between democracies but it can be argued that they are more likely to be solved peacefully.[40]

On the state level one of the most popular theories connected with the power of states assumes that the more the absolute power of a state increases, the more likely it is to expand externally.[41] The power-political view is most closely associated with the idea of the organic nature of state territoriality, which was presented by the German geographist Friedrich Ratzel. According to his theory a state was a living organism which grew and decayed naturally. Thus the border of the state was always dynamic and each fixed position was only temporary in character.[42] In this connection one might also recall the theory called 'lateral pressure', set out in the study by Nazli Choucri and Robert North, according to which growth in population and national capabilities leads states to expand their activities beyond their own borders.[43]

When regarding interests on the state level, the idea is often expressed that developed states or well-established democracies are less interested in expanding their territories. Typical assumptions are also ideas that nationalist states with some irredenta are more likely to initiate a territorial dispute than are multicultural states or ethnically homogeneous but unified states.[44] Furthermore, it can also be suggested that norms at the societal level can regulate the willingness to put forward territorial claims – for example that liberal democracies, because of their adherence to honour shared norms, are less likely than dictatorships to conduct expansionist policies.

The likelihood of territorial claims being presented can also depend on the power of various interest groups in the state. A relevant interest group in territorial disputes is, for example, an organization of an expelled population, an industrial bloc which wishes to have control over raw materials in some border area, or military organizations which aim at having strategic borders beyond existing ones. According to the recent study by Jack Snyder the existence of a coalition of such groups best explains the tendency of states to overexpand.[45]

Finally, also on the individual level, various kinds of possible explanations of territorial disputes can be invented. On the one hand, there are those sociobiological studies which stress the inherent nature of territorial competition.[46] On the other hand, there are those psychological explanations which direct attention to specific personalities and their belief systems. It can be argued that there are personal motives and territorial conceptions behind every decision to initiate or respond to a territorial conflict – historically Adolf Hitler and his conception of 'Lebensraum' is perhaps the best-known example.[47]

To sum up, none of the proposed theories alone can explain territorial disputes. In order to understand the causes of territorial disputes properly we ultimately need specific historical studies on them. Some people also hope to synthesize various plausible theories and give each of them some weight, although we do not have a definitive conclusion. For example, Goertz and Diehl have argued that territorial conflict, especially over homeland territory between states, can properly be viewed through the conceptual lenses of power politics, although other explanations also have, according to them, some merits.[48]

Because power-political theories have had such a dominant position in theorizing about boundaries, special attention should be given to their problemacy. It is true that power politics has often been involved in territorial disputes, but it is not true that territorial changes always follow power-political imperatives. Surely, there is no natural law determining such a connection. If the power of a nation is not defined tautologically i.e. in terms of territory, territorial changes have not followed changes in power relations.[49] Although military might has often been a necessary condition for successful expansion, not all powerful states have tried to enlarge their territories. Territorial expansion is not a necessity, and it is unclear why states should always aim at territorial enlargement.

What is stressed here is the view that we should reject general theories of territorial conflicts such as the power-political explanation, which treats boundaries merely as a reflection of the power position of states. In its simplest form, it does not give independent value to state interests which it regards as constantly targeted towards expansion, neither does it regard norms as anything more than a corollary of power relations. Therefore it is important to keep in mind other possible explanations, not just the power relationship, when evaluating various territorial claims and possibilities for resolution of territorial conflicts. More emphasis should be given therefore to interest formation and the norms which regulate and direct the behaviour of states.

5. HISTORICAL CLAIMS IN TERRITORIAL DISPUTES

On the surface, territorial disputes consist of conflicting claims to territory. To consider the claims to territory is important, because neither the explanation nor the resolution of territorial disputes can transcend these claims easily. Expansionist policies might be nothing but selfish, but it has always been regarded as necessary to legitimate territorial claims for a wider public in world politics. Legitimation efforts typically refer to some supposed common rationale or moral principles that are based on concepts such as needs and rights. Two types of territorial disputes appear to be dominant: the disputes resulting from questions of self-determination on the one hand, and the disputes that rise from historical changes of territory on the other hand. Of course, legitimation has not always corresponded to the original reasons for the expansion, but there is no inevitable reason to think that the justification would never include the real motives.

Historical justification has been in the forefront of territorial claims throughout the centuries. Together with claims for self-determination, the preference for historical justification has probably been growing during recent decades as strategic and economic claims have been regarded as discredited. As Norman Hill points out, 'the types of claims made by a state to territory reflect the doctrines and conditions dominant in international relations at the time'.[50] Indeed, according to Alexander Murphy territorial claims against neighbouring states after World War II have almost always been justified as attempts to recover land that had been wrongfully taken away.[51] With the exception of claims for self-determination, other claims are often either left unstated or are offered as support for the historical claim.

There are at least three forms of historical claims. One is the idea that any historical possession can serve as a basis for historical claims and sometimes it is assumed that states always try to maximize their national territory with the help of historical claims.[52] Clearly, this kind of argumentation leads to difficulties, because many boundaries have been altered several times in history. Furthermore, such an idea is often very backward-looking and sees history typically through some kind of rose-coloured spectacles. The second is the claim that the land belongs to those who came first or who cultivated it first. This claim is also hard to sustain because people have no eternal home. Third is the idea which refers to past violations of international law and justice. This form of historical claim comprises the idea that past violations of international norms should not be forgotten. Among these three forms of historical claims it is usually the third that is most commonly used and it is also the strongest, although as time goes by the right becomes harder to establish. Even if historical claims are sometimes fairly invalid both morally and legally speaking, sometimes the world community does not seem to accept the idea that past wrongdoings concerning borders should be totally ignored.[53]

6. RESOLUTION OF TERRITORIAL DISPUTES

If territory is a major source of wars, the prevention and resolution of territorial disputes become important for achieving peace in general.[54] Of course, if territorial disputes resulted merely from history, we could just wait until the historical disputes have been forgotten and eliminate all territorial changes that could then result in territorial disputes later. However, the idea that time is the best healer of territorial disputes is unsatisfactory because territorial disputes seem to be long-standing. Furthermore, it makes territorial changes that might be regarded as inevitable difficult to execute. As George Kennan has argued, 'the national state pattern is not, should not be, and cannot be a fixed and static thing'.[55] In other words, if territorial disputes are difficult to bury or prevent totally, we have to think seriously about their resolution. According to Kennan, this is the task for diplomacy, not for law, for 'law is too abstract, too inflexible and too hard to adjust to the demands of the unpredictable'.[56]

In the post-Cold War international society, however, there seems to be a firm belief according to which territorial disputes should be resolved on the basis of international norms. Yet, norms as such do not make territorial questions easy to resolve since both the meaning and the significance of the norms might be contested. But if there exists a consensus between the parties about the implementation of rules and norms of international law and morality, the prospect of transferring a disputed territory and resolving the conflict peacefully will increase.[57] Anyway, mutually agreed borders are likely to be more legitimate and thus more durable than borders that have been imposed.[58]

Most of the contemporary international norms sustain the territorial status quo, independently of what it is.[59] Along with general prescriptions of international law that shield the territory of a state by emphasizing its integrity, and the finality and stability of international boundaries, the most important norms regulating territorial disputes in a European context are those of the CSCE (now the OSCE), agreed at the Helsinki meeting of 1975.[60] The CSCE process reflected especially the concern of the Soviet Union to stabilize the territorial status quo in Europe. Hence, the norms of the CSCE stress the inviolability of borders, and states pledged not to make territorial demands to each other. Accordingly, peaceful changes of borders are not excluded but they should occur only on the basis of mutual agreement.

The emergence of territorial disputes after the end of the Cold War has raised the question as to whether the status quo can survive and whether current norms of international law and the CSCE, especially, are sufficient to manage the difficulties posed by the territorial questions or whether the disputes will just blow up violently.[61] Some people feel that the time has come for a general review of borderlands and boundaries in Europe,[62] but the principles on which such a review should be based are not easy to share. It is doubtful if general formulas of legitimate borders can be found, such as borders based on natural frontiers, self-determination or historically just borders. The theory of natural frontiers is fallible, because there can hardly be any objective way to define natural frontiers. Self-determination is very much debated, because it raises fears of fragmentation and the principle is difficult to execute.[63] Historically just borders are almost always contested by the question, which decisive moment in history established borders for all time?

Because a normative conception of just borders has been difficult to achieve, theories of conflict resolution usually emphasize a pragmatic approach. According to them conflict resolution must build on the principle of voluntary consent and a solution should not be imposed. It aims at transcending the incompatibilities as they are perceived by the parties themselves. The role of third parties remains to facilitate the solution by helping to create congruent perceptions and to harmonize principles, but they should not impose any solution. Various theories of conflict resolution suggest means to achieve a mutually acceptable solution.[64] A.O. Cukwurah contends that 'direct negotiations between disputing parties seem to offer the widest opportunity for reaching an effective settlement' in territorial disputes.[65] Because of the intransigence of popular sentiments attached to territory, such negotiations are often most fruitful when they involve only the highest level of decision-making.

There is no reason to feel that a settlement of territorial disputes would always be an impossible task. Neither does every change of borders necessarily lead to future conflicts and wars. There are several historical cases of a successful resolution of territorial conflict or just examples when historical changes of borders are simply not disputed. According to the statistics, territorial disputes are no more difficult to resolve than some other types of disputes.[66] But by the same token it can be stressed that conflict resolution practices do not necessarily lead to a successful solution, especially when parties see the dispute in competitive terms. So long as states stick to rigid conceptions of sovereignty and territorial integrity, resolution of territorial disputes is difficult and their military potential can remain high.

An often suggested model for resolving territorial conflicts is based on status quo and the improvement of minority rights. It should be clear, however, that minority rights cannot be an answer to territorial disputes when the claims are historical. Instead, historical disputes should be resolved by developing a common understanding of history and then resolving the question of what history means in the present-day situation. Historical rights, if they are valid, can be taken into account in different ways. A revindication of territory is one but not the only way to overcome historical injustices.[67] In other words, compromises on territorial disputes do not necessarily include changes of border, but from the perspective of problem-solving, the possibility should not be ruled out.[68]

7. CONCLUSIONS

The purpose of this chapter has been to discuss theories of territorial conflict. It was pointed out that before we can construct a theory of territorial disputes we should investigate their nature, which seems to be more complex and fluid than has usually been assumed. In every respect, theories of territorial dispute have to be historically as well as spatially connected. There is no single theory of territorial conflicts but every conflict has a variety of different causes. Traditionally, power relations has been the most important variable in explaining territorial disputes and especially territorial changes. However, the degree of saliency of territorial disputes may also depend on international norms that regulate the issue. We also need to take a closer look at the processes of interest formation since it is too often assumed that states value territory only for strategic or economic purposes rather than because of historical affiliation or for reasons of experienced injustice.

Theories of the causes of territorial conflict affect the ways we try to deal with them. Prevention rather than resolution has been traditionally the dominant attitude towards territorial disputes. But territorial disputes can hardly be eliminated entirely. If we think that conflict is a natural phenomenon and that territoriality in human life cannot easily be avoided, the focus should be laid on procedures which help to resolve them. Discussion and mutual argumentation which aim at problem-solving could possibly be trusted much more than is often dared.

This book will concentrate on historical territorial disputes. It will be asked, what are the causes of the saliency of historically-based border disputes? Why do some historical changes of borders not evolve into territorial disputes even if power relations change? Alternatively, how do states learn to live with imposed borders? This question, it is believed, can be approached on the basis of the following case studies and their comparison.

NOTES

1. Ladis Kristof, 'Frontiers and Boundaries', *Annals of the Association of American Geographers*, vol. 49, no 3, 1959, p. 278.
2. J.R.V. Prescott, *Political Frontiers and Boundaries* (London: Allen & Unwin 1987).
3. Quincy Wright, *A Study of War* (Chicago: Chicago University Press 1965 [1942]), p. 772.
4. Alan J. Day (ed.), *Border and Territorial Disputes* (2nd edition) (Harlow: Longman 1987), pp. 1–2.
5. See e.g. Colin Williams and Stephen Williams, 'Issues of Peace and Security in Contemporary Europe', in Colin Williams (ed.), *The Political Geography of the New World Order* (London: Belhaven Press 1993), p. 127.
6. Gary Goertz and Paul Diehl, *Territorial Changes and International Conflict* (London: Routledge 1992), p. 20.
7. Alexander B. Murphy, 'Historical Justification for Territorial Claims', *Annals of the Association of American Geographers*, vol. 80, no. 4, 1990, p. 531.

8. See e.g. Marc Weller, 'The International Response to the Dissolution of the Socialist Federal Republic of Yugoslavia', *The American Journal of International Law,* vol. 86, no. 3, 1992, pp. 569–607, p. 606.

9. See e.g. István Deák ,' Uncovering Eastern Europe's Dark Histor', *Orbis,* vol. 34, no. 1, 1990, pp. 51–66; Robert Jervis, 'The Future of World Politics. Will It Resemble the Past?', *International Security* vol. 16, no. 3, 1991/92, pp. 39–73 and Peter Sugar, 'Quo Vadis Eastern Europe?', *Nationalities Paper,* vol. 22, no. 1, 1994, pp. 35–48.

10. George Curzon, *Frontiers* (Oxford: Clarendon Press 1908), p. 53.

11. Paul Diehl, 'What They Are Fighting For. The Importance of Issues in International Conflict Research', *Journal of Peace Research,* vol. 29, no. 2, 1991, pp. 333–44, p. 342.

12. Robert Mandel, 'Roots of the Modern Interstate Border Dispute', *Journal of Conflict Resolution,* vol. 24, no. 3, 1980, pp. 427–54.

13. See Richard Mansbach and John Vasquez, *In Search of Theory. A New Paradigm for Global Politics* (New York: Columbia University Press 1981).

14. James N. Rosenau, 'Pre-theories and Theories of Foreign Policy', in *The Scientific Study of Foreign Policy* (New York: The Free Press 1971).

15. See e.g. Morton Deutsch, *The Resolution of Conflict. Constructive and Destructive Processes* (New Haven: Yale Univesity Press 1973), p. 15.

16. Friedrich Kratochwil et al., *Peace and Disputed Sovereignty. Reflections on Conflict over Territory* (Lanham: University Press of America 1985), p. 53.

17. Kratochwil et al. (1985), p. 27.

18. Robert Sack, *Human Territoriality* (Cambridge: Cambridge University Press 1986).

19. John Ruggie, 'Territoriality and Beyond: Problematizing Modernity in International Relations', *International Organization,* vol. 47, no. 1, 1993, pp. 139–74.

20. For such a theory, see Robert Ardrey, *The Territorial Imperative* (London: Collins 1967).

21. See David Knight, 'Identity and Territory: Geographical Perspectives on Nationalism and Regionalism', *Annals of the Association of American Geographers,* vol. 72, no. 4, 1982, pp. 514–31.

22. Jean Gottmann, *The Significance of Territory* (Charlottesville: The University Press of Virginia 1973).

23. See Joseph Camilleri and Jim Falk, *The End of Sovereignty? The Politics of a Shrinking and Fragmenting World* (Aldershot: Edward Elgar 1992) and Alan S. Milward et al., *The Frontier of National Sovereignty. History and Theory 1945–1992* (London: Routledge 1993).

24. John Herz, *International Politics in the Atomic Age* (New York: Columbia University Press 1959) and Herz, 'The Territorial State Revisited. Reflections on the Future of the Nation-State', in James Rosenau (ed.), *International Politics and Foreign Policy* (New York: Free Press 1968).

25. Norman Angell, *The Great Illusion* (London: Heineman 1914).

26. Marcel Merle, *The Sociology of International Relations* (Leamington: Berg 1987), p. 121.

27. Susan Strange, 'States, Firms and Diplomacy', *International Affairs,* vol. 68, no. 1, 1992, pp. 1–15, p. 7.

28. Richard Rosecrance, *The Rise of the Trading State. Commerce and Conquest in the Modern World* (New York: Basic Books 1986).

29. For this kind of view, see e.g. Johan Galtung, 'A Structural Theory of Integration', *Journal of Peace Research,* vol. 5, no. 4, 1968, pp. 375–95.

30. Peter Liberman, 'Spoils of the Conquest', *International Security,* vol. 18, no. 2, 1993, pp. 125–53.

31. See F.S. Northedge and M.D. Donelan, *International Disputes. The Political Aspects* (London: Europa 1971) and David Welch, *Justice and the Genesis of War* (Cambridge: Cambridge University Press 1993).

32. See for instance Tägil (coord.) (1977) and Goertz and Diehl (1992).

33. The international state, and individual levels come from Kenneth Waltz, *Man, the State and War* (New York: Columbia University Press 1955). For the importance of dyadic pairs see e.g. Neil Richardson, Charles Kegley and Ann Agnew, 'Symmetry and Reciprocity as

Characteristics of Dyadic Foreign Policy Behaviour', *Social Science Quarterly*, vol. 62, no.1, 1981, pp. 128–38.

34. Robert Gilpin, *War and Change in World Politics* (Princeton: Princeton University Press 1983).

35. Evan Luard, 'Introduction', in Evan Luard (ed.) *The International Regulation of Boundary Disputes* (London: Thames and Hudson 1970), p. 12.

36. Nicolas Spykman and Abbie Rollins, 'Geographic Objectives in Foreign Policy', *American Political Science Review*, vol. 33, no. 3, 1939, pp. 391–410.

37. Mandel (1980).

38. See Erich Weede, 'Nation–Environment Relations as Determinants of Hostilities Among Nations', *The Papers of Peace Science Society* (International), vol. 20, 1980, pp. 67–90 and Mandel (1980); for a contrary view on this hypothesis see Kratochwil et al. (1985).

39. Mandel (1980).

40. See William Dixon, 'Democracy and the Peaceful Settlement of International Conflict', *American Political Science Review*, vol. 88, no. 1, 1994, pp. 14–20.

41. It can be remarked that power should not be conceived only in terms of military power. Neo-Marxist theory can be seen as an economic variant of the deterministic power–political view. According to a crude neo-Marxist theory, organized space represents anything more than a reflection of the social relations of production, and neo-Marxists tend to view the territorial system and its changing state borders as a consequence of the capital circulation and accumulation. For neo-Marxist interpretations of territorial organization see Immanuel Wallerstein, *The Modern World-System* (San Diego: The Academic Press 1974) and R.J. Johnston, J. O. Loughlin and P.J. Taylor, 'The Geography of Violence and Premature Death: A World-Systems Approach', in Raimo Väyrynen in collaboration with Dieter Senghaas and C. Schmidt (eds), *The Quest for Peace. Transcending Collective Violence and War Among Societies, Cultures and States* (Beverly Hills: Sage 1987).

42. Friedrich Ratzel, *Politische Geographie* (München: von R. Oldenburg 1923 [1908]).

43. Nazli Choucri and Robert North, *Nations in Conflict. National Growth and International Violence* (San Francisco: W.H. Freeman 1975).

44. See e.g. Mandel (1980); Rosecrance (1986) and Arie M. Kacowicz, *Explaining Zones of Peace: Democracies as Satisfied Powers?* Paper prepared for Presentation at the XVth World Congress of IPSA, August 21–25, Berlin. On irredentism, see Naomi Chazan (ed.), *Irredentism and International Politics* (Boulder: Lynne Rienner 1991).

45. See Jack Snyder, *Myths of Empire. Domestic Politics and International Ambition* (Ithaca: Cornell University Press 1991).

46. See e.g. Ardrey (1969).

47. See e.g. Robert Jervis, *Perception and Misperception in International Relations* (Princeton: Princeton University Press 1976) and Michael Dillon, 'Thatcher and the Falklands', in Richard Little and Steve Smith (eds), *Belief Systems in International Relations* (Oxford: Basil Blackwell 1986).

48. Goertz and Diehl (1992).

49. See e.g. Richard Hartshorne, 'Political Geography in the Modern World', *Journal of Conflict Resolution*, vol. 4, no. 1, 1960, pp. 52–66 and Michael Mann, *The Sources of Social Power*, Volume II (Cambridge: Cambridge University Press 1993), p. 258.

50. Norman Hill, *Claims to Territory in International Law and Relations* (Greenwood Press, Westport 1976 [1945]), p. 35.

51. Murphy (1990), p. 537.

52. See Weede (1973), p. 71.

53. See Murphy (1990).

54. See John Vasquez, *The War Puzzle* (Cambridge: Cambridge University Press 1993).

55. George Kennan, *American Diplomacy 1900–1950* (Chicago: The University of Chicago Press 1951).

56. Kennan (1951), p. 98.

57. See Arie M. Kacowicz, 'The Problem of Peaceful Territorial Change', *International Studies Quarterly*, vol. 38. no. 2, 1994, pp. 219–54.

58. See Kjell-Åke Nordquist, 'Peace After War. On Conditions of Durable Inter-State Boundary Agreements', *Reports of the Department of Peace and Conflict Research*, no. 34, (Uppsala: Uppsala University 1992).

59. See e.g. A.O. Cukwurah, *The Settlement of Boundary Disputes in International Law* (Manchester: Manchester University Press 1966) and Evan Luard, 'Conclusions', in Luard (1970).

60. *European Conference on Security and Cooperation. The Final Act* (1975).

61. See e.g. Carl Jakobsen, 'On the Search for a New Security Order: "The Inviolability of Borders": Prescription of Peace or War?', *European Security*, vol. 1, no. 1, pp. 50–58 and Pavel Baev, 'The Principle of Inviolability of Borders Will Have to Be Rejected', *New Times*, no. 37, 1993, pp. 25–7.

62. See Michel Foucher, 'The New Maps of Europe. Fresh or Old Perspectives?', in Carl Grundy-Warr (ed.), *Eurasia. World Boundaries*, vol. 3 (London: Routledge 1994), p. 70.

63. See e.g. Amitai Etzioni, 'The Evils of Self-Determination', *Foreign Policy*, no. 89, 1992, pp. 21–35.

64. See especially Kratochwil et al. (1985) and Luard (1970). For conflict resolution in general, see e.g. Deutsch (1973); John Burton, *Conflict: Resolution and Prevention* (London: Macmillan 1990); Raimo Väyrynen (ed.), *New Directions in Conflict Theory. Conflict Resolution and Conflict Transformation* (London: Sage 1991) and Dennis J. D. Sandele and Hugo van der Merwe (eds), *Conflict Resolution Theory and Practice. Integration and Application* (Manchester: Manchester University Press 1993).

65. Cukwurah (1966), p. 230.

66. See e.g. M.D. Donelan and M.J. Grieve, *International Disputes, Case Histories 1945–1970* (London: Europa Publications 1973); Richard Butterworth and M. Scranton, *Managing Interstate Conflict 1945–74: Data with Synopses* (Pittsburgh: University Center for International Studies, University of Pittsburg, 1976); Hugh Miall, *The Peacemakers. Peaceful Settlement of Disputes since 1945* (Hampshire: MacMillan 1992) and Kacowicz (1994).

67. See Jeremy Waldron, 'Superseding Historic Injustice', *Ethics*, vol. 103, no. 1, 1992, pp. 4–28; Gidon Gottlieb, 'Nation against State. New Approaches to Ethnic Conflicts and the Decline of Sovereignty', (New York: Council on Foreign Relations Press 1993), p. 47.

68. In another context I have developed this theme at greater length. See Tuomas Forsberg, *Territorial Disputes and the Possibility of Peaceful Change* (Unpublished paper, Forthcoming).

3. Constructing Territories, Boundaries and Regional Identities

Anssi Paasi

This chapter examines both conceptually and empirically the construction of territories, boundaries and regional identities. The aim is to consider the relation of borders to the social and historical construction of territories. It will be argued that such a viewpoint is more fruitful in understanding changing attitudes towards borders, identities of border areas, and conflicts over territories than the approaches of traditional political geography which have rather ahistorically concentrated on borderlines and border landscapes as empirical contexts or points of contacts between territorial power structures.[1]

Boundaries have always carried a special significance in *political geography* – Peter Taylor for example regards the border as perhaps the crucial concept in this branch of geography.[2] Yet, traditional geographical research concerned with borders has often been regarded as limited in scope and empirical in nature. This may be connected partly with the fact that political geography carries a certain 'risk of subjectivity' with it, and part of the lack of theoretical discussion may also be attributable to the belief that each border is a unique case, so that generalizations will not be particularly fruitful.[3] Thus, the state of research can be seen as unsatisfactory, and increasing demands have indeed been expressed recently that borders should be understood as the spatial outcomes of various societal processes and not simply as empirically observable phenomena.[4]

An attempt in this direction will be made below when outlining new points of departure for the geographical study of borders. The key argument is that boundaries may be simultaneously historical, natural, cultural, political, economic, or symbolic phenomena and each of these dimensions may be exploited in diverging ways in the construction of territoriality. Instead of discussing boundaries as mere empirical pheno- mena that hinder or support interaction, they can be interpreted as manifestations of *socio-spatial consciousness*. By this is meant collective forms of consciousness and ideologies, which have developed in the course of the history of a specific territorial unit, and which cannot thus be reduced to the ideas of single individuals living in some specific period of time. Socio-spatial consciousness is an abstraction which aims to conceptualize the social and historical construction of spatial (and social) demarcations. It points to the socialization into various territorial demar- cations and the adoption of territorial identities.

By stressing the role of socio-spatial consciousness, we can better see the significance of historical borders that might otherwise be easily disregarded by geographers who see the world from the perspective of the present day.[5] As Yi-Fu Tuan has put it, 'to know a place is also to know the past'.[6] Even if the physical characteristics of an ancient boundary have disappeared, the socio-spatial consciousness 'stretches' an individual actor as part of the continuity that a territorial community constitutes. Through various institutional practices it provides one basis for the identity of the actors. These territorial identities emerge from tradition and collective memory that always have a link with the community.[7]

1. REGIONAL TRANSFORMATION AND BORDER AREAS

From the perspective of everyday life of most European peoples it has for a long time been common to interpret territorial structures as if they were relatively stable.[8] This illusion of stability, however, seems to have vanished. For many discussants it has become obvious that where nations or ethnic minorities and majorities cannot live together, the result is the displacement of borders, people or both.[9] Seldom have such changes occurred peacefully. During the present century the displacements have typically taken place through violence, which has led to forced migration, the loss and reconstruction of identities or, at the extreme, the death of masses of people. In recent years the struggle over social and political power has led to violence, particularly in the territories of the former Soviet Union and Yugoslavia, and contested aims to redefine and signify the boundaries and contents of social space with new cultural and political terms, i.e. to transform the contents of socio-spatial consciousness.

The territorial system of states, nations and various administrative and cultural regions has been, however, in continual transformation throughout history. This transformation has reflected economic, political, military and administrative passions, evaluations and decisions made by the rulers and various social groups of those societies. Hence territories are not eternal: they are social and historical products both in their physical materiality and in their socio-cultural meanings. They emerge as a result of diverging institutional practices (within politics, administration, economy, culture), exist for some time and disappear as part of regional transformations. This appears to hold good in the case of sub-state territories as well as in the case of nation-states and supra-state entities.[10]

The current political map of the world simultaneously displays both stability and dynamism. Stable boundaries exist where states have signed and honoured treaties recognizing their sovereignty and where various social groupings agree on the delimitation and demarcation of a common border. Where the political situation is more unstable, the boundaries and their locations are typically potential sources of territorial conflicts and border disputes.[11] In present-day Europe the roles of boundaries are changing as a consequence of both economic and political integration and the collapse of the strict division between 'East' and 'West'. These changes seem to open up spaces as well as to create needs to redefine the boundaries of some territories and the territorial identities of border areas. Boundaries are once again back on the agenda.

The key question concerning the existence of regions in territorial transformation is the maintenance of a correspondence between the physical and social boundaries of territories. The production and reproduction of territorial identities occurs through contested efforts over the right to define specific identity units and to locate boundaries between them. The struggle over a redefinition of space is always an expression of the restructuring of economic, political and administrative practices but also of the restructuring of the contents of social consciousness, inasmuch as one obvious aim of various ethno-regional groups is to establish a territorial counterpart for social boundaries.[12]

The various elements of territorial identity are always shifting, but their transformation can undergo very different time spans.[13] Whereas the economic orientation in border areas can change relatively rapidly, cultural traditions prevailing in border areas usually take a much longer time: they may be hidden for some time in the course of history and be revived again as a consequence of local or national activism. Undoubtedly, one such cultural factor is the history of the locality, which can be different from the history of its inhabitants.

Territorial transformation takes place simultaneously on all spatial scales, i.e. at the local, regional, national and global level. Although territorial identities are often organized hierarchically, this hierarchy may be seriously challenged as a consequence of boundary changes. For example, for different people Vyborg may be a Finnish town or a Russian town, but some people rely more clearly on an autonomous identity of the town which is essentially multicultural and one that bears a tradition of having belonged to different states in the course of history.[14]

Also the role of the border and possible disputes over it may be viewed differently at the national and local level. The location of a border may be of major importance to the states involved but of minor importance to people and places located in the immediate vicinity of the boundary, or vice versa.[15] Typically it is thought that borders have much more symbolic value for states than for local communities. It is sometimes felt that boundaries are barriers for the local communities and they exist only for the sake of geographical centres. On the other hand, borders can be functional for the local communities living around borders if border areas develop into vital contact zones. Tight local and regional ties can evolve across the boundary in a process of regionalization. Thus, a borderland is not necessarily a political, economic or cultural periphery but can grow into an important centre of human activities. In many places cooperation rather than conflict characterizes border areas.[16] Against this background, Julian Minghi has suggested that the study of border landscapes can fruitfully benefit from shifting the analytical focus from conflict to harmony.[17] Although this perspective does not fit well with most disputed borders, a contested border area can also be transformed into a cooperative zone.[18]

2. THE INSTITUTIONALIZATION OF TERRITORIES AND THE CONSTRUCTION OF IDENTITIES ON VARIOUS SPATIAL SCALES

The construction of territories of various kinds is part of the continuous change or transformation taking place in the spatial system. This formation and dissolution of territories is taking place all the time and at varying spatial levels, being observable just as well at the local, regional or national level as it is on a broader scale (e.g. Europe as a whole).[19] Also, the construction of territories carries with it many historical relics, so that the formation of the borders and the process by which this takes place will differ markedly in significance, depending on whether it is examined from the viewpoint of an individual inhabitant of the border area or that of the political history of the territorial entity in question.

National boundaries may be regarded as part of a project by which the physical and symbolic construction and maintenance of the territories concerned and their internal social integration takes place.[20] The ideological foundation for this process is usually nationalism, through which the physical and political territory of a nation is transformed and expressed symbolically as a cultural state. Nationalism has a dual outlook with respect to space.[21] It looks inwards in order to unify the nation and its constituent territory; it looks outwards to divide one nation and territory from another. As Colin Williams and Anthony Smith have argued, whatever else nationalism may be, it is always concerned with a struggle over the control of land; it is equally a form of constructing and interpreting social space.[22]

The process of nation-building aims at binding the state and its inhabitants together. Nation-building is a metaphorical concept which should not be interpreted mechanically. Crucial instruments in the nation-building process are the socialization mechanisms developed by the state, particularly the school system, through which new generations can be integrated into a certain national community, as members of a 'we'.[23] We can think that social consciousness manifests itself materially in texts, maps, drawings and memorials, for instance, which reveal and strengthen the element of historical continuity in social consciousness.

As far as the parameters of regional transformation are concerned, the construction of the territories on different spatial scales can be labelled as the *institutionalization of regions*. In principle all territories emerge through the process of institutionalization, which refers to the process during which specific territorial units – on various spatial scales – emerge and become established parts of the regional system in question and the socio-spatial consciousness prevailing in the society. All societies are themselves being simultaneously transformed as part of the larger context, as recent tendencies in Europe aptly indicate. Territories are hence not 'organisms', that would develop, have a life-span or evolution in the manner that some biological metaphors – so typical in Western social thought – would suggest. Rather in this framework territories are understood as being a complex synthesis or manifestation of objects, patterns, processes, various social practices and inherent power relations that are derived from the simultaneous interaction between different levels of social processes.[24] Through the institutionalization process and inherent struggles the territorial units in question 'receive' their boundaries, their symbols and identities which distinguish the territory in question from other territories.

From this process we can abstract four stages: the formation of the territorial, symbolic and institutional shape and the establishment of an entity in the regional system and social consciousness of the society.[25] As regards the concrete territories, the order of these stages can vary. As far as the role of boundaries is concerned, both the territorial, symbolic and institutional shaping are significant in the construction of the physical and symbolic roles of boundaries and the establishment of boundaries in various social practices, such as politics, economics and administration, for instance. The existence of boundaries is thus important in the creation of territorial identities and they are especially significant in the case of local border landscapes.

During its institutionalization a region achieves a specific identity (the identity of the region), which cannot be reduced merely to the regional consciousness (regional identity) of the people living in the territory or to some symbolic values.[26] The identity of the region includes the production and reproduction of regional consciousness in the inhabitants and other people living outside a territory and, further, material and symbolic features of the region as part of the ongoing process of social reproduction. This points to the fact that the formation of social identity and social reproduction are one and the same.[27]

Since territorial identities are always constituted on the basis of social, cultural and/or physical demarcation (i.e. boundaries are an essential element in the construction of identities), in regional transformation some of these identities, their material and symbolic base, can be represented to be in danger because 'their' identities are expanding into 'our' territory. This situation can create territorial conflicts between various territorial entities whether they are states or some supra- or sub-state territories. This also makes visible the connection between territory-building and power relations: some individuals, groups and classes are always more active in the production of territories and identities while most people are rather reproducers. These activists can exploit the elements of historical experience, tradition and ethnicity, for instance, in mobilizing collective feelings and action.

Language and its expressions are often employed to depict territorial identities. Probably all languages contain some emotionally laden expressions illuminating the relationship between human beings and the ties with their environment, native localities and native country.[28] In diverging local contexts there usually exist locally coloured vocabularies of identities and the adoption of them is part of the territory-building process on various spatial scales. Naming – giving a name to someone or something – always means a withdrawal from a troubling anonymity; it means a settled position in the culture's identity matrix. Cohen and Kliot point out that names are part of the process of attaching meaning to one's surroundings.[29] The power of place names in the historical construction of territorial identities has become obvious in the recent dispute over the right to use the concept of 'Macedonia' in naming one part of the territory of the former Yugoslavia. The debate over the area is a fitting illustration of the fact that territorial identities can be based on a variety of even contradictory arguments emerging from history, ethnicity, language, and so on. Similar disputes over territorial symbols and boundaries have occurred in the case of former Soviet boundary areas, e.g. the Kurile Islands/Northern Territories, Kaliningrad/Königsberg or Moldova/Moldavia/Bessarabia.

The discussion regarding the socio-cultural construction of socio-spatial communities or territories will lead us to evaluate the role of language and discourse in the social construction of spatial demarcations and boundaries: how the ideas regarding 'us' and 'them' or the 'other' are created, signified and represented. In fact, the question is about an analysis of signification, i.e. how economic, political and cultural processes become part of the social construction and reproduction of communities; how landscapes, heritage, cultural products and rhetoric, metaphors and images are exploited in this process.

The symbolic construction of space, territoriality and boundaries is based on a dialectic between two 'languages', the language of integration and the language of difference, which emerge and are reproduced in various social practices. The former aims at homogenizing the contents of spatial experience and it includes, typically, narratives of 'our' history, culture, heritage, and so on. The latter strives to distinguish this homogenized experience from other territorial groupings. The use of this language involves the construction of social distinctions between 'we' and the 'others' and a spatial distinction between inside/outside or here/there.[30]

3. THE CHANGING REPRESENTATIONS OF THE FINNISH–RUSSIAN BOUNDARY

As a brief illustration of the construction of socio-spatial consciousness we will analyse how the Finnish–Russian boundary has been represented in the symbolization and signification of the cultural and political differences between the two states. This boundary is an interesting example of the social construction of boundaries and identities. It is located in the cultural area where Western and Eastern cultures meet each other and its location has changed many times as a consequence of territorial disputes. As such it is a fitting illustration of the transformation of the Europe of territories.

From the viewpoint of the institutionalization of the Finnish territory, the existence of the Finnish–Russian boundary may be logically interpreted in a historical framework which consists of four stages: 1) the period of the autonomous Grand Duchy of Finland, 2) the gaining of independence in 1917 and the period between the two World Wars, 3) the post-World War II period extending up to the disintegration of the Soviet Union and, finally, 4) the post-Soviet period. During these periods several representations of the border, based on natural, cultural or political features, have appeared simultaneously while some of them have been dominant.

The Idea of Historical Boundary

The Finnish State gained her independence in 1917 but the boundaries of the new state had already been drawn fairly clearly in people's minds well before that. During the rise of the Finnish nationalist movement, for example, the maps and textbooks used during the Grand Duchy period incorporated both the boundaries themselves and the notion of Finland as a distinct territorial unit. This caused annoyance in Russian circles, especially during the oppression years.[31] One might say, therefore, that the geography of Finland or the country's territorial existence and identity, began to represent itself more and more clearly in the socio-spatial consciousness of the Finnish people.[32] This boundary was mainly *historical*: it was an expression of the rising self-consciousness after a long period of Swedish and Russian rule. Even if the symbolic existence of the border was clearly realized, in practice the border between Finland and Russia was very much an open one during the 19th century and there was intensive interaction across the boundary. It can be argued that a formal border was created in 1859 when some customs stations were established to control goods traffic between Finland and Russia.[33] Nevertheless, these stations were rather local manifestations of the increasing control over space than expressions of boundaries dividing the space. In a way, they were an expression of the interaction between states in the course of a slow development of a frontier to a boundary.

The Idea of Political Boundary

During the autonomy period the border between Finland and Russia was above all legal. In the second phase, the rise of the socialist Soviet Russia and the establishment of Finnish independence were the events that triggered the drawing of a clear *symbolic* and closed *political* boundary in the east.[34] For the new independent State of Finland this demarcation was an essential part of the nation-building process of the new state.

The territorial aim of the boundary reinforcement in the 1920s and 1930s was therefore the national integration within Finland. The formation of a national territory and the conferring of symbolic value on it may involve conflicting motives and aims on the part of individuals or groups,[35] so that a major part of the process of producing a nationalistic ideology consists of presenting the state of the nation as being as united as possible and pointing to clear differences (and boundaries) with respect to other territories.[36] In Finland a great effort was made, in the course of developing the peripheral border areas and improving the living conditions of their inhabitants, to foster a spirit of nationalism and increase the political reliability of the population. These activities are a good expression of the *nationalization of peripheries* in order to create an overall national integration. At the same time it was difficult for the local people to comprehend why their rights which once extended fairly freely across the border now had to be curtailed.[37]

The Idea of Cultural Boundary

A typical feature to emerge as a result of independence was the construction of a *cultural* boundary between Finland and the Soviet Union. Although it was customary to make mention of the Eastern roots of the Finnish people in a historical sense (e.g. linguistically), there now emerged a need to create an image of Finland as a Western country, often as the last outpost of Western Europe. The justification given for this Western role was usually Finland's long connections with Sweden and Central Europe.

The intensifying physical and psychological separation from the new Soviet Union was one part of the general international geopolitical trend. Relations in the 1920s and 1930s were liberally tainted with visions of the Soviet Union as the hereditary enemy of Finland and of Finland as the last bastion of Christianity and Western ideals. The eastern border gradually became a mythical and symbolic expression of a historical and evidently eternal opposition between the two states.[38] This opposition was actively implemented in the collective memory of successive generations, e.g. through the textbooks used in schools.

The Idea of Natural and Artificial Boundaries

Whereas one tendency prevailing in Finland was the construction of social integration within the existing boundaries of the state and cultural and political integration towards the West, simultaneously there existed a tendency to achieve a cultural and natural boundary based on the physical geography of the area that extended far across traditional boundaries to Russian Karelia. The territorial aim was to transform 'our territory' to include 'us there', i.e. the Finnish-speaking Karelian population, and hence to create a Greater Finland.

In the same geopolitical spirit justifications were sought for extensions to Finland's territory in the east. One source for such arguments lay in the ideas, first raised in the 19th century, regarding the existence of natural boundaries for Finland, and these were adopted as part of everyday political thinking particularly during the 1920s and 1930s. The question of natural and artificial boundaries, so important in the tradition of political geography,[39] now began to emerge ever more clearly as an aspect of Finnish political geography, and soon came to dominate the terminology of this branch of geography in Finland.[40] Now it was thought that the natural resource base provided a country with its natural boundaries, while human activities provided the artificial boundaries. In this light the eastern border of Finland was commonly interpreted as artificial. This line of thought reached its culmination in 1941, when these geopolitical ideas were put forward as a 'scientific' justification for Finnish territorial expansion, at the moment when the troops engaged in the Continuation War were advancing over the old boundary to occupy the Russian areas in Eastern Karelia.[41]

The Ideological Boundary Between East and West

The new geopolitical order that arose out of World War II meant a vast upheaval as far as the regional integrity of Europe was concerned. A new worldwide spatial scale could be distinguished in the context of international conflicts as a result of the East–West dichotomy. The world gradually separated out into three parts: 'ours', 'theirs', and a set of disputed areas which had no obvious 'owner' or reference group.[42] Looked at on a world scale, Finland undeniably belonged to the disputed, indeterminately neutral camp.

During the Cold War the border between Finland and the Soviet Union was the longest boundary between the leading socialist state and a Western capitalist state. In spite of the neutral status of Finland it was still a typical illustration of an ideological boundary although its effects differed from the pre-war era. On the one hand Finland lost certain essential territorial, cultural and historical, elements of her Eastern character and of the Eastern legacy but on the other hand, the Eastern, political presence in Finnish society was strengthened. Nevertheless, in Finland the boundary was defined symbolically, running between East and West, rich and poor, democracy and totalitarianism.[43]

The Post-War Soviet Representation

Whereas the boundary has been typically represented in Finnish ideology as 'the outpost of the West', the interpretation given by Soviet historians to the history of the border area has been at least as ideological: in that

Karelia was for long regarded as an outpost of Russia against attacks from Sweden.[44]

The new boundary with Finland and the areas that Finland ceded as a consequence of World War II were also objects of redefinition in the Soviet Union. This redefinition took place, at first, in the form of concrete activities, such as the settlement policy, according to which the dominant part of the population of Russian Karelia finally consisted of non-Karelian people. But, the annexed areas had also to be integrated or written into the common discourse and practice constituting the territory. Both the loss and the gain of the territory had to be legitimized for the inhabitants of Finland and the Soviet Union. The signification of new spaces and landscapes occurred through the creation of new symbols of territoriality. In the case of the former Soviet Union these were typically the symbols of the socialist ideology, which manifested themselves in the form of monuments and statues, as well as in the renaming of social space by using the names of the key-figures of socialist ideology as a basis for this. This ideological landscape was a concrete and constant manifestation of state power at the level of everyday life.[45]

The redefinition of territorial space also took place through historical manipulation. One Soviet geographical textbook, published in Finnish in 1950, contains several ideological comments which clearly aim at creating specific 'territorial truths' for the readers. Hence, the areas located to the west and north of Lake Ladoga were now 'returned' to the Soviet Union in 1940 and the boundary of the Soviet Union was moved some twenty kilometres to the west.[46] In fact, the border was moved about one hundred kilometres to the west and the ceded Karelian areas had never been part of the Soviet Union – though they had been a part of Russia, of course.

Maps are undoubtedly among the most important instruments that can be employed in the creation of representations of a specific territorial order of the earth's surface. Maps not only depict but also construct the world and put forward power relations and ideologies.[47] A fitting illustration of the political and ideological exploitation of cartography is an atlas of the history of the Soviet Union, published in 1990.[48] It contains, for example, a map of the most remarkable industrial achievements during 1928–40. In the map the location of the Finnish–Soviet boundary in Karelia is represented as it has been since World War II. The areas that belonged to the Finnish territory during this period are represented as if they belonged to the territory of the Soviet Union. In general, Soviet textbooks and historic maps do not tell the reader anything about the Soviet attack on Finland in autumn 1939 or the Winter War and the Continuation War in general. The examples make it clear that whereas the boundary between Finland and the Soviet Union was taboo on the Finnish side after World War II, its representation was also a difficult problem on the Soviet side.

The Boundary as a Sphere of Contact: Back to a Frontier?

The political and economic changes in Eastern Europe have been crucial also as far as the recent idea of the Finnish–Russian border is concerned. The end of the Cold War has meant a period of rapid economic growth for many border areas located between Eastern and Western Europe. The previously tightly closed boundaries have now developed into *spheres of contact* between countries. Seventy years of almost no transborder activity made areas on both sides of the Finnish–Russian border more dependent on their own national political and economic centres. Although the aim of regional policy in Finland has been to keep rural areas inhabited, the population in the border areas diminished. In Russian Karelia conscious investment and industrial policy led even more clearly to rapid urbanization. In this process more than 2,000 villages became empty and only 18 per cent of the population lives in the rural areas.[49]

After the collapse of the Soviet Union, the interpretation of the roles of the boundary and emerging economic practices between Finland and Russia are clearly at a new stage. It can be argued that now the idea of the border is developing into an interface, a contact surface or even back to the notion of a *frontier* with a new social and economic significance based on personal interaction between traders, and its economic implications are now being realized increasingly extensively on both sides.[50] Many of the local authorities on the Finnish and Russian sides have been ready to play an active role in this, hoping to open up routes and connections in the future and thereby develop the economy of both areas. Nevertheless it is a fact that the border is still a line between two completely different societies and the gap between the standards of living prevailing on each side is among the largest in the world. It is probable that the Finnish–Russian boundary will also be, in the near future, relatively strictly controlled on both sides.

4. GENERATIONAL AND GEOGRAPHICAL ASPECTS OF TERRITORIAL IDENTITIES

Generations and the Changing Experience of Space

Whereas national identities are expressions of general socio-spatial consciousness, at the local level and in daily life the dimensions of identity and the meanings of history and heritage become complicated. The idea of *generation* appears to be useful in understanding some clear differences in territorial identities. Generation provides peoples' spatial consciousness with common cultural elements, identity and frames for interpreting experiences.[51] Yet, regional identities form a continuum across generations, since memory is furnished not only from the recollections of events which an individual has experienced but memories of older associates. Personal histories always include elements of the history of a 'larger self' – family, neighbourhood, locality, nationality[52] – which unites individuals as a part of the histories of these entities.

The idea of generations is of crucial importance in understanding the diverging attitudes towards space when borders have been changed and/ or people migrated.[53] The generations which have experienced their old community, the establishment of a new border and the loss of their home locality may still keep the memories of the old community as part of their territorial identity. Although the older people have tried to transmit their memories of the past, the generations which have not experienced the war clearly live in a socio-spatial context which is characterized and limited by present geopolitical facts. For them the boundary has always been where it is now and they simply have no experience of other situations. Whereas older generations after the war were afraid of the new border, for younger generations it has been a much more neutral phenomenon. Some representatives of younger generations are also well able to analyse this situation, as the following example from the Finnish border commune Värtsilä shows:

> The situation is what it is: the boundary is there and we have had to get used to it. There have not been any problems with this, since it has always been there – for this generation. But the previous generations have a completely different attitude towards it. The most extreme opinions are expressed by those who had to leave all they had and in practice begin from scratch. Isn't this quite a unique situation, that also the inhabitants escaped the occupation? This does not occur all around the world, that people will leave their home region. ...The attitude towards the boundary

is ambiguous. The former generation who have personally experienced the situation and know the effects of the new boundary think consciously that the old days were golden times for Värtsilä, and very often they return to those days. Our generation takes a slightly different attitude. We have the present Värtsilä and we have to struggle on this basis – our views of the world vary somewhat. (A man aged 34 years).[54]

For the refugees who had to move from the ceded areas to inner Finland after the war, it has sometimes been easier to adapt to the new situation, since they could not visit their old homes and thus realize how the landscape beyond the border had become foreign. When the border between Finland and the Soviet Union was opened in the late 1980s, an immediate boom in nostalgic journeys to Karelia ensued, with a total of 1.26 million crossings of the Finnish–Russian border in 1991–92.[55] Most Finns are now familiar with television programmes and newspaper photographs showing former refugees searching the fields of Karelia for their lost homes and past spatial identities which were broken off as a consequence of the war. These were journeys into the past as much as journeys undertaken in the present; they were journeys in time as much as in space.

For the first time since World War II hundreds of old inhabitants of Värtsilä Commune have also visited their old home on the other side of the border. Whereas younger generations are used to the geopolitical fact that the present boundary has been located during their whole lifetime in the same place, older generations still have a strong Utopian identity which is directed to the past lost community. The old Värtsilä community is the one they identify themselves with, not the present one. Many visitors have been of the opinion that they will never go back to Russian Värtsilä: it is no more their place. Their place is old Värtsilä that has been preserved, over the years, deep in the collective memory of the community – this memory has been strengthened over the years in common discussions and in dreaming of 'the return'.[56]

Local and National Experiences on the Border Between East and West

Analytical dichotomy between socio-spatial consciousness at the national level and local experience is important in understanding the nature of the mobilization of people in connection with border disputes. The background for territorial conflicts between states is seldom found in specific local contexts themselves; rather a more general consciousness has to be created of the 'false distinction' between socio-cultural and physical territories and of the need to mobilize 'us' in order to correct this distinction, which can be based on different arguments: tradition, history, ethnicity, language, religion, and so on. Communities which have ceded their land or sovereignty preserve their traditions and experience in their memory and the lost world becomes idealized and sacred,[57] whereas those communities that have received new land or sovereignty strive to symbolize these and internalize them as part of the national and local identities.

It is obvious that many of the representations and meanings that people living elsewhere in a territory attach to the boundary reflect more socio-spatial consciousness than their own experiences. This must be true especially in instances where the boundary is located far away from the context of daily life and experience. Those who live in the border area have a personal contact and experience of the immediate border landscape, and its elements and possible restrictions. In addition they usually have experience of the reactions of those living elsewhere towards the boundary.

As was seen above, during the existence of the Soviet Union the Finnish–Soviet boundary was often represented as an ideological boundary between the capitalist and socialist worlds. The boundary was also represented for tourists as the cultural boundary between West and East. As regards the foreigners and people from Western and Southern Finland, the boundary was a mysterious place during the existence of the Soviet Union. A couple of people that were interviewed in Värtsilä in 1987 described this in the following way:

Especially for tourists, the boundary raises their curiosity. This is clear, so as you know this tourist route is the Route of the Bard and Boundary. During summertime plenty of tourists and foreigners stay here and take photographs of the prohibitory sign. So they are interested in the boundary, but few of them go into the zone without permission. (A man aged 70 years).

They cannot understand how someone can live so near the boundary, a couple of hundred metres from the settlements of the superpower, the Soviet Union. These people are not necessarily foreigners. My friend from military service, for instance, visited us once and when we were walking beside the barbed wire fence, he wanted to go away from it because it sent a cold shiver down his spine. (A man aged 24 years).

The idea that the boundary marks the division between East and West was and still is much more invisible among local people, whether they belong to older or younger generations. This is due to the fact that for them the border is an essential part of daily life and not merely a representation reflecting a wider historically constructed socio-spatial consciousness that prevails in Finnish society. In 1988 one interviewed person expressed this as follows:

> I do not regard this boundary as a boundary between east and west. Of course it is fact that there is a break within two economic systems within two kilometres, a socialist and a capitalist. It is a kind of boundary but I have never seen any other boundary. (A man aged 30 years).

Now, when it has become possible to visit the ceded Karelian areas, it is also possible to get a local perspective of everyday life on the Russian side of the border. Russians who inhabited Värtsilä only after World War II do not have such a historical consciousness of the territory as do the older Finnish generations. In such circumstances the local territorial identity often lies on a thin base, especially if the migration has been involuntary and the land that is settled is not in its natural state.[58] So the new land may feel alien or even hostile. The lack of historical continuity together with ethnic heterogeneity has made it difficult to develop a local identity on the Russian side of the border. But it is a fact that many people who were settled in the Russian areas after the war, and especially their descendants, have in many cases lived there for the whole of their lives and identify themselves as much with these areas as did previous Finnish inhabitants. For those people the pre-war Finnish history of the area had been almost totally unknown and for them the sense of unity across the present border is hard to establish.[59] This fact doubtless makes the distinct features of their local identity stronger than those of the corresponding Finnish Värtsilä.

5. CONCLUSIONS

Even if it can be argued that borders no longer have such a role in distinguishing space and place as they sometimes did before, this is hardly true for the former Soviet Union and Eastern Europe in general. However, the very idea of boundary has been rendered problematic, although it has certainly not been erased. Nevertheless one essential dimension of the territorial transformation still appears to be the perpetual restructuring of various demarcations and boundaries and the struggle over the right and means to define the new ones as part of the control of the territorial space of a state or some sub-state entity.[60]

Markedly different representations and ideological meanings can be attached to the borders that divide nation-states. These may then be exploited in the construction of territorial identities and in the mobilization of people in order to change the locations of boundaries so that various components of social and territorial identities would coincide. Traditionally, boundaries have been important especially for states and their territorial identities, but people living in border areas often develop their own regional or local identities that may look at the boundary more from a cooperative than an antagonistic perspective.

Boundaries make a difference. Social life is full of boundaries which give direction to existence, and which locate that existence. Also the boundaries between nation-states make a difference on the scale of both everyday life and collective national identities. The meanings connected with the latter are rarely expressions of the boundaries or border landscapes themselves, rather they are expressions of tradition, heritage and culture – territorial identity – which is bounded by certain boundaries. The boundaries between nation-states hence receive their meanings in the continual nation-building process, in the social reproduction of the nation-state and in the socialization of the citizens into specific territorial frames. Boundaries can hence be understood profoundly only in a historical and social context. This is also the context that renders the understanding of territorial disputes possible.

NOTES

1. Julian Minghi, 'Boundary Studies in Political Geography', *Annals of the Association of American Geographers*, vol. 53, no. 3, 1963, pp. 407–28.
2. Peter J. Taylor, 'Contra Political Geography', *Tijdschrift voor Economische en Sociale Geografie*, vol. 84, no. 2, 1993, pp. 82–90.
3. J.V.R. Prescott, *The Geography of Frontiers and Boundaries* (Chicago: Aldine 1965), pp. 9, 24 and J.V.R. Prescott, *Political Frontiers and Boundaries* (London: Unwin Hyman 1987), p. 8.
4. Cf. the compendium of articles in Dennis Rumley and Julian V. Minghi (eds), *The Geography of Border Landscapes* (London: Routledge 1991).
5. See Eric Fischer, 'On Boundaries', *World Politics*, vol. 1, no. 2, 1949, pp. 196–222.
6. Yi-Fu Tuan, 'Place: An Experiential Perspective', *The Geographical Review*, vol. 65, no. 2, 1975, pp. 151–65.

7. David Morley and Kevin Robins, 'No Place Like Heimat: Images of Home(land) in European Culture', *New Formations*, no. 12, Winter, 1990, pp. 1–24.

8. Immanuel Wallerstein, *Geopolitics and Geoculture. Essays on the Changing World-System* (Cambridge: Cambridge University Press 1991), p. 49.

9. Pierre Hassner, 'Beyond Nationalism and Internationalism: Ethnicity and World Order', *Survival*, vol. 35, no. 2, 1993, pp. 49–65.

10. Anssi Paasi, 'The Institutionalization of Regions: A Theoretical Framework for Understanding the Emergence of Regions and the Constitution of Regional Identity', *Fennia*, no. 164, 1986, pp. 105–46 and Peter J. Taylor, 'A Theory and Practice of Regions: The Case of Europes', *Environment and Planning D: Society and Space*, vol. 9, no. 2, 1991, pp. 183–95.

11. Stanley Brunn, 'Peacekeeping Missions and Landscapes', in Rumley and Minghi (1991).

12. Frederick Barth, 'Introduction', in F. Barth (ed.), *Ethnic Groups and Boundaries: The Social Organization of Cultural Difference* (London: Allen & Unwin 1969), p. 15.

13. Minghi (1963), p. 414.

14. See Rainer Knapas, 'Viipuri', in Wiipurilainen Osakunta (ed.), *Ikuinen Viipuri. Kaukomieli XV* (Helsinki: Otava 1993).

15. Minghi (1963), p. 415.

16. See e.g. Raimondo Strassoldo and Giovanni Delli Zotti (eds), *Cooperation and Conflict in Border Areas* (Milano: Franco Angeli 1982).

17. Julian V. Minghi, 'From Conflict to Harmony in Border Landscapes', in Rumley and Minghi (1991).

18. See Feliks Gross, *Ethnics in a Borderland. An Inquiry into the Nature of Ethnicity and Reduction of Ethnic Tensions on a One-time Genocide Area* (Westport: Greenwood Press 1978).

19. See Paasi (1986) and Taylor (1991).

20. See Paasi (1986).

21. James Anderson, 'On Theories of Nationalism and the Size of States', *Antipode*, no. 18, 1986, pp. 218–32.

22. Colin Williams and Anthony D. Smith, 'The National Construction of Social Space', *Progress in Human Geography*, vol. 7, no. 4, 1983.

23. Edward F. Bergman, *Modern Political Geography* (Dubuque, Iowa: WBC 1975), pp. 270–274 and Anssi Paasi, 'The Construction of Socio-spatial Consciousness: Geographical Perspectives on the History and Contexts of Finnish Nationalism', *Nordisk Samhällsgeografisk Tidskrift*, no. 15, 1992, pp. 79–100.

24. Michael Dear and Jennifer Wolch, 'How Territory Shapes Social Life', in J. Wolch and M. Dear (eds.), *The Power of Geography* (London: Unwin Hyman 1989), pp. 6–7.

25. Paasi (1986) and Anssi Paasi, 'Deconstructing Regions: Notes on the Scales of Spatial Life', *Environment and Planning* A 23, 1991, pp. 239–56.

26. Paasi (1986).

27. Philip Abrams, *Historical Sociology* (Peth: Pitman Press 1982), p. 262.

28. Paasi (1986).

29. Saul B. Cohen and Nurit Kliot, 'Place-Names in Israel's Ideological Struggle over Administrated Territories', *Annals of the Association of American Geographers*, no. 82, 1992, pp. 653–80.

30. Anssi Paasi, 'Constructing Boundaries, Representing Otherness: The Changing Representations of the Finnish–Russian Border' (Unpublished paper, 1994).

31. Tuomo Polvinen, *Valtakunta ja rajamaa: N. I. Bobrikov Suomen kenraalikuvernöörinä 1894–1904* (Porvoo: WSOY 1984), pp. 200–203.

32. Paasi (1992).

33. Tapio Hämynen, 'Liikkeellä leivän tähden: Raja-Karjalan väestö ja sen toimeentulo 1880–1940', *Historiallisia tutkimuksia*, no. 170 (Tampere: The University of Tampere 1993).

34. Hämynen (1993).

35. Karl W. Deutsch, 'Some Problems in the Study of Nation-Building', in Karl W. Deutsch and William J. Foltz (eds), *Nation-Building* (New York: Atherton Press 1963).

36. John MacLoughlin, 'The Political Geography of Nation-Building and Nationalism in Social Sciences: Structural vs. Dialectical Accounts', *Political Geography Quarterly*, vol. 5, no. 4, 1986, pp. 299–329.
37. Paasi (1994).
38. Anssi Paasi, 'The Rise and Fall of Finnish Geopolitics', *Political Geography Quarterly*, vol. 9, no. 1, 1990, pp. 53–65.
39. Minghi (1963).
40. Paasi (1994).
41. Antti Laine, *Suur-Suomen kahdet kasvot. Itä-Karjalan siviiliväestön asema suomalaisessa miehityshallinnossa 1941–44* (Keuruu: Otava 1982) and Paasi (1990).
42. Peter J. Taylor, 'Geopolitics Revised', *Seminar Papers*, no. 53 (Newcastle: Department of Geography of the University of Newcastle 1988) and Jean Gottmann, *The Significance of Territoriality* (Charlottesville: The University Press of Virginia 1973), p. 143.
43. Whereas before World War II Finland was still frequently regarded geopolitically as one of the Western countries, many post-war accounts of political geography now regarded her as an anomalous case in the world order – and placed her in Eastern Europe. See for example Saul B. Cohen, *Geography and Politics in a Divided World* (London: Methuen 1964).
44. Hannes Sihvo, 'Karjala rajamaana', *Karjalainen viesti*, no. 1, 1992, pp. 104–5.
45. John Pickless, 'Texts, Hermeneutics and Propaganda Maps', in Trevor Barnes and James Duncan (eds), *Writing Worlds* (London: Routledge 1992).
46. Nikolai N. Mihailov, *Kotimaamme kartan ääressä* (Petroskoi: Karjalais-suomalaisen SNT:n Valtion kustannusliike 1950), p. 39.
47. Dennis Wood, *The Power of Maps* (London: Routledge 1991).
48. *Atlas Istorii SSSR* (Moscow, 1990).
49. Eira Varis, 'Gridino ja Virma – kaksi Karjalan kylä', *Terra*, vol. 105, no. 4, 1993, pp. 316–23 and Pekka Nevalainen, 'Karjala 1900–luvulla.', *Terra*, vol. 105, no. 4, 1993, pp. 291–8.
50. Pertti Joenniemi, 'Regionality and the Modernist Script: Tuning into the Unexpected in International Politics', *Occasional Papers*, no. 57 (Tampere: Tampere Peace Research Institute 1994).
51. Paasi (1986) and (1991).
52. Edward Shils, *Tradition* (Chicago: The University of Chicago Press 1981), p. 51.
53. Zdzislaw Mach, *Symbols, Conflict, and Identity* (Albany: State University of New York Press 1993), p. 204.
54. The examples in this article are from the interviews I conducted with both Finnish and Russian inhabitants of Värtsilä Commune, an area that was divided by the new Finnish–Russian boundary after World War II.
55. Liisa Lehto and Senni Timonen, 'Kertomus matkasta kotiin: Karjalaiset vieraina omilla maillaan', *Kalevalaseuran vuosikirja*, no. 72, 1993, pp. 88–105.
56. Paasi (1994).
57. Mach (1993).
58. Ibid., pp. 180–81.
59. This became obvious during my visit to Russian Värtsilä in June 1992.
60. Stanley Brunn, 'The Future of the the Nation-State System', in Peter J. Taylor and J. W. House (eds), *Political Geography: Recent Advances and Future Directions* (London: Croom Helm 1984).

4. Expansionism and the Russian Imperial Tradition

Jyrki Iivonen

The aim of this article is to find out how the expansion of Russia and the Soviet Union has proceeded, and to explain the factors that, at various times, have given rise to this expansion. This is done because certain historical consistencies can be found from this expansion as a process. In the first part, the Russian imperial tradition from medieval times to 1917 is described. After that, attention is paid to the relationship between Soviet foreign policy and expansion. In the third part, the basic principles and causes for the Russian/Soviet expansion are put forward. Finally, in the fourth part, the role played by border disputes in the post-communist era will be analysed.

1. RUSSIAN EXPANSION IN A HISTORICAL CONTEXT

The starting point of Russian expansionism can be located in the late Middle Ages.[1] The so-called Tatar Yoke, lasting to the fifteenth century, effectively divides Russian history into two parts. Before the Tatar expansion, the territory today known as Russia was actually divided into independent or semi-independent city-states, usually governed by local warlords though in some cases a republican system was adopted.[2] The population in the area was not purely Slavic: northern parts were populated by Finno-Ugric tribes, south of them there was a belt of various Baltic tribes and then came the area that today is known as Ukraine, a home base for the proto-Slavs.[3] The basis of these pre-Tatar communities was an agricultural one; it is therefore possible to say that Russian society at that time was a feudal one, although not identical with the Western

European feudal system.[4] The adoption of the Christian faith in its Byzantine form at the end of the tenth century gave a new spiritual basis for the rule of the sovereign *vis-à-vis* the nobility and peasantry. The idea of the territorial system of government, encompassing several tribes, had also emerged by then. But because of the Tatar expansion into the Russian steppes, territorial unification of Russia could only start after the Tatars were pushed back into the interior of Asia.

Several events emerging in the middle of the fifteenth century gave a decisive impetus to Muscovy's rise as the constructor of a new Russia. It is not only the overexpansion and the weakening of the Tatar Empire that must be noted here. Another important factor was the collapse of the Byzantine Empire which gave Muscovy's rulers a firm ground to declare themselves as the only true holders of the Orthodox religion and church. To achieve this, the rulers of Muscovy had first to suppress other Russian states and then to occupy territories left unruled by the Tatars. At this stage her expansion was mainly directed to the north and east, sometimes even assisted by the Tatar rulers.[5] Some of the areas were also acquired by purchase and foreclosure for debts. In about 160 years, from 1300 to 1462, its territory grew from 20,000 to 430,000 square kilometres. The last purchase made by its rulers took place in 1474 (the principality of Rostov north of Muscovy) – after that expansion proceeded through conquest only, a process lasting for more than five centuries.

The main target of Muscovy's expansion during the latter half of the fifteenth century was Novgorod, and its final conquest started in 1471 and lasted for six years. By 1477, Novgorod was annexed by its ruler, Ivan III. His methods in ruling the occupied territories were similar to those adopted by Soviet leaders in the annexed territories five centuries later (mass deportations, numerous arrests, and so on).[6] In this way, serious uprisings against Muscovy's rule were effectively prevented. In the same way as Novgorod, other semi-independent city states such as Pskov were annexed during the next few decades. When Ivan's heir, Vasili III, died in 1533, Muscovy's territory had again grown considerably, this time more than sixfold, from 430,000 to about 2.8 million square kilometres. At that time, Muscovy bordered Poland–Lithuania in the west, Sweden in the north-west and the Arctic Sea in the north. The acculturation of the scattered Finno-Ugric tribes, living in a belt stretching from Scandinavia all the way to the Urals, had also started at that time, to be continued up to modern times.

For about 150 years, from the mid-sixteenth century onwards, Russian expansion was mainly directed to the east and south, where rather under-developed nomadic tribes and groups lived. The single most important event was the conquest of Kazan from the Tatars by Ivan IV ('The Terrible') in 1552. This not only meant the collapse of the Golden Horde but also made it possible for Ivan to continue the expansion into Siberia. In addition to territorial gains, Ivan also introduced some reforms to the Russian administrative system that made the autocratic features even stronger than before.[7]

During Ivan's reign, that is, in about forty years, Russia was able to conquer virtually the whole of Siberia, thus again doubling its territory, from 2.8 million to 5.4 million square kilometres. At the beginning of the seventeenth century, Russian fur traders moved almost unopposed from the Ural Mountains across Siberia to the Pacific and to the Chinese border, making these vast steppes virtually Russian lands as well. And the expansion was not confined to Asia but continued over to the American Continent. It is actually quite obvious that Russian fur traders would have continued even across North America, if the European emigrants had not been there earlier. Now their furthest colonies were founded on the Pacific coast in California.[8] In this way, Russia within a relatively short period of time became the largest country in the world.[9] What is worth noting is that simultaneously with the Siberian expansion Russia, however, remained internally very weak due to an internal power struggle (*smutnoe vremya* or 'Time of Troubles') and suffered several losses in her relations with her western neighbours Poland and Sweden. The coming to power of the Romanov dynasty in 1613 ended this contradictory period. Till the end of that century, Russian rulers were mainly interested in strengthening the internal unity of the country: in solving the conflicts in the relations between the Tsar and the aristocracy, in reconstructing the economy, in establishing relations with her militarily stronger rivals Poland and Sweden, in reforming the Russian Army, in suppressing peasant uprisings, and so forth. Because of this, Russian rulers were not yet really interested in or able to continue the expansionist policy of the previous two centuries.

Although Peter I ('The Great') in a formal sense only continued the expansionist policy started by Ivan III, he actually created a new and much more stable basis for Russia's expansionism through his extensive economic and administrative reforms. What is also worth noting is that for the first time in her history, Russia became an important actor in the

European political theatre. As a new kind of a ruler, Peter was making distinctive calculations on power relations and concluded that the main threat towards Russia most likely would come from the west and south-west rather than from the east. Knowing European conditions better than any of his predecessors, he created a twofold strategy: on the one hand, to adopt Western technology and administrative innovations and, on the other hand, to acquire for Russia such external borders – in the west in particular – as could be regarded as strategically and economically more profitable than hitherto.[10] Peter found it very important to acquire an access to the sea in the west as well as in the south. Without breaking out of her continental isolation, Russia would remain economically weak and militarily vulnerable. After the war against Sweden, which started in 1700 and ended with the Treaty of Nystad in 1721, Russian borders reached the Baltic Sea through the annexation of Livonia, Estonia, Ingria and Karelia. In the south, Russia was unable to shatter the Turkish domination. Conquests in the north-west therefore gave Russia her only access to the sea so far, an access that during the winter time was often very difficult to manage.[11]

After Peter's death in 1725, a period of weaker rulers followed, under which his acquisitions were not much enlarged. It was the foreign-born Catherine II ('The Great'), who was first able to strengthen the Russian Empire both domestically and internationally. From 1774 Catherine II directed Russia's military efforts especially against the Islamic control of the Black Sea. The fighting continued to the 1790s and led to the Russian annexation of the whole Crimean Peninsula. In addition the border in Southern Ukraine was pushed to the River Dnestr. New harbours were founded in Odessa and in Sevastopol, in this way making access to the Mediterranean much easier.[12] It is interesting to note that simultaneously with the military expansion in the west, peasant uprisings and rebellions continued in the east, the most dangerous of them being that of Yemelyan Pugachev in the 1770s.[13] In spite of these rather serious social disturbances, Russia's autocratic system of rule was able to preserve its virility.

The European political balance was badly shaken by the French Revolution of 1789 and its consequences, leading to an all-European war that was concluded by the Vienna Congress in 1814–15. Russia was, without any doubt, one of the main winners of the war, playing a central role in fighting Napoleon and his troops. But Russia had already participated in some negotiated territorial divisions. Between 1772 and 1795, on three separate occasions, Russia, Prussia and Austria divided Poland, which during the previous centuries had been Russia's main rival in the struggle for control of Eastern Europe. The largest part of Poland's territory was annexed by Russia.[14] Soon after that, Russia continued her growth at the expense of Sweden. In two peace treaties, in 1721 and 1743, Russia had been able to annex some territories from South-Eastern Finland. In 1808 a new war broke out between Sweden and Russia. This time the fighting again took place in various parts of Finland and ended in 1809 with a new treaty, which led to the annexation of the whole of Finland by Russia. Finland's annexation, as well as that of Bessarabia three years later (1812) based partly on the Tilsit Treaty (1807) between the Russian and French emperors, virtually divided Europe into their spheres of interest.[15]

Napoleon's attack on Russia did not ruin her position but rather made it stronger than ever, so that in 1815 Russia's political influence was even more extensive than her actual political borders. Being the main gainer of the Napoleonic Wars, Russia became the main bastion of the European status quo.[16] While Russia in this way became a European power, Russian nationalism was also encouraged, leading to the birth of a new national philosophy, Slavophilism, where Russia's unique nature and her valuable contribution to the whole world's civilization was elaborated.[17] When at about the same time the economic basis of political and military power became more and more important and while Russia was still very underdeveloped in this respect, her apparent strength was now even more illusory than before the Congress of Vienna.[18] Russia's expansion continued, but from now on the inputs required became larger and larger all the time. After 1815, the anachronistic nature of Russia's economic development *vis-à-vis* her international aims led to several national and social conflicts.

After the annexations of Poland, Finland and Bessarabia, Russia had reached her desired border in the west. The main emphasis in Russia's territorial expansion was again shifted to the south, aiming at establishing her power among Central Asian Islamic nationalities. The expansion ended up in Afghanistan, where the British Army, concerned with Britain's position in India, decided to stop the Russians.[19] One of the messianic goals was the religiously legitimized duty of reoccupying the city of Constantinople, the birthplace of the Orthodox Church and of great strategic importance.

While in the west Russia's policy was based on the idea of status quo, included the suppression of national uprisings in Poland and intervention in the uprising of 1848 in Central Europe, in the south Russia took effective advantage of the continuing decline of Turkey and Persia: Azerbaijan and Armenia were occupied, the resistance of mountain tribes in the North Caucasus was suppressed and Russia's grip on Georgia was made tighter.[20] In the East, an agreement was made with China on the mutual border, an agreement that a hundred years later was questioned by the Chinese leadership of Mao Zedong. In 1867, the impoverished Russian Czar made a surprising decision to sell Alaska to the United States for seven million dollars.[21] The border with China was also redrawn in the mid-nineteenth century, when Russia acquired the area today known as Primorye (Russian Far East).[22] In spite of several gains in the south, growing internal disturbances and the defeat in the Crimean War against Britain and France were already symptoms of Russia's growing internal weakness. The decline was only encouraged by the dissolution of the serf-system in agriculture and the birth of national separatism and ruthless terrorist movements against the tsarist autocracy.

In World War I, Russia again had her own expansionist goals, mainly at the expense of Turkey. In 1877–78 Russia had already participated in a victorious war against Turkey in the Balkans.[23] In the Treaty of San Stefano, Russia not only received additional areas from Turkey but was also able to dictate some state borders in the Balkans. The treaty was, however, never effectively executed. Because of that, the religiously finspired dream of capturing the Turkish Straits and Constantinople remained alive, becoming one of the main motives in Russia's decision to enter World War I. Russia's alliance with Serbia also dates back to those days. By the beginning of the twentieth century Russia's imperial expansion had already stopped. In a war against Japan in 1904–5 she had lost some territories acquired earlier. In the Great European War as well, instead of having new territorial gains, the whole monarchist system collapsed.

2. EXPANSION IN SOVIET POLITICAL THOUGHT

Marxism–Leninism has basically been an expansionist ideology, aiming at the globalization of its influence. It can therefore be argued that after 1917 Russia's expansionist policy continued although it adopted new political forms. Traditional imperial argumentation based on religion (the vanguard of the Orthodox faith), nationalism (the idea of *narodnost*, Russian uniqueness) and ideology (czarism, and the autocratic system of government) was replaced by a twentieth century variant. Bolshevik Russia was presented as a carrier of the new socialist faith, with the messianic duty of extending this correct faith across the whole world. The October Revolution was immediately followed by Russia's decline in terms of state borders: for the first time since the sixteenth century its territorial area clearly became smaller. The situation was most difficult in early 1919, when Soviet leaders controlled an area hardly larger than Muscovy's Principality five centuries earlier.

Abroad the Bolshevik political system was believed to be exceptionally unstable and temporary ('a giant on clay feet'). Numerous compromises were therefore necessary for its survival. Lenin in particular emphasized that for the present a policy of status quo was necessary for a future victory. He also believed that the proletariat inside the lost territories would soon rejoin the Russian proletariat. In various peace treaties concluded after the civil war, Soviet Russia lost several territories: Finland, Estonia, Latvia, Lithuania and Poland became independent, Romania and Turkey annexed areas they had lost at the beginning of the nineteenth century, Japan confirmed her possessions in the Pacific area, and so on. These losses were acceptable because it was believed that they were only temporary. Instead of the horizontal division into states the Soviet leadership looked forward to a new international system, where the role earlier played by states would be replaced by the international cooperation of the world proletariat.[24] Along with the unavoidable global victory of the socialist revolution the states and their borders would gradually wither away and the Russian proletariat would eventually be greeted everywhere as a new emancipator.[25] Instead of changing the borders, the original Leninist aim was to step over them and let them wither away.

As stated above, the territorial losses after the revolution were believed to be temporary. To the great disappointment of the Soviet-Russian leadership, the world revolution did not come about according to the scheduled timetable. While the expansion was, due to Russia's weakness, excluded for the time being, the more effective incorporation of territories and national groups within the borders of Soviet Russia (internal expansion) was activated. Any new separations were not allowed. Since the early 1920s, it was made absolutely clear that national self-determination did not mean independence but a union with the victorious Russian proletarian state.[26] This was, quite obviously, a violation of the Wilsonian interpretation of the term that had created the basis for the reorganization of the post-war European state system.[27] But quite soon, under Stalin's reign, Soviet Russia started to become more stabilized and active. At the end of the 1930s, a new period of traditional expansion was launched. In the same way that Napoleon and Alexander I had done at the beginning of the nineteenth century, Hitler and Stalin in 1939 made a treaty dividing Europe into their own spheres of interest. From Stalin's point of view, this Molotov–Ribbentrop Pact actually meant a replacement of the consequences of the post-revolutionary treaties: Finland and the Baltic states as well as eastern parts of Poland and Bessarabia (Moldova) were declared as falling inside the Soviet sphere of interest.[28] All earlier losses, with Finland notwithstanding, were compensated for during the first months following the signing of the treaty.

It is often said that history does not, after all, repeat itself. In the Soviet case the resemblance to the events of the early 1800s is striking, however. Like Russia in 1812, the Soviet Union was attacked in 1941 by the other party to the 'sphere of interest' treaty. And in the same way, the Soviet Union was able to stop the invasion and gain a victory over the European rival in cooperation with other European states. When the war ended in 1945, Stalin was able to realize the expansion to an extent never seen before. Most of the territories that Soviet Russia had lost in the revolutions of 1917–18 were now rapidly reannexed.

At least three different explanations were given for this rearrangement of borders. Especially in Eastern Poland the idea was to unite two divided nations, the Belarusians and the Ukrainians. The second explanation was to correct some historical injustices: Soviet Russia was in 1918–20 forced to conclude some peace treaties, e.g. with the Baltic states, which Lenin and other Bolshevik leaders saw as highly unjust. The third explanation was a strategic one: the Soviet Union wanted to have more secure borders and therefore annexed for example the Karelian Isthmus and Moldova, although both territories were populated by non-Russians. The annexation of the Kaliningrad (Königsberg) area was also mainly a strategic measure, giving a good naval base for the Soviet navy. It is good to remember, however, that in Teheran in 1943, when the allied leaders met for the first time, Stalin demanded the possession of the northern part of East Prussia not only for strategic reasons (it was a large ice-free port) but also because he felt that the Soviet Union deserved a small piece of German territory, because it had suffered from German aggression.[29]

In addition to these border changes, an alliance system of formerly independent non-sovereign people's democracies was created in Eastern

Europe.[30] The Soviet Union was no longer interested in a purely territorial expansion as such but rather wanted to enlarge her semi-independent sphere of interest (alliance system) as much as possible and to tie independent states through military and economic bonds. Stalin seems to have believed that the incorporation of new states into the Soviet sphere of interest through this type of arrangement would be so effective that traditional outright annexation would no longer be necessary.

Post-war Soviet state borders as well as borders inside the country were believed to be permanent, of course. Although the final long-term goal was still the global transition to socialism, Soviet foreign policy in many regards became preventive and reactive, the main aim being the preservation of the post-war status quo in Europe. In the Third World, the Soviet Union was quite prepared, however, to acquire new allies and territories even if that included a military risk of becoming involved in extensive military conflicts as was to be the case in Afghanistan.[31] It was the considerable weakening and finally the collapse of the Soviet Union that made border issues viable again. If we include the above-mentioned non-sovereign states as well as former Soviet republics that lay within the Soviet sphere of interest, then the decline and collapse of this multinational empire has really been remarkable although a quite logical and unavoidable consequence of the military and political over-expansion typical of all historical empires.[32]

In Marxism–Leninism it has been presumed that economic factors are more decisive than political ones. Because of that, and although a global transition to socialism would inevitably materialize sometime in the future, territory as such was important for Soviet leaders as well. This was especially true of Stalin (after the revolution the Commissar for Nationalities Affairs), who, after the failure of world revolution and after what was eagerly interpreted as the 'deceit' of the so-called Western socialism in 1914 and again in 1918, adopted a policy of gradual expansion, in both a horizontal and a vertical sense. In other words, according to Stalin, socialism had to be expanded both inside the territory already under socialist control (class struggle against the residues of the bourgeois elements, forced collectivization in agriculture, cultural revolution and the adoption of socialist realism in literature and arts, etc.), and internationally through the action programme of proletarian internationalism as well as through military operations. To be able to exert influence by military means, Soviet Russia also needed an effective army which was possible only if her economic basis was reformed and strong. In this sense, territorial expansion, even a modest one, was essential from the point of view of the Soviet leadership. To achieve all these goals, Soviet power had to be strong.[33]

From the Soviet perspective, the international system consisted of various circles according to the level of Soviet political influence in each of them.[34] The existence of these circles can also be used when explaining Soviet territorial expansion. Their nucleus was the original Russian territory or national area, the so-called Russian heartland. It covered most of the then Russian Federation (RSFSR).[35] This first circle was rather centrally organized under Soviet rule, with a limited cultural autonomy granted to those minority nationalities that lived within the same territory as the Russians. Most of the constitutional arrangements concerning this circle were included in the Soviet Constitution of 1924.

Outside this Russian core area there was the circle of larger dependent nations, in most cases Slavic (Ukraine, Belorussia) or historically and culturally already more or less connected to Russia during the imperial era (Caucasus, Transcaspian Islamic republics). Their separate national existence was openly recognized, but their right to constitute themselves as independent states was prohibited. The annexation of these territories was carried out during the last phases of the Russian civil war. Cooperation between local communists and the all-union armed forces was an integral part of the whole project. In the Soviet Constitutions their relationship to the Soviet Union was explained on a basis of a voluntary agreement so that in the framework of international law, all fifteen Soviet republics were defined as sovereign members of the world community.[36] In spite of their formally declared sovereignty, in practice it was not possible for them to separate from the Soviet Union before the autumn of 1991 when the Soviet system had already virtually collapsed. If the first circle was marked by centralization, the second circle was marked by federative linkages.

The third circle is the most interesting for us. It consisted of those areas that had temporarily been parts of the Russian Empire but had also shown their capacity to become truly sovereign units within the international system. Already before 1917 they were regarded as being capable of a separate existence, at least for a while. This circle included Poland, Finland and the Baltic states. When national independence in 1917–20 was granted to these territories, it was believed to be a temporary solution only, pending the all-European victory of the socialist revolution. It was even officially declared that the proletariat in these countries should replace their national governments and voluntarily join socialist Russia.[37] In other words, it was firmly believed that quite soon a socialist revolution would break out in these countries as well, after which they would rejoin Russia but on a socialist basis. This might have been one reason why the Soviet leadership made such generous concessions in peace negotiations with these countries at the beginning of the 1920s. It is also worth noting that even then concrete efforts were made by the Bolshevik leadership to contribute to the revolutionary transformations in these countries.[38] The independence of these states was never genuinely accepted – one of Stalin's main aims in foreign policy was to resettle those disputes he regarded as remaining unsolved. It was the Molotov–Ribbentrop Pact that first gave him the opportunity he had expected since the early 1920s. After World War II, the Soviet Union was able to preserve the territorial gains of the German–Soviet treaty and even to enlarge them. The Baltic states were directly incorporated while Finland and Poland lost large areas. By emphasizing the ethnic principle in drawing interstate borders Stalin was also able to annex Transcarpathia and even Northern Bukovina and Moldova. In most annexations the justification was strategic rather than ethnic, however. The south-eastern part of Finland as well as the Baltic states were essential factors in Leningrad's security, while the possession of the Kurile Islands gave additional protection to Vladivostok. The Soviet Union also emphasized the annexations as compensation for her losses in the war.

The fourth circle consisted of countries within the Soviet sphere of interest that, however, had never belonged to the Russian Empire. Their relationship to Russia in the post-war era was that of 'non-sovereign sovereignty'. They were formally acknowledged as members of the world community, connected to Russia through various alliance arrangements. In reality their room of manoeuvre was extremely limited as was shown in 1956 in Hungary and in 1968 in Czechoslovakia. Although independent as such, even they can therefore be regarded as targets of expansionist Soviet policy.[39]

Outside these four circles there were developed capitalist countries that were seen as rivals and therefore as countries towards which a policy of peaceful coexistence was adopted. But it was believed that one day even they would join the Soviet Union. Before that it was crucial to preserve the status quo and further improve the capabilities of the Soviet economy. Throughout the post-war period, Soviet foreign policy towards Western Europe was based on this idea.[40] While the situation in Europe was thus stabilized, Soviet expansionist ambitions were more and more directed to the Third World countries, where possibilities for continuous expansion still existed. In Europe the Soviet Union tried to convince other countries of the permanent nature of the post-war border changes. Soviet leaders believed they had received the final seal on this aim in Helsinki in 1975 at the Conference on Security and Cooperation in Europe, where the inviolability of post-war borders was solemnly confirmed. At that time Soviet policy in Europe had already become very restrictive and rigid by nature; it was not until the years of Gorbachev's *perestroika* that new forms were adopted.[41]

3. PRINCIPLES OF RUSSIAN EXPANSIONISM

As shown above, Russian territorial expansionism has been a long historical process, in which several stages and principles can be separated. First of all, it is quite clear that in Soviet (and Russian) foreign policy the principles of expansion and coexistence have existed side by side so that one of them is always dominating at any one time.[42] From the fifteenth century up to the 1980s, the Russian/Soviet policy on borders has clearly followed a three-step scheme: from expansion through stabilization (coexistence) to a new expansion. It has been rather well understood by Russian leaders that after each new expansion a period for gathering new strength (a breathing spell, as Lenin called it in 1918) was needed and that the acculturation of newly annexed territories was started before new territorial achievements became possible. But a new expansionist act was always included in their political programmes. In spite of periods of status quo, the international system was always seen in a state of constant flux.

When analysing the patterns of Russian expansionism, a separation between borders and frontiers should be made. In other words, for a long time what Russia had in the east and south was not a border but a frontier, a territory which 'civilized people did not yet dominate'.[43] As long as occupied territories were populated by 'inferior tribes' it was more convenient to speak of frontiers in the same way as in the American expansion to the west. It was after Russia had reached the Pacific Ocean that her expansion was directed to the west, which means that the expansion to Siberia was in a certain degree similar to the American expansion to the west. In spite of scattered local tribes both territories were interpreted as free spaces. This 'compelled' expansion had a certain impact on the development of political and social institutions as well.[44] During this stage frontiers also started to change into borders, into politically defined treaty-based demarcation lines between different ethnic groups and governments. Because of the existence of the frontier concept as distinct from the border concept, after 1917 it was easy to combine the Communist messianism and expansionism with these old Russian traditions: from now on, the Soviet Foreign Ministry dealt with the borders and the Soviet Communist Party with the frontiers. It is, in other words, possible to see two comprehensive Russian policies *vis-à-vis* expansion, to be called the frontier-seeking policy and the border-moving policy. The expansion started as frontier seeking, changed into border moving and at the beginning of the twentieth century again changed back to frontier seeking.

Third, military and material calculations have been important when planning Russian expansion. The imperial expansion was usually directed to territories where the resistance was believed to be smallest. In the beginning, ethnically related neighbouring tribes were acculturated and after that other Slavic groups and city-states surrounding Muscovy. After Muscovy's leading position among scattered Russian administrative units had become indisputable, attention was shifted to the acculturation of rather small and scattered national groups – some of the Slavic and some Finno-Ugric or nomadic tribes. Siberia was also easily annexed, because local ethnic groups living there were small, unorganized and underdeveloped and therefore unable to provide any effective resistance to the Russian expansion. It was only after this that Russia's expansion became a military project and not only that of filling relatively empty territories and proclaiming them Russian property. When moving to the west and south, Russia quite soon ended up in lasting military conflicts with her much stronger neighbours. From then on, borders were also more clearly defined than before. After that, what has also been typical of Russian expansion has been the growing use of military strength in annexing new territories.

Fourth, for a long time there has been a distinct ideological legitimization for the expansion. Already in the sixteenth century, a doctrine of Moscow as the Third Rome was created.[45] In 1917, the duty to protect the Orthodox Faith changed to the duty to protect the socialist ideology and Soviet Russia, the country where it was put into practice. And in both cases it was believed that the best way to defend it was through territorial expansion, to include, at a certain stage, the whole world within the influence of the correct faith.

Fifth, the Russian Empire made deliberate efforts to mould the ethnic composition in the border areas. The rulers in the Russian centre wanted to acculturate all new territories as rapidly and as effectively as possible. Three political solutions were widely adopted to achieve this. First, deliberate labour and industrialization policies were used. Because in the occupied rural areas there was no factory industry or working class, skilled manual workers had to be imported from outside. A large proportion of them were from Russia and other Slavic parts of the Soviet Union. Second, not only the industrial labour force but also the political and cultural elite were often imported. The interests of the central administration were secured so that the highest officials in the republics were either Russians or Russified locals. Republican communist parties, the army and security organs especially were under Russian control. The educational system was also used in Sovietization. Third, in some cases during Stalin's reign, whole ethnic groups were the targets of forced deportations.[46] Only some of these groups have been allowed to move back, thus creating growing ethnic tensions in those territories where they now live and from where they were deported.

This planned and forced transformation of the ethnic composition in the border areas led to several political problems after the collapse of the Soviet Union in 1991. While the local national identity was forcefully suppressed for decades, the counterreaction, emerging along with *perestroika*, gave an opportunity for a new extremely powerful national awakening. The decades of Russification in the disguise of Sovietization led to a growing anti-Russian atmosphere. In a case where 25 million Russians live in these ex-republics, the situation may become a very difficult one, especially because Russia has declared that the status of all Russians belong to her vital national interests. In spite of certain pressures existing in at least some ex-republics, the majority of Russians living there are very reluctant to move back to Russia.[47] On the basis of the following table, giving the per centage of Russians in former Soviet republics, it is easy to conclude that in those republics that right now have political disputes with Russia (Estonia and Latvia and also, in a certain way, Moldova), the share of the Russian population is relatively high, in the same way as in Ukraine and Kazakhstan, where the situation is potentially tense as well but where the dependency on Russia is so strong

that serious conflicts have not yet emerged.[48] Russia has also avoided
making any direct territorial claims upon these two republics (with the
exception of some nationalist politicians like Vladimir Zhirinovsky).

Table 4.1. The per centage of Russians in various Soviet republics in 1989

	%		%
Russia	81.5	Estonia	30.3
Latvia	34.0	Lithuania	9.4
Belorussia	13.2	Ukraine	22.1
Moldova	13.0	Georgia	6.3
Armenia	1.6	Azerbaijan	5.6
Kazakhstan	37.8	Kyrgyzstan	21.5
Uzbekistan	8.3	Turkmenistan	9.5
Tajikistan	7.6		

What other, is the main explanation for Russia's permanent desire for
territorial expansion? First of all it must be noted that Russia's whole
existence has been determined geographically and/or territorially.[49] Because of the severe natural conditions, the limited amount of cultivable
soil, *zemlya* (with the exception of the so-called Black Earth belt in
Ukraine), and the non-existence of natural borders (rivers, mountains,
seas), Russia tried to expand as widely as possible at the expense of her
weaker neighbours. Russia has had one bad harvest out of three, in most
cases because of the temperature and the distribution of rainfall.[50] The
absence of natural borders made Russia militarily vulnerable. Once
foreign troops invaded the country, the consequences were always long-
lasting and burdensome. Territorial size – connected to the construction
of an effective military apparatus – was believed to be the best guarantee
against any foreign occupation. Russia, in other words, aimed at the
domination of Mackinder's world-island, that is, of the Eurasian landmass.[51]

Various religious and political slogans in legitimizing expansion were
only an excuse to hide these real reasons: access to the sea in the west
(Atlantic Ocean, Black Sea) and east (Pacific Ocean) as well as securing
a mountain border against the Asiatic and Islamic masses in the east
(China, Mongolia, Japan) and south (Persia, Afghanistan, Turkey). When
she had achieved these goals, Russia felt less vulnerable to external
attacks(by Tatars in medieval times, Poles in the fifteenth century,

Napoleon in 1812 and finally Hitler in 1941) which earlier had several times ruined the country and caused a recession that usually lasted for decades, sometimes even for centuries.[52] But because of her large size, the fear of internal threats increased, leading for example to the Stalinist purges of the 1930s. From this perspective, Russian expansionism was rather logically motivated: Russia expanded at the expense of her re-source-poor underdeveloped neighbours, which were relatively weak and had several local rivals and were therefore unable to resist Russia. Because these neighbours in addition lacked any central power, they were also spatially small. When these territories finally started to increase their resistance to central rule after the dissolution of the Soviet Union, they proved to be quite successful.[53]

On the other hand, the border issue has never been an absolute one for the Russian (Soviet) leadership. This means that in addition to shifting borders to new places, other methods, in addition to outright annexations to secure Russian interests, have also been adopted. Already before 1917 but especially after that, at least three different forms of incorporation or expansionism can be identified: outright annexations into the Russian/ Soviet Empire, various federative solutions with the central power and finally an arrangement of non-sovereign sovereignty through alliance linkages. Only the first two of these three types have actually included concrete changes in the state borders. In the third case, the main respon-sibility of representing Soviet interests was in the hands of the loyal local authorities and only in exceptional cases – as in Hungary in 1956, in Czechoslovakia in 1968 and in Afghanistan in 1979 – were external military measures adopted. The weakness of the domestic power appara-tus (which after all was imported from abroad), however, led to a permanent Soviet military presence, further consuming her already restricted economic resources. It also created a favourable ground for strong anti-Russian feelings, evident everywhere after the dissolution of the socialist bloc.

When it comes to Finland's case, her relationship with Russia in the nineteenth century as well as with the Soviet Union after World War II has been a rather special one. Even today it is argued whether Finland in the nineteenth century, as an autonomous unit within the Russian Empire, was a separate state or not.[54] In a certain way, the Finnish–Russian border was already a border between two states. After 1944, Finland's foreign policy line was changed to one of neutrality. This policy was sometimes questioned during the Cold War, and finally labelled 'Finlandization', meaning a special form of limited sovereignty and subjection to Soviet domination.[55] From this viewpoint, it is quite indisputable that the Soviet Union was at that time able to exert some political influence on Finland, but in a very cautious way, wanting it to be an example to other countries. Finland's relationship with modern Russia is completely different from its relationship with the Soviet Union.[56]

4. BORDERS IN THE POST-SOVIET ERA

Since the fall of the Soviet Union in 1991, the question of borders inside its territory has rapidly developed into a heated political issue, having an impact on three different levels: Russia's relations with some of its older neighbours, Russia's relations with the 'near-abroad' and ethnic relations inside the Russian Federation. While on the one hand demands have been made for Russia to retreat inside her own national borders, on the other hand some of the former Soviet republics (e.g. Tajikistan and Azerbaijan) have been unable to organize their own border troops and have therefore been forced to rely on Russian peacekeeping troops and other support.[57] Because of this, Russia has somewhat unwillingly intervened in armed struggles on the Afghan–Tajik border as well as in the war between Armenia and Azerbaijan over the future of Nagorno-Karabakh.

Six reasons for regional conflicts inside the former Soviet Union can be listed:[58]

1. heterogenization caused by internal emigration;
2. the artifical nature of borders drawn up during the Soviet period;
3. the growth of national consciousness;
4. the unilateral transfer of regions from one territorial unit to another (a very illustrative example of this is the case of Crimea, which in the 1950s was transferred from Russia to Ukraine, although national relations in the area did not give any real grounds for such a decision so that today the dispute over the Crimean Peninsula is one of the most difficult problems in Russian–Ukrainian relations[59]);
5. the forced deportations of some ethnic groups;
6. multidimensional historical disputes in some areas (Armenia's and Azerbaijan's war over the Armenian-populated but Azeri-governed Nagorno-Karabakh autonomous area is an example of this[60]).

In recent studies on Russia's internal problems it has been estimated that the total number of regional conflicts in the former Soviet Union is now 176 and that new conflicts are appearing all the time

The dominant feature in the drawing of internal administrative borders was, of course, an ethnic one. Inside the former Soviet Union, several autonomous republics, areas and districts existed. But when drawing their borders the ethnic principle was not always followed.[62] Sometimes political motivations prevented the Soviet leadership from following this schema, for example in the Caucasus. Sometimes it was also difficult for purely technical reasons to decide the location of ethnic borders, mainly owing to the scattered diffusion of various ethnic groups. An additional difficulty has been created by the deportations of whole national groups. Along with their rehabilitation, their resettlement in the original areas has proved to be very difficult.[63] Their original territories have often been settled by Russians and other Slavic peoples, who should be deported if the original situation were to be recreated. This poses, therefore, quite a number of personal and humanitarian problems.

In today's Russian foreign politicy discussion, two separate schools of thought can be separated: the Western and the Eurasian (national ones). The former emphasizes Russia's need to cooperate with the West while the latter has a much more reserved attitude and would like to have a more nationally oriented Russian foreign policy, trying to find allies rather from Asia and from the Islamic world.[64] Those criticizing Yeltsin's foreign policy have argued that Russia has actually made an act of surrender, creating a situation where it has become possible for the West to intervene in Russia's internal affairs.[65] At least two reasons have been mentioned: that people working in the foreign ministry are 'incompetent amateurs'[66] and that Yeltsin has forgotten Russians living abroad and is ready to give away territories belonging to Russia.[67] This means that Yeltsin's opponents at quite an early stage took the question of certain territories as an issue to be used against him, leading to a situation where Yeltsin has also had to adopt a tougher line especially in relations with the near-abroad.[68] The critics argue that the formation of separate national territories was a mistake right from the beginning and that Russia should be changed into 'a unitary state of all peoples living in its territory'.[69]

A certain division has therefore occurred regarding the targets of Russia's foreign policy. In addition to the traditional objects of foreign policy (USA, developed European countries, Eastern Asia, Third World countries, etc.), there are now also the so-called 'near-abroad' countries. The role of the former is quite clear. Those in possession of adequate economic resources are partners that could and should assist Russia in her economic reforms. In other words, these countries do not pose any kind of real security threat to Russia's economic and political development. The role of the 'near-abroad' is much more complicated. In each former Soviet republic there is, as a consequence of the Soviet industrialization policy, a large Russian minority. As mentioned earlier, the Russian foreign policy establishment has been a bit uncertain whether its task is to defend the interests of Russian minorities in the 'near-abroad' areas or not. They clearly live beyond the borders of the new independent Russia, but still, from a psychological point of view, they form a group of people that feel the need for Russia's protection. Even quite moderate Russian politicians have recently emphasized that the position of Russian minorities in various former Soviet republics is a crucial factor in their relations with the independent Russia.[70] An additional problem has arisen, because some of the Russian minorities live in a very defined area inside former Soviet republics – for example, in Kazakhstan in its northern parts, in Estonia in the Narva area and in the coastal area up to Tallinn, in Latvia especially in Riga, and in Ukraine in the industrialized eastern parts of the republic. The existence of Russian minorities has already led to a vivid discussion on the necessity of Russia's geopolitical control over the former Soviet Union.[71]

The Russian leadership, being in a weak political position even after October 1993, had consistently opposed all internal and external demands for redrawing the borders. There have been several reasons for this kind of attitude. First, Russian leaders have been worried by the possible domino-effect: that agreement on border changes in one instance would precipitate several new demands. This has been true with internal as well as external borders. Second, as noted, the conservative opposition in Russia has adopted the unity of Russia as one of its main slogans. It has also accused Yeltsin's leadership of too soft an attitude towards erosive trends inside Russia. It has therefore been assumed that yielding to demands for border changes would considerably strengthen the position of conservatives and weaken that of the present leadership. Third, governments in countries that have territories once annexed by Russians, have so far been rather modest in putting forward their territorial demands. The Finnish foreign policy leadership, for example, has been very careful not to make any direct territorial claims on Russia and has rather emphasized that the borders were decided in the peace treaties concluded after the war. Because of this attitude, public opinion in some countries is not campaigning openly for regaining these territories.[72] Instead of direct ownership change, Russia has made several proposals of cooperation in these areas, of lowering the borders, of special economic zones, and so forth. So far the measures taken in this respect have been quite limited. The Russian leadership has rather wanted to be quiet on all territorial disputes.[73] The activities of former Soviet republics have, on the other hand, been contained by their own Russian minorities which – so they believe – could be manipulated by the Russian Government.

The territorial issue is very important for Russia. After losing most of the gains of her expansion during the last two centuries, Russia is unwilling to make any changes to her present borders. In a couple of years, Russia has declined from a socialist superpower to a regional troublemaker, the future of which is more than uncertain. Because of the existence of several destabilizing factors, the Russian leadership has been very cautious on all territorial questions, including the territories annexed by the Soviet Union in World War II. The critical remarks concerning the legitimization basis of these annexations are understood and even, to a certain degree, accepted, but in spite of this territorial unity is something that should be preserved by all possible means. This is a fact which makes future negotiations on the annexed territories very difficult. As long as domestic instability in Russia continues, real discussions on territorial disputes almost certainly will remain minimal.

NOTES

1. For a general introduction to Russia's history, see, e.g., Nicholas V. Riasanovsky,*A History of Russia* (New York: Oxford University Press 1977).
2. This communal system of government, the proto-communist Russian village community, was later used as an argument for the messianic idea of Russia as a legal birthplace of communism. It also gave birth to the idea of Russia's direct transition to socialism, skipping over the capitalist stage of development. See Andrzej Walicki, *The Controversy over Capitalism. Studies in the Social Philosophy of the Russian Populists* (Oxford: Oxford University Press 1969).
3. On the relationship between the Finno-Ugric and Slavic tribes within this region, see, e.g., Jüri Selirand, 'Itämerensuomalaiset ja itäslaavilaiset', in Kyösti Julku (ed.), *Suomen varhaishistoria* (Rovaniemi: Pohjois-Suomen historiallinen yhdistys 1992), pp. 530–39.
4. See Karl August Wittfogel, *Oriental Despotism. A Comparative Study of Total Power* (New York: Vintage Books 1981), pp. 201–2.
5. In 1392, for example, the acquisition of Nizhni-Novgorod (known as Gorki during the Soviet period), north of Moscow, was actually a gift of the Khan of the Golden Horde as

an expression of gratitude after Moscow had assisted him in his fight against his rivals. As a general introduction to Russian expansion, see Walter Kolarz, *Russia and Her Colonies* (New York: Archon Books 1967).

6. Richard Pipes, *Russia Under the Old Regime* (Harmondsworth, Penguin Books 1977), p. 82.

7. Perry Anderson, *Lineages of the Absolutist State* (London: Verso 1980), pp. 330–31. On the peculiar relationship between old Russian traditions and more recent Soviet practices, see Tibor Szamuely, *The Russian Tradition* (London: Secker Warburg 1974).

8. The importance of the fur trade is due to the fact that it was one of the main sources of revenue of the Russian state and was also at the time of Siberian expansion its main export. See Paul Johnson, *The Birth of the Modern World Society 1815–1830* (London: Weidenfeld Nicholson 1991), p. 268.

9. As an illustration of the speed of Russia's territorial expansion it can be mentioned, for example, that for 150 consecutive years, Russia annexed approximately 35,000 square kilometres of new territory every year. In spite of the size of territorial expansion, Russia's population remained small, partly explaining the relative weakness of the Empire, see Pipes (1977), pp. 83–4. Russia's expansion was so easy partly because there was no serious threat to the home base, see Paul Kennedy, *The Rise and Fall of the Great Powers. Economic Change and Military Conflict from 1500 to 2000* (London: Fontana 1990), p. 120.

10. It can be argued – and not without grounds – that Stalin had a similar starting point in his foreign policy. This kind of realist thinking has been thoroughly described by Henry Kissinger in his new work *Diplomacy* (New York: Simon Schuster 1994).

11. Anderson (1980), p. 341.

12. It is interesting to note that after the independence of Ukraine, Russia is again about to lose these harbours.

13. On Pugachev, see Paul Avrich, *Russian Rebels* (Cambridge: Harvard University Press 1973), pp. 196–225. Aleksandr Pushkin wrote his famous novel *Captain's Daughter* on this uprising.

14. On Poland's partitions in 1772–95, see, e.g., Norman Davies, *Heart of Europe. A Short History of Poland* (Oxford: Oxford University Press 1987), pp. 306–11. Throughout the whole nineteenth century, Poland with two extensive uprisings, in 1830 and 1863 respectively, was the most turbulent of Russia's border provinces.

15. Anderson (1980), p. 345.

16. It has been emphasized by several authors, and indeed quite correctly, that the Holy Alliance very soon became 'a bond by which the signatories agreed to combine to resist popular pressure for constitutions', see Johnson (1991), p. 115.

17. On the philosophical and historical roots of Slavophilism in Russia, see, e.g., Andrzej Walicki, *The Slavophile Controversy. History of a Conservative Utopia in Nineteenth Century Russia* (Oxford: Clarendon Press 1980). On their appearance in today's Russia, see, e.g., Thomas Parland, *The Rejection in Russia of Totalitarian Socialism and Liberal Democracy. A Study of the Russian New Right* (Helsinki: Finnish Society of Sciences and Letters 1994).

18. See Kennedy (1990), passim.

19. Afghanistan has, in other words, been an area where Russian and Western spheres of interest already collided over one hundred years ago.

20. See Ronald Grigor Suny, *The Making of the Georgian Nation* (London: I. B. Tauris 1989), chapter 4.

21. It is interesting to note that Vladimir Zhirinovski, the chairman of the maveric nationalistic Liberal-Democratic Party, has included Alaska in the list of territories that must be returned to Russia in the future.

22. On the history of the Russian–Chinese border, see, e.g., George Ginsburgs, 'Recent History of the Territorial Question in Central Asia', *Central Asia Monitor*, no. 2, 1992, pp. 31–41; no. 3, 1992, pp. 21–9 and no. 4, 1992, pp. 32–40.

23. Riasanovsky (1977), p. 429.

24. Walter Connor, *The National Question in Marxist-Leninist Theory and Strategy* (Princeton: Princeton University Press, 1984), p. 5.

25. See, e.g., V. Kubalkova and A.A. Cruickshank, *Marxism–Leninism and Theory of International Relations* (London: Routledge Kegan Paul,1980) and Margot Light,*The Soviet Theory of International Relations*(Brighton: Wheatsheaf Books 1988).

26. As a general introduction to this problem, see Richard Pipes,*The Formation of the Soviet Union. Communism and Nationalism, 1917–1923* (Cambridge: Harvard University Press 1954) and Samad Shaheen, *The Communist (Bolshevik) Theory of National Self-Determination* (The Hague: W. van Hoeve 1956).

27. Charles W. Kegley, 'The Neoidealist Moment in International Studies? Realist Myths and the New International Realities', *International Studies Quarterly*, vol. 37, no. 2, 1993, p. 137.

28. For an account of the Nazi–Soviet Pact and of Hitler's and Stalin's roles in concluding it, see Alan Bullock, *Hitler and Stalin. Parallel Lives* (London: Fontana Press 1992), pp. 661–9.

29. Ibid., pp. 890–91. Stalin also promised to accept the Curzon Line as Poland's eastern border, if his demand on Kaliningrad (Königsberg) were accepted.

30. Of crucial importance here is the relationship between the principle of national self-determination and actual political decision-making – in other words, national self-determination could have quite different manifestations in different instances, depending on the political aims of the political leadership. The purpose of national self-determination was, in other words, purely an instrumental one. See Jyrki Iivonen, *Independence or Incorporation? The Idea of Poland's National Self-Determination and Independence within the Russian and Soviet Socialism from the 1870s to the 1920s* (Helsinki: The Finnish Institute of International Affairs 1990).

31. In Afghanistan the issue was not one of borders or access to the Indian Ocean but only of helping to power a government that would not violate Soviet aims and efforts in the Islamic world after Islamic fundamentalism had become a real political power in Iran. As events in today's Tajikistan have shown, this fear is a real one and has led to a similar development as in Afghanistan fifteen years earlier. No wonder then that in Russia it has been emphasized that the withdrawal from Afghanistan will not continue in Tajikistan. This was emphasized by Foreign Minister Andrei Kozyrev during his visit in the area in September 1993. See *Izvestiya*, 11 September 1993.

32. Jyrki Iivonen, *Neuvostovallan viimeiset vuodet* (Helsinki: Gaudeamus 1992), p. 8.

33. Light (1988), pp. 32–3.

34. Iivonen (1990), pp. 235–6.

35. Separatist movements inside Russia since 1991 show that even this core circle is not as uniform as was expected immediately after the collapse of the Soviet Union. What is also worth noting is that this modern Russian separatism is not only ethnic by nature but also territorial, i.e., Russian-dominated areas in Siberia, e.g., have demanded wider autonomy and have therefore declared themselves independent itals Moscow, although they have not separated as states yet. Their aim has rather been to get some economic gains from the central administration.

36. See *Konstitutsiya SSSR. Politiko-pravovoj kommentarij* (Moskva: Izdatelstvo politicheskoj literatury 1982), p. 206 and Jyrki Iivonen and Juha Tolonen, 'Perustuslain kehitys Neuvostoliitossa',*Turun yliopiston oikeustieteellisen tiedekunnan julkaisuja. Julkisoikeuden sarja*, C: no. 1 (Turku: University of Turku 1987), pp. 172–5.

37. See, e.g., *Dokumenty vneshnej politiki SSSR*, tom 1 (Moskva: Izdatelstvo politicheskoj literatury 1958), p. 565.

38. In Finland, Russian troops participated in some military operations during the Civil War in 1918 (although the main fighting took place among the Finns), Estonia ended up in a war with Russia a bit later and in 1920 Russia and Poland fought a war where neither side gained a victory. It was only after these failed military operations that the Russian leadership was ready to conclude peace treaties. In the German uprisings of 1921 and 1923 the Comintern (Third International) was very active as well, but behind the scenes.

39. In order to avoid these events repeating themselves in the future, some Central European countries are now looking for security guarantees from the West. Czech President Václav Havel, for example, has declared that 'the postcommunist countries of Europe should seek

membership in NATO', see Václav Havel, 'New Democracies for Old Europe', *New York Times*, 17 October 1993.

40. On peaceful coexistence, see, e.g., Light (1988).
41. On this, see the articles in Jyrki Iivonen (ed.), *The Changing Soviet Union in the New Europe* (Aldershot: Edward Elgar 1991).
42. This is also the title of Adam Ulam's much acclaimed classical book *Expansion and Coexistence. Soviet Foreign Policy 1917–1974* (New York: Basic Books 1974).
43. On the difference between 'frontier' and 'border', see Ellwyn R. Stoddard, 'Frontiers, Borders and Border Segmentation: Toward a Conceptual Clarification', *Journal of Borderland Studies*, vol. 6, no. 1, 1991, p. 2. Stoddard refers to the TV series 'Star Trek', where the task of the space ship crew is to 'seek new frontiers, to boldly go where no one has gone'.
44. The famous US historian Frederick J. Turner wrote in 1893 of the American westward expansion as follows: 'The existence of an area of free land, its continuous recession, and the advance of the American settlement westward, explain American development. Behind institutions, behind constitutional forms and modifications, lie the vital forces that call these organs into life and shape them to meet changing conditions.' Cited in Tiziano Bonazzi, 'Frederick Jackson Turner's Frontier Thesis and the Self-Consciousness of America.', *Journal of American Studies*, vol. 27, no. 2, 1993, p. 151. On Turner's contribution to the study of Russian expansion, see Mark Bassin, 'Turner, Soloviev and the "Frontier Hypothesis": The Nationalist Signification of Open Spaces', *Journal of Modern History*, vol. 65, no. 3, 1993, pp. 473–511.
45. Mikhail Agursky, *The Third Rome. National Bolshevism in the USSR* (Boulder: Westview Press 1987).
46. Eleven nations were the targets of forced deportations: Balkars, Chechens, Crimean Tatars, Georgian Greeks, Ingushes, Karachais, Koreans, Kurds, Meshkets, Volga Germans and Kalmykians. See N. L. Zhukovskaia, 'The Republic of Kalmykia. A Painful Path of National Renewal', *Anthropology & Archeology of Eurasia*, vol. 31, no. 4, 1993, p. 87.
47. V. I. Perevedetsev, 'Migratsiya naseleniya v SNG: Opyt prognoza', *Polis*, no. 2, 1993, p. 75.
48. Channey D. Harris, 'The New Russian Minorities: A Statistical Overview', *Post-Soviet Geography*, vol. 34, no. 1, 1993, pp. 4–6.
49. Wittfogel (1981), pp. 219–25.
50. Even good harvests were usually quite low. Typical British yields during the first half of the nineteenth century were tenfold compared to those of Russia and even Scandinavia produced more than Russia. However, climate is not the only reason for problems in Russian agriculture. See Johnson (1991), p. 271.
51. James F. Burke, 'Gorbachev's Eurasian Strategy', *World Affairs*, vol. 155, no. 4, 1993, p. 157
52. The influence of these historical examples has been twofold. On the one hand, they showed the need to secure safe borders to avoid large human and economic losses. On the other hand, however, they showed that Russia had always survived external attacks even when they lasted for years or decades.
53. Cf. David V. Waller, 'Ethnic Mobilization and Geopolitics in the Soviet Union: Towards a Theoretical Understanding', *Journal of Political and Military Sociology*, vol. 20, no. 1, 1992, p. 46.
54. See Osmo Jussila, *Maakunnasta valtioksi. Suomen valtion synty* (Helsinki: WSOY 1987).
55. International suspicions towards the genuiness of Finland's neutrality were increased by several statements by Soviet leaders since Khrushchev. These statements openly presented Finnish–Russian relations 'as a positive example of peaceful coexistence between countries belonging to different social systems', see Jyrki Iivonen, 'Perestroika, Neutrality, and Finnish–Soviet Relations', in Hanspeter Neuhold (ed.), *The European Neutrals in the 1990s. New Challenges and Opportunities* (Boulder: Westview Press 1992), p. 144.
56. On recent changes in Finnish foreign policy and her relations with Russia, see Jyrki Iivonen, 'Finnish–Russian Relations after the Cold War' Presentation at the 35th ISA National Convention, Washington DC, 29 March–2 April 1994.

57. Gabriel Schoenfeld, 'Outer Limits', *Post-Soviet Prospects*, no. 17, 1993. The principles on which Russian peacekeepers operate in the former Soviet territory is, of course, of vital interest here.

58. See Charles Demko, 'Panel on Patterns of Disintegration in the Former Soviet Union', *Post-Soviet Geography*, vol. 33, no. 6, 1992, pp. 349–50.

59. On the Russian–Ukrainian dispute over the Crimean Peninsula, see Suzanne Crow, 'Russian Parliament Asserts Control over Sevastopol', *RFE/RL Research Report*, vol. 2, no. 31, 1993, pp. 37–41.

60. See, e.g., Claire Mouradian, 'The Mountainous Karabakh Question: An Inter-Ethnic Conflict or Decolonization Crisis?', *Armenian Review*, vol. 43, no. 2–3, 1990, pp. 1–34.

61. Demko (1992), p. 351.

62. See Pavel Baev, 'The Principle of Inviolability of Borders Will Have to Be Rejected', *New Times*, no. 37, 1993, p. 25 as well as his chapter in this book.

63. One example of the present problems connected with the deported nations is the discussion on the re-establishment of the German autonomous republic. See Barbara Dietz, 'Anders als die anderen. Zur Situation der Deutschen in der Sowjetunion und der deutschen Aussiedler in der Bundesrepublik', *Osteuropa*, vol. 42, no. 2, 1992, pp. 147–59.

64. See Heinz Timmermann, 'Die Aussenpolitik Russlands: Ausdruck der Suche nach einer neuen Identität', *Berichte des Bundesinstituts für ostwissenschaftliche und internationale Studien*, no. 20, 1993; Fred Halliday, 'Russian Foreign Policy: Who's Driving the Troika?', *The Nation*, 8 March 1993 and S. Neil MacFarlane, 'Russia, the West and European Security', *Survival*, vol. 35, no. 3, 1993, pp. 3–25.

65. *Pravda*, 16 December 1992 and 14 January 1993 and *Rossiiskaya gazeta*, 31 December 1992.

66. *Pravda*, 3 December 1992.

67. Igor Shafarevich in *Pravda*, 2 November 1991.

68. MacFarlane (1993), pp. 13–15.

69. Alexander Rutskoi, 'We Need Each Other', *New Times*, no. 10, 1993, p. 16.

70. See, e.g., Sergei Stankevich, 'Russia in Search for Itself', *The National Interest*, vol. 28, 1992. On the near-abroad in Russian foreign policy, see Roger E. Kanet and Brian V. Sounders, 'Russia and Her Western Neighbors. Relations Among Equals or a New Form of Hegemony?', *Demokratizatsiya*, vol. 1, no. 3, 1993, p. 449.

71. Arkady Chereshnia, 'Big Brother as an Equal', *New Times*, no. 17, 1993, p. 12.

72. In an opinion poll carried out in Finland in the autumn of 1992, only 25 per cent agreed with the argument that Finland's government should start official negotiations with Russia on the return of Karelia. See, Jyrki Iivonen, 'The Attitude of Finns towards Current Developments in Russia and Finnish–Russian Relations', *Yearbook of Finnish Foreign Policy* (Helsinki: The Finnish Institute of International Affairs 1992), pp. 30–31.

73. One proof of that was that Yeltsin several times postponed a visit to Japan that finally took place in mid-October 1993. During that visit Yeltsin was very reluctant to speak publicly of the dispute over the five Kurile Islands. See *New York Times*, 14 October 1993.

5. Old and New Border Problems in Russia's Security Policy

Pavel K. Baev

The breakup of the Soviet Union could be interpreted as a two-dimensional catastrophe: defeat of the communist ideology (in its Leninist version) and collapse of the state structures. Both dimensions are of relevance for the borders of the successor-states, and first of all for Russia which presents herself as the main heir-in-law of the USSR. Actually, this political heritage confers few privileges, and brings with it many responsibilities for unresolved or quasi-resolved problems including those involving borders. Soviet leaders were able to impose their geopolitical will on their neighbours, but now Russia is faced with a natural wish or even demand for the undoing of past injustices.

Another part of the heritage is the unique perception of the state borders as something sacred and inviolable, but at the same time expandable. Despite the fact that the new Russian political elite loudly rejects Marxist–Leninist ideology and totalitarian methods, it is not difficult to find the origin of the modern perception of territory and frontiers in the former and the roots of current border politics in the latter.

1. EVOLUTION OF SOVIET BORDERS

The Soviet policy of border-building experienced a remarkable evolution during the 75-year lifetime of the 'real' socialist state. In *the initial phase* the borders were not only considered to be temporary, but were actually moving rapidly as the front-lines of the 'permanent revolution' that was proclaimed by Trotsky and pushed forward by the Red Army's bayonets. Ideologically motivated Bolsheviks were eager to accept seemingly humiliating territorial compromises and create some buffer-states (such as the Far-Eastern Republic) in order to concentrate forces for the next breakthrough.[1] To some extent – as far as Ukraine and Crimea, Far East and Caucasus were concerned – this approach worked though the reconquest of Central Asia took some ten years more. But the Polish campaign in 1920 convincingly revealed the exhaustion of revolutionary energy. A theoretical conclusion on the possibility of the victory of socialism in one particular country was drawn from this, and it in turn actually justified the beginning of real state-building, which also meant a political and territorial settlement with the capitalist neighbours of the Soviet Union.

One of the necessary steps in establishing relations with a reluctant West was to demarcate the boundaries and in so doing recognize formally the priority of traditional borders over the 'revolutionary frontiers'. This marked *the first stage* of the evolution of 'communist' borders (which could be called 'recognition'), which was determined by a sheer lack of power in the fledgling Soviet regime. At this stage ideology still played the key role and provided the idea of a border as a divide between two historical epochs: the imperialist past and a communist future – as materialized in the first 'state of workers and farmers'. It is perfectly accurate to say that the borders of the USSR not only ran across space, but – in essence – across time.[2] Thus the territorial expansion of the 'state of the future' was presented as a linear function of time, and the 'frontier' remained open for new adventures. Their planning became a task for the Comintern which was organized to reach across the formal borders and, as Lenin put it, 'to strengthen the connection between one temporarily isolated section of international socialism and other sections'.[3]

The second stage of the evolution of the 'communist' borders, which could be called one of consolidation began approximately with the twelfth anniversary of the October 1917 coup, named by Stalin as the Year of Great Change. It was marked by a striking reverse in the state-building process from a Europe-oriented internationalism to a centre-oriented nationalism, and subsequent transformation of the state as such from an ideological to a bureaucratic entity. The role of ideology while remaining pivotal became primarily functional: to justify the hyper-centralization of state structures. Accordingly the content of the ideology was changing in the direction of traditional empire-building and -saving concepts enriched with a new image of a 'Besieged Fortress'. Romanticism gave way to a new pragmatism: while the goal of conquest of the world was moved to the indefinite future, a more practical task was set for the near term – to get back the lost territories.

The third stage of evolution (it could be called 'expansion') started in the late 1930s when a political alliance with Hitler was suddenly undertaken. The lack of any ideological justification for this alliance was striking and painful for many in the USSR, but the imperial ideology that already dominated the Kremlin (though maybe less so at the grassroots level) did not actually need any justification for territorial enlargement.

The westward expansion started with the return of several areas lost in the first stage (thus creating six of the eight border problems that are the subject of this book), of which the most difficult was to win back some territory from Finland. The legitimacy of a return to the pre-1914 borders was taken for granted and the expulsion of either a part or the whole (as in Karelia) of the indigenous population was intended to preclude any further border revisions. The expansion continued after the victory over the treacherous ally, but acquired a new quality that influenced the character of the borders. While the pre-war acquisitions and the two new trophies – East Prussia and Sakhalin/Kuriles – were fully integrated in the state (social and ethnic homogeneity was achieved through severe repression and resettlement), after 1945 priority was given to the creation of an external 'security belt' that was legitimized by the Yalta and Potsdam agreements.[4] Even the most rigid control from Moscow provided the 'peoples' democracies' in Eastern Europe with a status essentially different from those of the Soviet republics.

The role of ideology as a state-building factor became remarkably formal as the cult of Stalin turned the 'world revolution' into a purely abstract idea. The new borders were fortified to make them impenetrable and to minimize the contacts with 'outsiders' who were all treated as enemies; even the Comintern – which in the previous stage had been transformed into an intelligence and propaganda structure – was dissolved. The Future was finally captured inside the state borders, and a popular slogan 'Frontier is under Lock!' confirmed that there was no escape.

The fourth stage of evolution, whic lasted from the mid-1950s to the mid-1980s, could be defined as the crystallization and subsequent erosion of 'communist' borders. During this long period the Soviet leadership tried to preserve Stalin's heritage while avoiding extremes. Some attempts to revitalize the role of ideology were considered of crucial importance, but its diminishing persuasiveness dictated the necessity to maintain the 'information border'.

A strong new factor was created by the deep traumas in national (and particularly in military) mentality caused by the shock of the German invasion in 1941. No further proof of the inherent aggressiveness of 'Imperialism' was needed, and the obsessive idea of Defence made the claims on the monopoly on the Future indeed ritual.[5] The two epochs were engaged in a sort of trench warfare; for 40 years Defence remained the best justification for the efforts to encircle the 'Socialist camp' with a bastion border – the Wall.[6]

The character of the borders within the 'Socialist camp' was determined by the recognition by the Kremlin leaders that homogeneity inside the empire was beyond their grasp. The social gap between the USSR and the 'brother-countries' was in real terms becoming less and less bridgeable, despite successful military interventions and their strong economic dependence on the USSR. Dangerous heterogeneity made it necessary to erect inner borders between the 'Socialist Citadel' and the outer strongholds, so that a multi-layer hierarchy of borders emerged in which the territory of the allies actually performed the functions of a 'military buffer' and a *cordon sanitaire* for the USSR. Some carefully planned expansion beyond the external perimeter of the Fortress was considered to be both strategically and ideologically important, so as to deliver some evidence that the Future was indeed coming. The successful enterprises in Cuba and Vietnam paved the way for adventures in Africa, but then followed the disaster in Afghanistan. In the mid-1980s the strategic overextension and ideological impotence became self-evident, and the heretical idea of a gradual retreat to 'defendable borders', which was implicitly influenced by Alexandr Solzhenitsyn, gained more and more supporters.[7]

2. RETREAT AND COLLAPSE OF EMPIRE

In the late 1980s a modest retreat – as a precondition for a new spurt – was recognized as unavoidable by a new generation of the Soviet political elite. Mikhail Gorbachev subscribed to the conclusion that the resources for modernization could be found only by diminishing the military burden and that this could be justified only by proportionally diminishing the external threat. So he boldly threw away dogmas like 'vigilance' and demonstrated a readiness for compromise and even sacrifice in order to guarantee the security of 'real frontiers' by political means.[8] A partial demilitarization of the borders was combined with a partial de-ideologization, but the rationale for the latter was the increased competitiveness of the Soviet social model (supposedly as a result of the expected economic upsurge) that would make the informational Wall redundant. This gave an impetus to negotiations on the border issue with both Norway and Japan, but the window of opportunity remained open for too short a period.

Transparency actually was fatal for this model, but it was only Erich Honecker who understood this clearly, while Gorbachev saw nothing but 'minor' vulnerable points in his logic – the questions concerning the limits to retreat and the demarcation of 'real frontiers'. Neither Africa, nor Afghanistan could provide the answer, because the real centre of gravity was in Poland where the remnants of socialism were held together only by martial law. Up to June 1989, Moscow was inclined to believe that a genuinely democratic regime on a 'socialist basis' would make Poland a more reliable ally – so all the more bitter was the disillusionment from the electoral victory of Solidarity.[9]

Poland sent the first clear signal that the power structures, not only in Eastern Europe but also in the USSR, were too rigid for modernization and on the verge of collapse. Gorbachev and other New Political Thinkers failed to interpret this signal adequately and let the DDR slip into chaos. Only when the locomotive of reunification reached full speed, did Moscow launch desperate efforts to stop it. The border question was a part of these efforts, and while the emphasis was on the Oder–Neiße border, Kaliningrad was obviously one of the real concerns. The FRG provided the required guarantees for the borders, but allowed only a four-year stay for the Soviet 'lost legion' on German soil.

The chain reaction of revolutions in Eastern Europe in the autumn of 1989 pushed the retreat significantly further than had been provided for by the New Political Thinking. Sharp debates at the CPSU plenum in February 1990 were a testimony that many in the leadership had arrived at the laboured conclusion that a partial 'Finlandization' of Eastern Europe would not endanger the Soviet borders. It was hard to swallow but actually only one option was left – to exchange the empire's frontiers for the state borders of the USSR, but the conservatives in Moscow were advocating a counteroffensive.[10] Shevardnadze, who remained an ardent non-interventionist, took the blame for 'losing Eastern Europe', and his resignation in December 1990 indicated that the chance to consolidate the Citadel had been lost.

In early 1991, another option remained open for the Soviet leadership – to treat the Baltic republics as a special case and concentrate on saving the state as such.[11] According to Michael Beschloss and Strobe Talbott, back in September 1989 US State Secretary Baker tried to persuade Shevardnadze of this, saying 'You'd be better off with three little

Finlands'.[12] But Gorbachev stubbornly followed the course – set out during his visit to Vilnius in January 1990 – of holding the Balts 'in' and preserving the 'sacred' imperial frontiers, which inevitably led to bloodshed, political polarization in Moscow and resentment in the Army.[13] In August 1991 everything was lost.[14]

Even from this abridged analysis it is possible to conclude: a) that the process of disintegration was not a continuum, but included discrete contraction stages; b) that the breakup of the USSR was by no means unavoidable. It seemed perfectly feasible for the democratic forces to use the slogan of self-determination in order to push forward the transformation and destruction of totalitarian structures. Russia was in the vanguard of this struggle and – after her President and Parliament defeated the coup in August 1991 – initiated the dissolution of the USSR in December 1991.

What is most striking about this event is 'how astoundingly, how unbelievably little damage has been done'.[15] But already during the following year the litmus test of democracy was turning more and more negative. The collusion of the leaders of Russia, Ukraine and Belarus was sufficient to dismantle peacefully the eroded political superstructure – so a breakup logically followed the breakdown. At first, it was even possible to interpret the collapse as yet another stage of contraction to some 'Slavic core', but the re-marriage with Central Asia and even more the escalation of tensions between Russia and Ukraine revealed the real picture. And when it came to societal rupture, it turned out to be violent and painful. As aggressive nationalism was gaining ground, awakened by the rhetoric of self-determination and released by the elimination of the 'centre', many liberal experts reevaluated the disintegration of the USSR as a grave mistake and a major setback for democratic modernization.[16]

3. BORDERS AND IDENTITY CRISES OF SUCCESSORS

The immediate result of the voluntary dissolution of the Soviet Union was the emergence of a dozen quasi-states with very limited historical legitimacy (if any), ethnically mixed populations (except in the case of Armenia) and growing social tensions. As the republican political elites enthusiastically started the process of state-building, they faced a problem of identity which inevitably brought the question of borders to the surface. Every attempt to increase the territorial integrity only emphasized the artificial and sometimes absurd character of the inherited boundaries and left the sovereign leaders with a question: can my state exist within these borders?

One can easily arrive at a negative answer to this question from the emotional rejection of the political heritage of Stalin which denies any moral validity for the old borders. On a closer look, his cartographic exercises are found to be far from capricious; the borders were drawn deliberately to generate ethnic tensions, to make each republic a sort of *matryoshka*-doll with minorities inside minorities – all dependent on Moscow.[17] The 'revisionist' answer was first presented in a statement by President Yeltsin's press secretary on 25 August 1991 (one week after the abortive coup) which said that Russia reserves for herself 'the right to raise the issue of the revision of borders' with those states that refuse to settle relations with Russia in bilateral treaties.[18]

This approach found an ardent supporter in Vice-President Rutskoi, who developed a habit of referring to history *per se* and insisted that the real Russia could not be contained within the borders of the current Russian Federation.[19] But officially the statement was quickly withdrawn as many experts argued about the self-damaging character of the *Regus Sic Stantibus* approach to the border problem.[20] Any attempt to redraw Stalin's map would immediately backfire through a chain reaction of territorial claims: indeed, by late 1991 there were some 168 ethno-territorial disputes in the former USSR and 73 of them directly concerned Russia; actually, only two of the 23 inter-republican borders in the former USSR are not disputed.[21] The old Soviet external borders could also become questionable, and of the eight cases under scrutiny here, the Kuriles, Kaliningrad and Karelia look the most vulnerable.

Bearing this in mind, the majority of the leaders of the new states arrived at a consensus to avoid any territorial resettlement. And, perhaps, inter-national recognition was another strong factor preventing an outbreak of territorial conflicts. The inviolability of borders inside the Common-wealth of Independent States was solemnly confirmed and President Yeltsin announced that 'The imperial period in Russia's history has ended'.[22] Nevertheless, Russia's approach to the sovereignty of the neighbour-states in general and to their borders in particular remains fundamentally ambivalent. Thus, the Sixth Congress of Russia's People's Deputies in April 1992 rejected a proposal to introduce a moratorium on border changes up to 1995.

This ambivalence is related to the dilemma as to whether Russia should commit herself to the protection of the former USSR borders or to concentrate on the erection of her own new borders that would prevent the spilling over of violence from the conflict areas in Central Asia and the Caucasus.[23] The acceptance of the latter option – however natural from the point of view of 'normal' international relations – is complicated by several considerations. First, Russia's land borders are estimated to be 3,000 kilometres longer than those of the Soviet Union. More than a half of the land border is with new neighbours (Russia has 14 neighbour-states – more than any other state), which means that an expensive new infrastructure would have to be built up from scratch, but the resources are not going to be available.[24] Second, the erection of a real border would damage relations with Kazakhstan, which is an important strategic ally, and would also mean abandoning more than 6 million Russians living in Northern Kazakhstan. Third, border-building along the Caucasus – which is the only 'natural' border for Russia – is not feasible owing to rather complicated relations with the North Caucasian republics, especially Chechnya. At the same time, Moldova and Azerbaijan insist on having absolutely transparent borders with Romania and Iran respectively and have refused to allow any Russian presence on the former USSR border.

These considerations dictated a flexible approach: to build new borders where necessary (first of all, with Estonia, Latvia and Lithuania) and to secure the former Soviet borders where possible. In the latter case, Tajikistan presents the most serious challenge: Russia has found herself supporting a clearly undemocratic regime in Dushanbe, and instead of protecting the border, the border troops are mostly defending their posts.[25]

Russian policy-makers initially were careful to avoid any Realpolitik arguments on 'power' and 'spheres of influence', but tried to stick to a 'normative' position placing the principle of the inviolability of borders at the foundation of their flexible border policy. This choice was determined primarily by two issues: Crimea and the Kurile Islands. Naturally, both cases were enmeshed in a fierce internal political struggle, and a detached observer would, perhaps, find it ridiculous that while demanding back the 'primordial Russian' Crimea, the opposition was insisting on the inviolability of territorial settlement with Japan. When the military joined the 'no-return' lobby, President Yeltsin had to abandon a compromise advocated by the Foreign Ministry and cancelled his visit to Japan in September 1992.[26] At the same time, the tensions over Crimea were instigated by a resolution of the Russian Supreme Soviet adopted in May 1992 declaring the transfer of Crimea from Russia to Ukraine in 1954 unconstitutional and 'without the force of law'. Only the principle of inviolability of borders provided President Yeltsin with a rope to walk between the two crises, so when the Russian Supreme Soviet in July 1993 adopted another resolution with a direct claim on Sevastopol, Yeltsin was able to denounce it and even refrained from blocking a pro-Ukrainian resolution in the UN Security Council.

During 1993, the problem of regional separatism and disintegration increased the sensitivity of the border issue, forcing Russia's leaders to consider seriously the option of a geopolitical retreat from the North Caucasus and the erection of a new border for Southern Russia proper.[27] Another consequence was a retreat from the idea of resettling ethnic Germans in the Kaliningrad Oblast which was turned into a garrison area instead.[28] On the other hand, the development of the Barents Initiative, launched at the meeting of Foreign Ministers of Norway, Russia, Finland and Sweden in Kirkenes, Norway in January 1993, provided a framework for cross-border cooperation that effectively marginalized the territorial questions as far as both natural resources (as with Russian–Norwegian delimitation in the Barents Sea) and ethno-historical aspects (as with Karelia) were concerned.[29]

The disintegration menace is even more a driving force in Ukrainian state-building, including its border policy. After he was elected in December 1991, President Kravchuk has been trying to build a new state identity by marrying nationalism with territorial integrity. Up to the spring of 1994, his balanced approach helped to avoid internal splits despite the deepening economic crisis. But the parliamentary elections in March–April 1994, and even more the presidential elections in July, provided evidence that the country remained ethnically divided in various ways: Eastern Ukraine is clearly pro-Russia oriented, Crimea rather seeks independence, Odessa solicits the free port status, and Western Ukraine considers itself part and parcel of Central Europe.[30] The latter case is particularly complicated: historical, ethnic and geopolitical borders make up a patchwork which is crossed by the dividing line between the Catholic and Orthodox Churches.[31] Any self-determination attempt from the Hungarian, Polish or Slovakian minorities could revive the deeply rooted territorial disputes in Transcarpathia, and the foreseeable reunification of Moldova and Romania could create the same effect.[32] This potential instability could, perhaps, explain the extremely nervous and sometimes paranoid attitude of the Ukrainian leaders towards any attempt at border revision.

Therefore, for both Russia and Ukraine the border question was inevitably placed in the context of national identity-building, which involved the revival of myths and the reconstruction of history. Hence the discovery that history matters and contains a direct challenge to the political survival of every fledgling state. And this makes every already painful border question an existential one with the possibility of resonating far beyond its actual setting. On the other hand, the poor results in improving the internal cohesion of these states allow every failure in keeping the borders intact to be used to unleash a chain reaction of disintegration.

4. BORDERS, THE RUSSIAN DIASPORA AND LOCAL CONFLICTS

Adopting the official policy of inviolability of both old and new borders, Russia finds its implementation increasingly difficult. Two main problems that are undermining the status-quo approach are the Russian population in the 'near-abroad' and the management of ethno-territorial conflicts. Initiating the dissolution of the USSR, the new Russian political elite obviously underestimated the explosive nature of the issue of the Russian diaspora. For most of 1992, Russia's foreign policy operated with a liberal concept of human rights and the promotion and protection of national minorities in general. Foreign Minister Kozyrev insisted that the only way to secure the rights of 25 million ethnic Russians who had suddenly found themselves in 'foreign' countries was building a 'belt of good-neighbourliness'.[33] Escalation of ethnic tensions in many new independent states made this 'Westernized' approach vulnerable to criticism from various 'patriotic' forces. Even more important, it allowed the military leadership to champion the rights of Russians and to establish a link between the withdrawal of troops and the protection of the Russian-speaking population in the Baltic states.[34]

Recognizing this vulnerability, President Yeltsin berated the Foreign Ministry in October 1992 for its lack of attention to the Russian diaspora and called for a more aggressive approach which was later formalized in a document 'The Russian Federation's Foreign Policy Guidelines'.[35] It marked a departure from a 'normative' approach based on the Paris

Charter and the introduction of a different set of 'norms' (historical and ethnic) and also a reintroduction of the mobilizing idea of 'great power' with its 'area of responsibility' and external interests challenged by other powers. The unexpected success of the ultra-nationalist Liberal-Democratic Party (the name could not be more misleading) in the parliamentary elections in December 1993 pushed the government even further to assume the role of 'protector' of Russians against the states they are living in.[36] This course inevitably involves direct interference in the internal affairs of these neighbouring states that are expressing strong concerns, but so far it has not included any indication of a possible territorial reshuffling.

There is no formal recognition of the fact that such a reshuffling is already taking place in at least several regional conflicts, though actually Russia has substantially contributed to this. The first conflict in this list – and so far the only one directly involving a Russian minority – is the secession of Transdnestria from Moldova that led to bloody clashes in December 1991–July 1992. General Lebed, the commander of the Russian 14th Army deployed in Transdnestria, actually took the initiative in recognizing the secessionist government and in defending it from Chishinau. When his crusade, encouraged by the Russian military leadership and by Vice-President Rutskoi, also found support in the Russian Supreme Soviet, President Yeltsin initiated a peace-making operation conducted in July–August 1992 under the aegis of the CIS. This operation effectively transformed the front-line along the River Dnestr into a new border which was duly consolidated during 1993. Ukraine carefully refrained from any involvement in the conflict and from any participation in the quasi-settlement, being concerned primarily about the possible linkage between a Moldovan–Romanian reunification (accelerated by the conflict) and territorial claims on Northern Bukovina and Southern Bessarabia.[37]

From mid-1992 the focus of Russia's conflict management shifted to the North Caucasus and resulted in several peace-making operations. Since this area remains beyond the scope of this book, suffice it to say that among the results of Moscow's activity were the secessions of both South Ossetia and Abkhazia from Georgia; while the former is moving along the road of unification with North Ossetia (which is the only pro-Yeltsin republic in the North Caucasus), the latter acquired a quasi-independent status similar to that of Chechnya.[38]

More relevant for this study are the closely interwoven ethnic, territorial and military problems between Russia and the three Baltic states. The initial benevolence of the Russian Foreign Ministry towards Estonia, Latvia and Lithuania left the Russian Army with an opportunity to take the initiative. Looking for any justification for slowing down the troop withdrawals, the Russian military leadership could not overlook the issue of the rights of the Russian-speaking population, which according to the laws and regulations adopted by Estonia and Latvia in late 1991–early 1992 was deprived of citizenship. Since its creation in May 1992, the Russian Ministry of Defence started to push forward the point that the troops deployed in the Baltic were the only guarantor of the physical security of the Russians. Thus, the Russian military presence in Estonia and Latvia was becoming a sort of peacekeeping operation. President Yeltsin subscribed to this position in October 1992 when he issued a directive suspending the troop withdrawals and linking this to the alleged violation of the rights of the Russian-speaking population.

The year 1993 witnessed a number of new developments in this controversy. While in the international arena Russia failed to raise any support for the 'linkage' approach, an attempt was made to split the Baltic unity by treating Lithuania on different terms. Praising Vilnius for the provision of citizenship to all residents (and implicitly acknowledging the absence of any territorial claims and the cooperation regarding Kaliningrad), Moscow completed the withdrawal of troops by 31 August 1993 even without any formal agreement. By contrast, the negotiations with Latvia (about 10,000 Russian troops remained at the beginning of 1994) and Estonia (about 3,000) remained deadlocked; the former managed to strike a deal only in April and the latter in August 1994.

Simultaneously, a fierce political offensive was launched against Estonia which in June–July 1993 adopted a rather controversial Law on Aliens labelled by top-ranking officials in Moscow as 'apartheid' and 'ethnic cleansing'. A protest campaign in the predominantly Russian-populated Narva region culminated in a referendum on territorial autonomy held on 17 July 1993. The results were not very convincing which made it easy for the Estonian Supreme Court to declare the referendum null and void. What was more important, the Estonian Government made several conciliatory steps and gestures towards the Russian residents, so the crisis was temporarily defused.

At the same time as the number of Russian citizens in Narva is steadily growing, the ethno-national conflict is acquiring a territorial dimension.[39]

The growth of social tensions and unemployment in the industrialized north-west of Estonia provides a support base for nationalistic leaders who advocate secession and unification with Russia.[40] In this case, the Russian Government would find it difficult to refer to the principle of the inviolability of borders, since the Estonian Government refuses to recognize the existing border and insists on restoring the provisions of the Tartu Treaty (1920). Currently, Moscow bluntly rejects any territorial claims from both Estonia and Latvia, and all the evidence shows that public support in these countries for keeping the border question open is diminishing.[41] It is perfectly possible to assume that these overlapping territorial problems could provide the Russian Army with another chance to seize the initiative and go forward with a peace-making intervention in north-eastern Estonia, presenting the politicians in Moscow with a *fait accompli*.

In general, the new political willingness to attach the highest priority to the protection of ethnic Russians in the 'near-abroad' and the chain of precedents of *de facto* redrawing of borders through peace-making operations create a fertile ground for new military adventures that could be directly aimed at the territorial expansion of the Russian Federation.

5. CONCLUSION

Since the beginning of 1993 Russia has started to claim special rights and responsibilities for preserving stability and managing local conflicts across the geopolitical space of the former Soviet Union. This course enjoys broad support in the political elite, while many experts are competing in presenting justifications and guidelines.[42]

What is particularly relevant to this study are the attempts to secure some international legitimization for such a course. They are conducted primarily by the Foreign Ministry which has abandoned its initial Euro-normative approach in favour of a Russo-centric one combining ethno-historical 'norms' with great-power 'rights'. Begging for blessings and support from the UN and CSCE, Foreign Minister Kozyrev places the emphasis on two points: that no one else can shoulder the burden of making peace (however imperfect) in the smouldering ruins of the USSR, and that Russia's behaviour still meets international standards, including the principle of the inviolability of borders.[43] The second point, obviously, contains a good portion of hypocrisy, since the political declarations fail to take into account the real results of Russian interventions in Transdnestria, South Ossetia and Abkhazia.

Even more obvious is the hypocrisy of the official rhetoric intended for domestic consumption which is becoming openly nationalistic and aggressive. Actually, neither Kozyrev nor Yeltsin himself can compete in the field of 'patriotic' statements with Zhirinovsky who feels absolutely free to make breathtaking territorial claims. If any logic could be found in his geopolitical vision (and it is going to be advertised by the parliamentary Committee on Geopolitics controlled by his party), it is that of 'historical rights' of major nation-states, particularly Russia and Germany.[44] Yeltsin's drift towards the nationalistic current, far from improving his buoyancy, results in a dangerous shift of foreign policy towards irrational territorial expansion.

At the same time, Russia's manoeuvres to obtain international support for her peace-making activities should not be treated just as a camouflage for a neo-imperialist course. To a substantial degree, they are intended to keep this course in check, to introduce certain limits for the foreseeable interventions and to create new levers of control. It is indeed a commonplace that President Yeltsin has failed to establish any effective political control over the Russian Army which has become an independent policymaker in the 'near-abroad'.[45] The international involvement could, presumably, contribute to a clarification of the political goals of the peace-making operations (including those related to borders) and could also be instrumental in transforming the political role of the Army.

On the other hand, any participation of the OSCE or, possibly, NACC in peace-making activities in the former USSR involves the necessity of revising the principle of the inviolability of borders. In a way, this principle has also been put under question by the UN peacekeeping operations in Cyprus and, more recently, in Croatia. It might be the case that conflict management in some post-USSR cases could only be effective if the border changes were introduced, even if the consent of the parties to the conflict would not be immediately available. The crucial challenge for the policy-makers is, therefore, to produce such a revised version of the inviolability of borders principle as would not provoke a chain reaction of territorial reshuffling.

NOTES

1. Even if formally recognized by Moscow, the independence of the newly-born states was not taken seriously. Stalin's article from 1919 provides a convincing testimony: 'The so-called independence of so-called independent Georgia, Armenia, Poland, Finland etc. is only a deceptive appearance masking the complete dependence of these – pardon the word – states on this or that group of imperialism'. See Stalin, *Sochineniya*, vol. IV (Moscow, Foreign Languages Publishing House 1950), p. 353.
2. Vittorio Strada elaborated this idea in a presentation at the conference of the Rome Movement in Moscow in October 1991. See *Nezavisimaya Gazeta*, 6 November 1991.
3. V.I. Lenin, 'Left-Wing Childishness and the Petty-Bourgeois Mentality', in V.I. Lenin, *Collected Works* (Moscow: Progress 1974[1918]), p. 331.
4. One example confirming this priority is the return of the Bialystok area to Poland. The security emphasis was introduced by the special Commission in the Soviet Foreign Ministry for the peace treaties headed by Maxim Litvinov. The papers of the Commission (634 files) are now available from the Foreign Policy Archive (Komissiya Litvinova po podgotovke mirnykh dogovorov i poslevoennogo ustroistva, Archiv Vneshnei Politiki Rossiiskoi Federatsii, file 512). I am indebted to Vlad Zubok, Senior Researcher, Nobel Institute, Oslo ,for sharing this information.
5. The prevailing of security over ideology was most evident on the border with China which, after the armed incidents in 1969, was fortified beyond rationale, despite the unquestionably 'communist' nature of the neighbour.
6. A brilliant analysis of the concept of the Wall as an element of European political philosophy can be found in Ola Tunander's forthcoming book *Murar. Essaer om Makt, Identitet och Territorialitet*. See also his article 'Frihet, Murar och "Frimmurare" i 90-talets Europa', *Internasjonal Politikk*, vol. 51, no. 4, 1993, pp. 419–34.
7. Solzhenitsyn later presented his ideas in the celebrated brochure 'How to Rebuild Russia' where he made an emotional point: 'We do not have a power for the Empire – and we don't need it, and let it fall from our shoulders: now it is smashing and sucking us, and fostering our downfall.' See *Komsomolskaya Pravda*, 18 September 1991.
8. As one astute observer puts it, 'For the 20th Congress generation, Eastern Europe was not an irreducible area of domination as much as a badly managed sphere of influence'. See Alex Pravda, 'Soviet Policy Towards Eastern Europe in Transition', in Alex Pravda (ed.), *The End of the Outer Empire* (London: Sage 1992), p. 2.
9. Soviet mass-media tried to play down the resonance of this defeat. Maybe the only voice calling the failure by its real name was that of Marina Pavlova-Silvanskaya. See *Literaturnaya Gazeta*, no. 29, 1989.
10. In January 1991, the International Department of the CPSU Central Committee prepared a document which set down guidelines for a more 'active' policy in Eastern Europe employing military instruments. See Suzanne Crow, 'International Department and Foreign Ministry Disagree on Eastern Europe', *RFE/RL Report on the USSR*, 21 June 1991.
11. Alexandr Yakovlev alone tried to prepare the ground for a compromise by pressing for a formal abrogation of the protocols to the Molotov–Ribbentrop Pact of 1939, but his personal diplomacy only instigated the crisis.
12. See Michael Beschloss and Strobe Talbott, *At The Highest Levels* (London: Little, Brown & Co. 1993), p. 111.
13. In early 1991 this author – as a columnist for such periodicals as *Radical* and *Rossia* – introduced a dilemma: '*Perestroika* or the Baltics – we cannot have both'. The inability to make a choice eventually resulted in missing both alternatives.
14. Enjoying a vacation in Crimea on the eve of the coup, Gorbachev argued in an article: 'Today a genuinely voluntary community of peoples is being put together and that will give unprecedented stability to our Union. ... In the course of 1000 years in one case, of 200 to 300 years in another and of 50 in the third case [i.e. the Baltic republics] such realities had taken shape for the healthy growth of which was required a vital, real federation and not

some loose community or association.' See Mikhail Gorbachev, *The August Coup* (London: HarperCollins 1991), p. 115.

15. See Tom Nairn, 'Demonizing Nationalism', *London Review of Books*, 25 February 1993.
16. Thus, Victor Kuvaldin argues that 'It was the swift and illegitimate elimination of the Union that has resulted in sharp increase of the armed conflicts and their death toll, and the end to this bloody bacchanal is nowhere in sight. Today the "Belovezh syndrome" is threatening the integrity of many new-born states, including Russia.' See *Nezavisimaya Gazeta*, 7 August 1993.
17. Paul Goble argued: 'By converting the ethnic identity of all groups into official nationalities with a clearly defined territorial dimension, Stalin institutionalized ethnic tensions, justifying his authoritarian regime and guaranteeing that the collapse of the Soviet Union would follow ethnic lines'. See Paul A. Goble, 'Russia and Its Neighbours', *Foreign Policy*, no. 90, 1993, p. 80.
18. This statement was addressed first of all to Ukraine, which was pushing forward the Uti Possidetis approach. As Sakwa pointed out, 'Yeltsin had hoped to make the other republics aware of the price and dangers of seeking full independence, but the plan had disastrously backfired, and fuelled the independence movements.' See Richard Sakwa, *Russian Politics and Society* (London: Routledge 1993), p. 384.
19. See *Pravda*, 30 January 1992.
20. Report 'Strategy for Russia' prepared by the Council on Foreign and Defence Policy providing the guidelines for an 'enlightened post-empire course' made it clear that 'Any rational policy demands for an unconditional recognition of the principle of inviolability of borders, despite their obviously artificial character. A rejection of this principle would pave the way for dozens of conflicts, to a national catastrophe'. See *Nezavisimaya Gazeta*, 19 August 1992.
21. For detailed information see a report of the Centre for Political-Geographic Research in *Politicheski Monitoring Rossii*, no. 3, 1992. See also Charles J. Dick, John F. Dunn and John B.K. Lough, 'Pandora's Box. Potential Conflicts in Post-Communist Europe', *International Defence Review*, no. 3, 1993, pp. 203–8.
22. New Year's Message, Russian Television, 30 December 1992.
23. Solzhenitsyn insisted that 'Central Asia and the Transcaucasus have their separate roads, which are far from us. Ukraine – with its short-sighted hatred – has been repulsing us. The only real encouraging entity, which can be stable, is the state union of Belarus, Russia and Kazakhstan.' From a letter to Vladimir Lukin published in *Moscow News*, 12 March 1993.
24. See *Voennyi Vestnik*, no. 7, 1992, p. 32.
25. Heavy casualties in July 1993 revived the 'Afghan syndrome', but in the debates the majority of influential experts, such as Sergei Blagovolin, insisted that Russia could not abandon her 'security frontier'. See *Moskovskie Novosti*, 1 August 1993. The Russian Security Council subscribed to such a position, so President Yeltsin told the leaders of the Central Asian states on 7 August that the border with Afghanistan is considered as 'essentially Russian'.
26. The negative assessments of the Russian General Staff were presented in *Nezavisimaya Gazeta*, 30 July 1992. In May 1993 the military leaders, including the commander of the Pacific Fleet, reiterated their opposition to territorial concessions (see *Vostok Rossii*, no. 17, May 1993), so Yeltsin had to postpone his visit for the second time. The official visit finally took place in October 1993, but every effort was made to avoid the territorial problem. See Stephen Foye, 'Russo–Japanese Relations: Still Travelling a Rocky Road', *RFE/RL Research Report*, vol. 2, no. 44, 1993.
27. For a more elaborate analysis see 'Ethnic and Political Conflicts in Georgia and North Caucasus', *Conflicts in the CSCE Area* (Oslo: PRIO 1994). See also Iver Neumann, 'The Caucasus between Russia, Turkey and Iran', *NUPI Working Paper*, no. 495, 1993.
28. See Phillip Petersen and Shane Petersen, 'The Kaliningrad Garrison State', *Jane's Intelligence Review*, February 1993.
29. For an elaborate analysis see Pavel Baev, 'Russian Perspectives on the Barents Region', in Olav Schram Stokke and Ola Tunander (eds), *The Barents Region – Regional Cooperation in Arctic Europe* (London: Sage 1994).

30. This situation was diagnosed by several Russian experts long before the alarmist US National Intelligence Estimate discovered it. See Andrei Kortunov, 'Should You Hit a Man when He Is Down?', *Moscow News*, 10 December 1993 and 'Dire US Forecast for Ukraine Conflict', *International Herald Tribune*, 26 January 1994.

31. Samuel Huntington emphasized this division line in his celebrated article 'The Clash of Civilizations?', while arguing that 'If civilization is what counts, however, the likelihood of violence between Ukrainians and Russians should be low.' See*Foreign Affairs*, vol. 72, no. 3, 1993, p. 38.

32. An interesting reflection on this split could be found in Stalin's Report to the XVIII Congress of the CPSU (March 1939): 'It is quite possible, of course, that there are madmen in Germany who dream of annexing the elephant, that is the Soviet Ukraine, to the gnat, namely the so-called Carpatho-Ukraine. If there really are such lunatics in Germany, rest assured that we shall find enough strait-jackets for them in our country.' (Thunderous applause). See Josef Stalin, *The Problems of Leninism* (Moscow: Progress 1953), p. 755.

33. At the Sixth Congress of People's Deputies in April 1992 Kozyrev advocated passionately a 'nonintrusive' approach to the protection of Russian-speaking populations in the CIS countries. See John Lough, 'Defining Russia's Relations with Neighbouring States', *RFE/RL Research Report*, vol. 2, no. 20, 1993.

34. The draft military doctrine released in May 1992 identified the violation of rights of Russians and 'those identifying ethnically and culturally with Russia' as a serious*casus belli*. See *Voennaya Mysl,* special issue, May 1992. A more cautious approach limiting the case only to the citizens of the Russian Federation could be found in the Military Doctrine that was approved in November 1993. What is also interesting is that the 'territorial claims of other states' are going on the top of the list of 10 'main existing and potential sources of military threat'. See *Jane's Intelligence Review*, Special Report, January 1994.

35. This document was prepared by the Russian Security Council and endorsed by President Yeltsin in early May 1993. It is certainly possible to trace its origin to the above-mentioned Report Strategy for Russia that argued that Russian minorities should be considered not only as a top priority problem, but also as an important asset for Russia's foreign policy. See *Nezavisimaya Gazeta*, 29 April 1993.

36. This new priority was presented in President Yeltsin's 1994 New Year Address where he defined Russia as 'the first among equals' in the CIS. It was elaborated in Kozyrev's controversial speech before the Russian ambassadors on 18 January 1994. The first reaction from German Chancellor Kohl and British Defence Minister Rifkind came two weeks later at a security conference in Munich. They made it clear that NATO had taken into consideration Russia's concerns on the enlargement issue and 'in return' expected that Moscow would respect the sovereignty of neighbours. See *Süddeutsche Zeitung*, 7 February 1994.

37. A referendum and parliamentary elections in Moldova in March 1994 showed strong public opposition to reunification; nevertheless, the survivability of the state remains highly questionable.

38. For a more elaborate analysis see Pavel Baev, 'Europeiske Utbryterstater og Nye Grenser', *Internasjonal Politikk*, vol. 51, no. 4, 1993, pp. 475–83.

39. Of Narva's 85,000 residents, about 11,500 are Russian citizens, while fewer than 6,000 are Estonian citizens. Ethnic Estonians make up only about 10 per cent of the population of north-eastern Estonia. See Philip Hanson, 'Estonia's Narva Problem, Narva's Estonian Problem', *RFE/RL Research Report*, vol. 2, no. 18, 1993.

40. A clear signal came from the December elections. Of about 10,000 Russians voting in Estonia (6,000 in Tallinn and 4,000 in Narva), 65.5 per cent opposed the new Constitution with 48 per cent supporting Zhirinovsky's LDP and 19 per cent the Communists.*Baltfax*, 13 December 1993.

41. A poll from December 1993 indicated that only 53 per cent of the Estonian respondents supported the restoration of the pre-World War II border, while 40 per cent were ready to accept a compromise. The attitude of non-Estonian respondents differed significantly: 69 per cent were for compromise and only 15 per cent backed the restoration of the Tartu Treaty line. See *RFE/RL News Brief*, 27 December 1993–4 January 1994.

42. For an early moderate version see Sergei Karaganov, 'Presentiment of Imperialism', *Moscow News*, no. 44, 1992. Andranik Migranian, another member of the Presidential Council, has recently declared himself the author of the Russian version of the 'Monroe Doctrine'. See *Nezavisimaya Gazeta*, 12 January 1994. Yuri Baturin, national security advisor to the President, declared that Russia as a great power had a duty to protect ethnic Russians in all new independent states. See *Der Spiegel*, 7 February 1994.

43. The best example could be found in Kozyrev's speech at the CSCE meeting in Rome in early December 1993, which had some peculiar reflections on his celebrated phoney speech at the CSCE 1992 meeting in which he tried to present a course of the post-democratic Russia. See William Safire, 'Russian Reform: Thanks, Kozyrev, for That Slap', *International Herald Tribune*, 18 December 1992.

44. What is most interesting in Zhirinovsky's recent cartographic exercise is his willingness to return Kaliningrad to Germany and to leave Russia's border with Finland unchanged. See *The European*, 4–10 February 1994.

45. Back in 1992, Kozyrev went as far as to accuse the military establishment of deliberately exploiting the conflicts in Transdnestria and Transcaucasia. See *Izvestiya*, 1 July 1992. But in 1993 he dared not repeat those accusations.

PART III

Cases

6. Bessarabia and Northern Bukovina

Ioan Chiper

One might say that the situation of the territories inhabited by Romanians in the east and north-east of the present political borders of Romania surpasses in its complexity that of the other territories the Russian Empire or the Soviet Union has 'reunited' over the past two centuries. The issue is about the Romanian territories of Bessarabia, Northern Bukovina, Herta District and the Isle of Serpents, that were gathered under Russian or Soviet domination at different times (see Map 6.1).The territories of Bessarabia, Northern Bukovina and Herta District, that were annexed by the Soviet Union in June 1940, had a total area of 50,800 square kilometres and they had a population of 3.9 million inhabitants.[1] The part of the Republic of Moldova on the left bank of Dnestr known as Transdnestria should also be added to the above list. All the aforementioned territories belonged once to the medieval Principality of Moldavia or evolved historically in close relation to this principality populated by ethnic Romanians. Today all these regions are in different situations.

1. HISTORICAL EVOLUTION

General Background

The Principality of Moldavia was formed in the 14th century. Her borders went along the River Dnestr in the east, the River Ceremush in the north, the Oriental Carpathians in the west and the River Milcov, the maritime Danube and the Black Sea coast in the south. In the second half of the 15th century and during the first decades of the 16th century the Romanian medieval principalities of Wallachia, Moldavia and Transylvania fell under the domination of the Ottoman Empire. They succeeded, neverthe-

Map 6.1. Bessarabia and Northern Bukovina.

less, in preserving their autonomy and maintaining their political, administrative and military structures.

Bessarabia

According to current practice Bessarabia is the designation for the territory bordered by the rivers Prut, Danube and Dnestr. However, until the 19th century the term Bessarabia designated only the southern part of the territory of Moldavia between the Prut and the Dnestr.

The Russian ambition to rule Moldavia became apparent in the 18th century. The Russian Empire wished to conquer the Romanian principalities in her expansion directed towards the Straits, and Moldovia became a battlefield for Russian and Turkish armies. As a result of the Russian–Turkish War at the beginning of the 19th century Russia eventually occupied Moldavia and Wallachia. In the Treaty of 1812 the territory between the Prut and the Dnestr was given to Russia.[2] The territory then annexed by Russia was 45,630 square kilometres in size.

In the Paris Treaty of 1856 after the Crimean War, Russia was compelled to return the southern part of Bessarabia to Moldavia. After the union of Moldavia and Wallachia (1859) and the creation of the Romanian State this part of Bessarabia fell within the Romanian borders. Under the terms of the San Stefano Peace Treaty twenty years later Southern Bessarabia, i.e. the districts of Bolgrad, Cahul and Izmail, were again given to Russia.[3]

In October 1917 the revolutionary turmoil in Russia and the collapse of tszarism prompted the Congress of the Moldavian Soldiers to proclaim the national and territorial autonomy of Bessarabia and decide upon the setting up of a representative body, the Country Council.[4] Bessarabia was proclaimed the Moldavian Democratic Republic within the Russian Democratic Federative Republic by the Country Council in December 1917.[5] The Country Council declared the Moldavian Republic independent in January 1918 and in March–April 1918 the same body, which also comprised representatives of the national minorities, voted for union with 'her Mother, Romania' (86 ayes, 3 noes, and 36 abstentions from voting).[6]

France, Britain, Japan and Romania recognized the union in the treaty signed in Paris in October 1920. The Soviet Government, however, never recognized the union of Bessarabia with Romania. In August 1939 in the Soviet–German Molotov–Ribbentrop Pact Germany gave her approval to the annexation of Bessarabia by the Soviet Union,[7] which took place a year later. In June 1940, through a note of ultimatum, the Soviet Government demanded the return of Bessarabia, accusing Romania of having detached the territory from the Soviet Union (Russia) 'thus breaking the century-old unity between Bessarabia, that is mainly inhabited by Ukrainians, and the Soviet Ukrainian Republic'.[8] Taking into account Romania's complete isolation on the international scene as well as German pressure and the threats from the military forces of her revisionist neighbours, the Romanian Government accepted these claims on 28 June 1940. That day and during the days that followed Soviet troops annexed Bessarabia.

Northern Bukovina

Bukovina started to emerge as an issue in the second half of the 18th century following the events engendered by the first division of Poland

(1772) and the Russian–Turkish War (1768–74). The Habsburg Empire had remained neutral during the war and the Court in Vienna required, from the Ottoman Porte, the northern part of the Principality of Moldavia as a reward. The Porte agreed to the request and in 1775 Bukovina fell under Habsburg rule. That is the territory where Suceava, the old capital of medieval Moldavia, was situated. The region had not had a special name while still belonging to Moldavia but the Court in Vienna adopted the name Bukovina (Buchenwald). Its area was 10,441 square kilometres and at that time it was inhabited by more than 71,000 people of whom Romanians made up the majority. Approximately 16,000 people were Guzuls, Ruthenians, Armenians, Jews and Gypsies. As in the case of Bessarabia, during the Habsburg domination a continuous modification of the ethnic structure of Bukovina took place through colonizations and considerable infiltrations of Germans, Ukrainians, Jews, and so on.

At the end of World War I Bukovina became part of the Romanian State as a result of the disintegration of the Austrian–Hungarian Monarchy. In November 1918 the General Congress of Bukovina decided unanimously on 'an eternal and unconditional union of Bukovina within its ancient borders up to the Ceremush, Calacin and the Dnestr' to Romania. The delegates of the Polish and German national councils joined this decision.[9]

Bukovina was not mentioned in the Molotov–Ribbentrop Pact but in June 1940 the Soviet Government let the German Government know that it intended to annex Bukovina. The same month the Soviet Government addressed a note of ultimatum to the Romanian Government, demanding Northern Bukovina. As a result it was annexed by the Soviet Union. No part of Bukovina had belonged to Russia, Ukraine, or the Soviet Union before the summer of 1940.

The Herta District

The Herta District is a territory situated in North-Eastern Moldavia between the Prut and the Oriental Carpathians. It has always been part of the Principality of Moldavia, and, after the 1859 union, the Romanian State. This territory, with its compact Romanian population, was annexed by the Soviet Union in June 1940. The territory was occupied after the Soviet notes of ultimatum in June 1940, without at even having been claimed. Even the most aberrant justifications were impossible.[10]

The Isle of Serpents

The Isle of Serpents, the largest island in the Black Sea, is situated about 45 kilometres out at sea in front of the Danube mouths. Its territory is only 0.17 square kilometres but it lies on the central axis of the Danube delta, facing a harbour. The Isle of Serpents has a certain strategic importance, but it is also important for the delimitation of territorial waters and continental plateau which can be exploited economically. The mouth of the Danube and the Isle of Serpents were under Ottoman rule together with the rest of the Romanian territories except for approximately a 30-year period before the Crimean War when they were occupied by Russia. Through the Berlin Peace Treaty of 1878, together with Dobruja and the Danube Delta, the Isle of Serpents again became Romanian territory. It continued to be Romanian territory even after the summer of 1940, as well as after the Paris Peace Treaty of February 1947.

However, on 4 February 1948 the Soviet Government forced Romania to give up the island, a protocol being signed to this end by Vyacheslav Molotov and Prime Minister Petru Groza. The island was yielded through an official report signed on 28 May 1948. These documents were never ratified either by the Soviet or by the Romanian parliaments, so the occupation of the island by the USSR was never valid in legal terms.[11]

A similar modification of the border took place in response to an official report dated 25 November 1949 when the frontier on the branch of Masura was displaced in the Danube delta.

Transdnestria

The territory of Transdnestria was never included within the historical boundaries of the Moldavian Principality or the Romanian State, but its evolution has been dependent on Moldavia. Up to the end of the 18th century the majority of the population was Romanian. The borders of the Russian Empire were moved to the Dnestr in 1793 and Transdnestria was put under Russian rule. The ethnic picture changed owing to colonization by Russians, Ukrainians, Germans, Bulgarians, and others.

During the socio-political turmoil in Russia in 1917 the community of Transdnestrian Romanians convoked their own Congress in Tiraspol in December and requested a union with Bessarabia. They also demanded the use of the Romanian language in schools and use of the Latin alphabet.[12] These efforts did not produce an effect, however. First, in October 1924 the presence of the considerable Romanian population was acknowledged and a distinct Romanian administrative union was created, on the eastern bank of the Dnestr, when the Soviet authorities decided to create the Moldavian Autonomous Soviet Socialist Republic (MASSR) within the Ukrainian Soviet Socialist Republic. The actual purpose of the decision was, however, to create an important political bridgehead for the Russian actions against Romania. Far from including the whole of the Romanian population living on the left bank of the Dnestr, the new autonomous republic was initially 7,516 square kilometres in size and comprised eleven districts. The population numbered 545,000 of whom, according to official data, 39 per cent were Romanians. After a few years the territory was extended to 8,434 square kilometres and three more districts were created.[13] The capital was established first at Balta and from 1929 at Tiraspol. Between 1932 and 1938 the Latin alphabet was introduced in the Romanian schools of the Moldavian ASSR.

2. THE STATUS OF THE TERRITORIES AFTER THE SOVIET ANNEXATION IN 1940

While the Soviet annexation of Bessarabia and Northern Bukovina was imposed by force, the next phase, the creation of the Moldavian Soviet Socialist Republic, represented an abuse. The Moldavian Soviet Socialist Republic was proclaimed by the Supreme Soviet of the USSR through a law of 2 August 1940. The new republic, decreed in Moscow, did not consist of all the annexed territories nor of all the districts of the former Moldavian ASSR. A part of the territories was given to the Ukrainian Soviet Socialist Republic, namely Hotin in the north and Izmail and Cetatea Alba (Akkerman) in the south. Out of the fourteen districts of the former Moldavian Autonomous Republic to the east of the Dnestr, eight were given to Ukraine.[14] Ukraine also received the territories of Northern Bukovina and the Herta District.

The annexation of Romanian territories by the Soviet Union had been a direct consequence of the agreement between Berlin and Moscow, inaugurated by the Ribbentrop–Molotov Pact. When relations between the two totalitarian states deteriorated and Germany attacked the Soviet Union in June 1941 Romania took part in the war on the side of the

German Army. By the end of July 1941, the Romanian–German forces had liberated Bessarabia, Northern Bukovina and the Herta District, which were reintegrated into the Romanian state. The Romanian Army continued military operations beyond the Dnestr.

The territory between the rivers Dnestr and Bug that bordered the rivers Niomjii and Rov in the north and the Black Sea and the bank of the Dnepr in the south passed under Romanian civilian administration in August 1941. The name of this administrative unity was Transdnestria.[15] This phase ended when the year 1944 brought the Soviet troops back to the Transdnestrian territory.

In August 1944 there was a *coup d'état* in Romania and as a consequence arms were turned against Germany. An armistice with the Soviet Union came into force in September 1944 and Romania was constrained to accept the frontier which it had had with the Soviet Union after June 1940. This frontier was confirmed in the Peace Treaty of February 1947.[16]

The end of World War II meant that the historical unity of Bessarabia was destroyed. The Moldavian Soviet Socialist Republic was corseted through Kiev in both a strategical and economic sense and the access to the Danube was now reduced to less than one kilometre. Important resources of raw materials had been lost and part of the economically structured zones were destroyed. The communist leaders of the Moldavian Soviet Socialist Republic had already addressed a letter to Stalin in the summer and autumn of 1940 and again after the war in 1946 asking for the three districts that had been given to Ukraine to be again incorporated into the rest of Bessarabia.[17] These efforts were ignored.

The occupied Romanian territories witnessed the introduction of the political-administrative and economic structures of the Soviet regime. The land, banks, industrial and commercial enterprises, the railway and water transports and other means of communication were nationalized. Also the collectivization of agriculture was initiated and state farms were created.

Until the 1970s, the Moldavian Soviet Socialist Republic was a territory with a mainly agricultural economy. The food industry, especially the production of wines and tinned products, was most significant. Industrial investments were considerably reduced compared to other Soviet socialist republics during the first two decades after the war. The most important industrial activities were concentrated on the left bank of the Dnestr. A strong dependence on Russia was created as regards the sources of raw materials, energy and fuels. A high percentage of the national product was also transferred to other parts of the Soviet Union.[18] The process of urbanization was accelerated more in Moldavia than in the rest of the Soviet Union, which can be explained by the lower level of the economic structure of Bessarabia. This also facilitated the policy of colonization practised by Moscow.[19]

It has been estimated that in the name of Sovietization one million ethnic Romanians were deported to labour camps or sent to distant regions of the Soviet Union. Many Romanians were executed. Simultaneously a systematic process of Russian and Ukrainian colonization took place in Moldavia.[20] The Russification of the Romanian population was promoted through imposing the Russian language, which was standard for all the territories annexed by the Soviet Union. In addition, partial attempts were made to create an artificial language, a Moldo-Romanian-Russian cant, by replacing words of Latin origin with Slavic words and the promotion of certain regionalisms, especially those on the left bank of the Dnestr.[21] The official point of view – presented and spread in the most diverse writings – was that there existed a Moldavian people and a Moldavian language, different from the Romanian people and the Romanian language. This aberrant theory, which obviously contradicted the historical reality, was officially recognized until the proclamation of the Republic of Moldova in 1991. The consequences of this theory still affect present developments.

The following three tables show the demographic development of those Romanian territories that today belong to the Republics of Moldova and Ukraine. Different political dominations and historical backgrounds naturally have left their traces. Bukovina was under Austrian domination in the years 1775–1918 and Bessarabia under Russian domination from 1812 to 1918. This was followed by the Soviet domination over Bessarabia, Northern Bukovina and the Herta District in 1940–41 and again from 1944 to 1989. During the Soviet regime the penetration of the Ruthenian and Ukrainian populations into Bukovina and of the Ukrainian and Russian populations into Bessarabia was favoured.

Table 6.1[22] shows the population of Bessarabia, the largest of the Romanian territories later to come under Soviet occupation. The figures are from the years 1817, 1897 and 1930. Ethnic structure has been estimated on the basis of mother tongue.

Table 6.1. The Population of Bessarabia by Nationality

Nationality	1817	%	1897	%	1930	%
Romanians	419,240	86.0	920,919	47.6	1,610,757	56.2
Ukrainians	30,000	6.5	379,698	19.6	314,211	11.1
Russians	6,000	1.5	155,774	8.0	351,912	12.3
Bulgarians	1,205	0.25	103,225	5.4	163,726	5.7
Gagauzians	1,205	0.25	55,790	2.9	98,173	3.4
Jews	19,130	4.2	228,168	11.8	204,858	7.2
Germans	–	–	60,206	3.1	81,089	2.8
Gypsies	–	–	8,636	0.4	13,518	0.5
Poles	–	–	11,696	0.6	8,104	0.3
Greeks	3,200	0.7	–	–	–	–
Armenians	2,650	0.6	–	–	–	–
Others	–	–	11,300	0.6	18,055	0.6
TOTAL	482,630	100.0	1,935,412	100.0	2,864,402	100.0

The structure of the population in the Republic of Moldova according to the 1989 census can be seen in Table 6.2.[23]

Table 6.2. The Population of Moldova by Nationality 1989

Nationality	No. of pers. (thousand)	%	Urban area (thousand)	%	Rural area (thousand)	%
Romanians	2,794.7	64.5	935.9	46.3	1,858.8	80.3
Ukrainians	600.4	13.8	379.0	18.9	221.3	9.5
Russians	562.1	13.0	483.7	23.9	78.3	3.4
Gagauzians	153.3	3.5	63.1	3.1	90.4	3.9
Bulgarians	88.4	2.0	40.2	2.0	48.2	2.0
Jews	65.8	1.5	65.3	3.2	0.5	0.02
Germans	7.3	0.2	4.5	0.2	2.8	0.1
Others	70.5	1.6	48.4	2.4	22.1	0.9
TOTAL	4,335.4	100.0	2020.1	100.0	2,315.3	100.0

The structure of the population according to the 1989 census in Chernovtsy Oblast that was formed out of the former Romanian districts of Chernovtsy and Stovojinetz, the Herta District and parts of the districts Radautzi and Hotin in the Ukrainian Soviet Socialist Republic is shown in Table 6.3.[24]

Table 6.3.   *The Population of Chernovtsy Oblast by Nationality 1989*

Nationality	Number	%
Ukrainians	666,095	70.8
Romanians	100,317	10.7
Moldavians	84,066	9.0
Russians	63,066	6.7
Jews	16,469	1.8
Others	10,355	1.0
TOTAL	940,801	100.0

One can meet Moldavians and Romanians – or in fact, only Romanians, since it was the Soviet census which made this artificial distinction – not only in Chernovtsy Region but also in other parts of Ukraine. In Odessa Oblast in Southern Bessarabia they numbered 144,500, in Transcarpathian Oblast 29,500 in the Nikolaev Oblast 16,700 and in the Kosovograd Oblast 10,700.[25]

These figures provided by the 1989 census do not reflect the real demographic situation, however. The Soviet authorities were interested in increasing the number of Russians and Ukrainians and many Romanian inhabitants did not dare to declare their real nationality. As already shown, according to some unofficial estimations of the Romanians living in Ukraine, their number is about 500–600,000.

3. THE ATTITUDE OF THE FORMER POSSESSOR TOWARDS THE ISSUE

After the installation of the Communist regime in Romania the fact that a part of Romanian territory had been annexed by the USSR was a taboo subject for almost two decades. It was re-opened once the communist leadership in Bucharest started to move away from Moscow in 1964 and later after the affirmation of an autonomous policy of Romania within the Warsaw Pact.[26] The official position of the leadership in Bucharest could be formulated as follows: Romania has no territorial claims towards either one of her neighbours, but the historical truth must be told unreservedly. Hence, during the period 1964–89, the publication of certain historical writings which dealt with the main claims disputed between the Romanian and the Soviet historiographies – 1812, 1918, 1940 – led to tensions between Bucharest and Moscow.

At the official level the idea of uniting Moldova with Romania was put forward at the end of the 1980s. At the 14th Congress of the Romanian Communist Party, Nicolae Ceausescu, the dictator of Romania since 1965, requested the repossessionss of the Molotov–Ribbentrop Pact, which implied the repossession of the lost territories. This took place on the eve of his downfall, and was a desperate effort to win over public opinion, which was almost totally against him.

4. AFTER THE COLLAPSE OF COMMUNISM

The disintegration of the Soviet Empire and the revolutions in the East-European countries generated a new framework for the relations between Romania, the newly created Republic of Moldova, Russia and Ukraine. The Republic of Moldova was proclaimed on 27 August 1991. Roughly speaking, the new state had two alternatives: a) to unify with Romania or b) to keep the status of an independent state.[27] The attitude of the local population towards these alternatives can be analysed at the level of a) the decision-makers, b) the Romanian population and c) the minorities (Russians, Gagauz and Ukrainians).

The Decision-Makers

The decision-makers in Chisinau act in the direction of maintaining the Moldavian statehood. 'The objective of state of the Moldavian leadership under President Snegur is an undivided, sovereign state, in which her own political position of power is safeguarded.[28]

This policy of maintaining an independent Republic of Moldova combines, in fact, two distinct trends. One of them is in favour of a progressive reintegration within the economic space of the former Soviet Union and cooperation with the 'centre' in Moscow. The other trend opposes this tendency and supports independence as a means of blocking any such integration, no matter what form it might take.

In December 1991 President Snegur signed an agreement to affiliate the Republic of Moldova to the CIS, the decision reflecting the economic realities that had resulted from the inclusion of Moldova, for almost five decades, in the Soviet Union. However, the opposition to this act was so strong that he did not present it to the parliament for ratification for nearly two years. When the affiliation agreement was eventually brought to the parliament in August 1993 it was not ratified. In order to circumvent this parliamentary refusal, President Mircea Snegur substituted a recommendation from the president of the parliament, who thereby exceeded his authority. Nevertheless, with such dubious authorization, President Snegur signed, on behalf of Moldova, the agreement on the constitution of the economic union of the CIS in September 1993.

An agreement of integration within the Rouble Zone within the framework of the cooperation policy with the Russian Federation had been signed by Moldova in September 1992.[29] In July 1992, to the surprise of the authorities in Chisinau, all banknotes issued between the years 1961 and 1992 were called in by the Central Russian Bank. This sudden decision by Moscow pushed the government of Moldova to accelerate the issue of a national currency. On 29 November 1993 the currency of the Republic of Moldova, the *leu,* was introduced, the name being identical to the Romanian national currency.

The Moldovan attitude towards Romania could be characterized as a preferential partnership. Being subordinate to the relations with the former Soviet zone, the economic and cultural relations with Romania have a preferential status compared with her relations with any other state. Although the planned Treaty of Brotherhood between the two countries has not yet been signed, Moldova and Romania are parties to numerous cooperation agreements in different domains. Since the second half of 1993 the Romanian Government has also adopted a set of measures with a view to the economic assistance of the Republic of Moldova. Their aim is to diminish the dependency of Moldova on the CIS.

Romanian Population

Within the Romanian population most of the intellectuals (a precise evaluation being, however, difficult to achieve) are favourable to the reunification with Romania. Grouped in the Popular Christian-Democratic Front (which has 78 seats in the parliament)[30] and the newly created Congress of Intellectuals, they criticize vehemently the position adopted by President Mircea Snegur, whom they accuse of being an opponent of unification with Romania.

The great majority of the rural population certainly retains a consciousness of its Romanian identity. It is however influenced by the long-lasting Soviet propaganda, which presented the 'royal, bourgeois-landlord Romania' as a power pitilessly exploiting Bessarabia during the period

1918–40. The economic difficulties that Romania is facing today do not yet make the 'mother-country' so attractive that unification with her is regarded as a means of getting rid of the difficult situation that the Republic of Moldova is experiencing. Thus, for the present, the majority of the Romanian population of Moldova is favourable to the maintenance of Moldovan independence. The union with Romania was fended off in a referendum organized in Moldova in March 1994.[31]

The Minorities

The attitude of the minorities of the Republic of Moldova is not unitary. Regarding the question of unification with Romania, they express reservations or firm opposition. The attitudes towards independence, integrity and the structure of the state are much more complicated. The 'separatists' – the Gagauz who dwell in the south of the Republic of Moldova and the Russian-speaking population from Transdnestria – have claimed the status of territorial autonomy. They are in favour of the federalization of Moldova and are thus becoming important instruments for the policy that not only aims to block the unification of Moldova with Romania but also prevents the consolidation of Moldovan independence. In August 1990 the Gagauz – a Christianized Turkish population that was settled in the south of the territory – proclaimed a 'Gagauz Soviet Socialist Republic' and conferred on itself an administrative and military framework. This structure is supported by the Soviet 14th Army and by the other separatist factions on the left side of the Dnestr.[32] In these regions on the left bank of the Dnestr, which have an area of 4,118 square kilometres, there is a population of 564,000 inhabitants. Romanians number 234,000 and their share is 40 per cent, Ukrainians 170,000 (28 per cent), Russians 153,000 (25 per cent), Bulgarians 11,000 (2 per cent), Gagauz 3,300 (0.5 per cent) and other nationalities 24,000 (4 per cent).[33]

A 'Dnestrian Moldavian Soviet Socialist Republic' was proclaimed on 2 September 1990, just a few days after the proclamation of the 'Gagauz Soviet Socialist Republic'. On 1 March 1992 it started military actions against the legal authorities. During the period 1 March–29 July 1992 these actions acquired the character of a real war, the military actions of the separatists in Tiraspol being supported by the Soviet 14th Army. Tanks, armoured vehicles and artillery were used. By the end of May there were recorded about a thousand dead and about 4,200 wounded.[34] Those fleeing from the conflict zone to the right bank of the Dnestr numbered 33,000.[35]

On 21 July 1992 Presidents Snegur and Yeltsin made an agreement on the peaceful settlement of the armed conflict in the Dnestrian zone. This agreement, which some people called President Snegur's 'capitulation', gave the separatists *de facto* recognition of their administrative structure on the left bank of the Dnestr, which was later extended to Tighina (Bendery) on the right bank of the Dnestr.[36] One of the main actions of the authorities of the self-proclaimed Dnestrian Republic to demonstrate their distinctiveness was the setting up of a trial in Tiraspol against six supporters of the Moldovan Popular Front in December 1993. The leader of the group, Ilie Ilascu, was sentenced to death.[37]

At the same time, the anti-unionist forces on the right bank of the Dnestr intensified their activity. Thus, when debating the issue of the new Constitution of the Republic of Moldova, a group of deputies of the faction 'Life of the Villages' required that instead of the formulation 'the official language of the Republic of Moldova is the Romanian language', the article on languages should read 'the state language of the Republic of Moldova is the Moldavian language'.[38]

The situation in Moldova is by no means stable. After the proclamation of independence the Republic of Moldova tried to create her own military structures. However, the measures taken were neither systematic nor sustained, so that the armed forces of the country are totally insignificant. Having in mind the events that took place, they proved unable to withstand the aggressive actions of the Russophone separatists who were supported by the Russian 14th Army.

The economic situation is characterized by the difficulties inherent in a period of transition from the socialist to the market economy. They are made even more acute by the fact that the region on the left side of the Dnestr came under the control of the separatist forces. Numerous industrial enterprises, which are vital for the normal development of the economic life of the republic, are concentrated here.

5. THE ATTITUDE OF THE PRESENT NEIGHBOURS TOWARDS THE ISSUE

Russia

The official Russian position is that after the collapse of the Soviet Union there exists no Russian–Romanian territorial dispute, since the former

Romanian territories situated beyond the borders of the Republic of Moldova belong now to the Republic of Ukraine instead of to the Russian Federation.

The withdrawal of the Russian frontiers from the Prut did not mean that Moscow had lost interest in the Dnestrian zone, however. The most convincing expression of this is the presence of the Soviet 14th Army on the territory of the Republic of Moldova. After the collapse of the Soviet Union parts of its army joined the Ukrainian Army but its nucleus remained on the territory of the Republic of Moldova, more precisely in the region on the left bank of the Dnestr and at Bendery (Tighina) on the right bank of the river.

The 14th Army fulfils a threefold role: a) it blocks the union of the Republic of Moldova with Romania, supporting the separatist forces of the former, especially the so-called 'Dnestrian Moldavian Republic', proclaimed on the left side of the Dnestr, b) it acts as a Russian outpost against Ukraine and c) it serves as a bridgehead for Russian policy in the Balkans. The commander of the army, Lieutenant General Aleksandr Lebed, underlined that the 'Dnestr area is the key to the Balkans', and consequently pointed out that 'if Russia withdraws from this little piece of land, it will lose the key and its influence in that region'. As a conclusion concerning the 14th Army's identification with the whole of Russia he said: 'if the peacekeeping Fourteenth Army withdraws from [there], then Russia itself has withdrawn'.[39]

Officially, Russia declares that she intends to withdraw the 14th Army, but the reality is that the 14th Army is the weapon of the neo-imperialist policy of Moscow. As Vladimir Socor points out: 'Among the newly independent states that emerged in Eastern Europe from the ruins of the USSR, Moldova is the only one to be confronted by a Russian army stationed on its territory without a legal basis and that fought against the host state, underwriting a Russian insurgency that aimes at the secession from that state'.[40] The Russian position towards the former Romanian territories – Bessarabia and Northern Bukovina – is determined by the fact that she no longer has zones of influence in Central, Eastern and South-Eastern Europe.

Ukraine

As a result of the disintegration ot the USSR the territorial problem, engendered by the Soviet occupation in June 1940 and the inclusion of

Northern Bukovina and the Bessarabian region within Ukrainian borders, has become an issue between Romania and Ukraine – and between Moldova and Ukraine.

On the one hand Ukraine is engaged in a latent confrontation with Russia, which now and then witnesses strong outbursts. On the other hand, as one analyst put it, 'with the exception of Russia, Romania looms as the greatest potential danger to Ukrainian borders'.[41] This ambiguity naturally has an effect on the Romanian/Moldovan–Ukrainian issue. The anti-Ukrainian function of the presence of the 14th Army close to the Dnestr cannot be ignored by Kiev as the diverging interests of Ukraine and Russia become manifest. At the same time, Kiev cannot sympathize with the movement of national unity of the Bessarabian Romanians that might result in the extension of Romania and the repossession of the formerly Romanian but currently Ukrainian territories.

The Ukrainian apprehension towards the Romanian position with respect to the territorial dispute found its expression in the position that the Ukrainian Supreme Assembly took with regard to the declaration of the Romanian parliament of June 1991. This declaration rejecting the Molotov–Ribbentrop Pact was considered in Kiev as an indirect formulation of territorial claims towards Ukraine. The Romanian parliament adopted in turn, in November 1991, a resolution with respect to the referendum concerning the independence of Ukraine, declaring that 'the referendum organized by the Kiev authorities in the Romanian territories forcibly incorporated in the former Soviet Union, namely Northern Bukovina, the district of Herta, the district of Hotin and the counties in Southern Bessarabia is null and void, as are the consequences of this referendum'.[42] As a result when the 5–600,000 Romanian minority in Ukraine tried to affirm its national identity and establish relations with Romania they were the object of offensive measures.

Until now, Ukraine's reservations towards Romania have prevailed. The authorities in Kiev are avoiding a clear policy against the self-proclaimed Moldo-Dnestrian Republic. The position of the government in Kiev is based on the principle of the respect of the integrity of the Republic of Moldova, bearing in mind the idea that the territory on the left side of the Dnestr enjoys a broad autonomy. In case the Republic of Moldova is reintegrated within the Romanian borders, the Ukrainian Government considers that the region could choose its own political status.[43]

Romania

The Romanian position concerning the territorial issues generated by the collapse of the Soviet Union was expressed in the aforementioned resolution of the Romanian parliament declaring the Molotov–Ribbentrop Pact null and void from the outset. Nevertheless the rejection of the Soviet–German pact and of its consequences was not followed by an explicit formulation of territorial claims towards Ukraine. Wishing to be a factor of stability in South-Eastern Europe – a region marked by tensions and conflicts – the Romanian government avoided generating new sources of dispute with its claims.

As to Moldova, the authorities in Bucharest took several opportunities to underline the special character of the relations between the two Romanian states. Numerous exchanges of presidential, governmental and parliamentary delegations took place between Romania and the Republic of Moldova. Their aim was to deepen the economic and cultural integration between the two countries. Thousands of pupils, students and candidates for doctor's degree from the Republic of Moldova are studying in Romania by dint of a programme of scholarships supported by the Romanian government.

For a short period of time during the spring of 1992 while the conflict in the region of the Dnestr was worsening, Romania participated in discussions (involving Moldova, Russia, Ukraine and Romania) aimed at putting an end to the hostilities and creating a quadripartite structure for monitoring the ceasefire. This collaboration ended when Boris Yeltsin requested that Romania should no longer take part in the discussions concerning the conflict in the region of Dnestr.[44] Bucharest let herself be excluded without protesting.

At present (autumn 1994), discussions are taking place with a view to concluding a Romanian–Moldovan Treaty of Brotherhood and Integration. However, beyond the official rhetoric nothing is being undertaken to further reunification. As was noted, 'neither the leadership in Bucharest nor Chisinau pursue such a goal. Chisinau backs the thesis coordinated with Bucharest of two independent Romanian states, Romania and the Republic of Moldova, in which one people, the Romanians, lives.'[45]

The Romanian opposition parties reproach the authorities in both Bucharest and Chisinau with what they consider an insufficiently firm attitude concerning the unification of Bessarabia with Romania. The

Romanian press and public opinion manifest a lively and constant interest
in developments in the Republic of Moldova. The Romanian press deals
broadly with news and comments concerning the events beyond the Prut,
setting them against the international background.

The diverging attitudes inherent in the political pluralism were overcome at the time of the conviction of the so-called Ilascu group in Tiraspol
in December 1993. All political factions were brought together in their
firm protest against this sentence. The President, the Senate and the
Chamber of Deputies as well as the Government of Romania all made
official statements. The attitude of the political establishment was joined
by a strong popular current. After the sentence was delivered, Bucharest
and other towns in Romania witnessed a restless wave of meetings,
demonstrations and declarations of protest. The national solidarity with
the Romanians beyond the Prut thus acquired the character of a mass
movement.

6. FUTURE PROSPECTS

The existence of the two Romanian states – Romania and the Republic of
Moldova – cannot be considered a natural situation. Yet their unification
appears today as a long-term process full of obstacles. The following
premises, at least from the Romanian point of view, are necessary in order
to achieve the unification: a) the reestablishment of integrity of the
Republic of Moldova by eliminating the separatist structures, b) the
withdrawal of the Russian 14th Army from the territory of the Republic
of Moldova and c) the development of economic and cultural relations
between the two Romanian states. The reunification should be the
expression of the will of the Romanians of both sides of the Prut to live
within the frontiers of the same state. This requires the Romanians on the
left side of the Prut to forget their reservations concerning their unification with Romania and to abandon the inheritance of the Soviet and
separatist propaganda.

One of the main impediments in the way of the reunification is the status
of the territory of the Republic of Moldova situated on the left side of the
Dnestr. Several proposals were advanced concerning its status: a) the
proclamation of a Dnestrian independent state, b) affiliation with the
Russian Federation, c) affiliation based on a federal formula with Ukraine,

d) the integration of the territory into a large Russian–Ukrainian–Belarusian union[46] or e) an exchange of territories between the Republic of Moldova and Ukraine, Moldova yielding the territory situated on the left bank of the Dnestr and receiving in turn the regions of historical Bessarabia that were incorporated into Ukraine in 1940.[47]

The settlement of the issue of the Romanian territories clustered today within the borders of Ukraine seems very difficult, too. However, military confrontation is out of the question. From a Romanian point of view, actions must be undertaken for the preservation of the ethnic identity of the Romanian minority in Ukraine as well as for the intensification of cultural contacts with Romania.

The results of the 12 December 1993 elections in Russia pointed out the unexpected strength of the ultranationalist trend. Also other political groupings have a large number of supporters of the neo-imperialist restoration. The destiny of Russia is at the crossroads. Depending on the political orientation that will prevail, which is currently difficult to forecast, means will be chosen for solving the territorial dispute inherited from the former USSR.

NOTES

1. For more details see George Cioranescu, *Aspects des relations russo-roumaines* (Paris: Minard 1967); Florin Constantiniu, *Intre Hitler si Stalin. Romania si pactul Ribbentrop–Molotov* (Bucharest: Danubius 1991); V. Florin Dobrinescu, *Batalia diplomatica pentru Basarabia* (Iasi: Junimea 1991) and Ioan Scurtu and Constantin Hlihor, *Anul 1940. Drama romanilor dintre Prut si Nistru* (Bucharest: Editura Academiei de Inalte Studii Militare 1992).
2. See George Cioranescu, *Bessarabia, Disputed Land between East and West* (München: 1985), pp. 22–3. For the changes that took place in the administration of Bessarabia, see A.V. Boldur, *Istoria Basarabiei. Sub dominatia ruseasca (1812–1918)* (Chisinau: 1940).
3. Barbara Jelavich, 'Russia and the Requisition of Southern Bessarabia, 1875–1878', *Südost-Forschungen*, vol. 28, 1969, pp. 199.
4. See George Tofan, 'Cum s-a alcatuit Sfatul Tarii', *Patrimoniu*, no. 1, 1990, pp. 154–60.
5. Vasile Nedelciuc, *The Republic of Moldova* (Chisinau: Foreign Relations Committee of the Parliament of the Republic of Moldova 1992), p. 25.
6. Ion Nistor, *Istoria Basarabiei* (Bucharest: Humanitas 1991), p. 282. See also *1918. Le récit du témoin Alexandru V. Boldur. L'Union de la Bessarabie avec la Roumanie* (Rome: 1978).
7. *Akten zur deutschen auswärtigen Politik*, D–7 (ADAP), p. 207.
8. See *Le pacte Molotov–Ribbentrop, et ses conséquences pour la Bessarabie. Recueil de documents* (Chisinau: Universitas 1991), pp. 18–19.
9. See for more details Ion Nistor, *Istoria Bucovinei* (Bucharest: Humanitas 1991).
10. Ion Gherman, *Tinutul Herta* (Bucharest: 1991).
11. See Vasile Cucu and Gheorghe Vlasceanu, *Insula Serpilor* (Bucharest: Viata Romaneasca 1991).

12. Nedelciuc (1992), pp. 25–6.
13. M. Movileanu, 'Din istoria Transnistriei (1924–1940)', *Revista de istorie a Moldovei*, vol. 4, no. 1, 1993, pp. 61–9; E. Diaconescu, *Romanii din rasarit: Transnistria* (Iasi: 1942), pp. 216–20 and cf. Matei Cazacu and N. Trifon, 'Moldavie ex-soviétique: histoire et enjeux actuels' and 'Notes sur les Roumains en Grèce, Macèdonie et Albanie', *Collection Cahiers d'Izotok*, no. 2–3, 1993, p. 97.
14. The frontiers of the Moldavian Soviet Socialist Republic were established by the Supreme Soviet of the USSR on 4 November 1940. See Nedelciuc (1992), p. 27.
15. Olivian Verenca, *Administratia civila romana in Transnistria* (Chisinau: Universitas 1993).
16. Valeriu Florin Dobrinescu, *Romania si organizarea postbelica a lumii, 1945–1947* (Bucharest: Editura Academiei 1988), pp. 41, 136. The Romanian delegation tried unsuccessfully to obtain a modification of the frontier between the points Peliheceni and Mihaileni.
17. *Le pacte Molotov–Ribbentrop* (1991), p. 119.
18. Nicholas Dima, *From Moldovia to Moldova* (Boulder: 1991), pp. 66–71.
19. Adrian Pop, 'Componente ale politicii de deznationalizare in Moldova Sovietica', in *Sub povara granitei imperiale* (Bucharest: 1993), pp. 38–9.
20. It is still difficult to establish exact details of the demographic and ethnic modifications produced as a result of deportations, transfers or withdrawals of certain national groups, of the terror inflicted and of the military operations. See Nicholas Dima, *Bessarabia and Bukovina. The Soviet–Romanian Territorial Dispute* (Boulder: East European Monographs 1982); Cioranescu (1985), pp. 207–22; Cazacu and Trifon (1993), pp. 113–14; Nedelciuc (1992), p. 27; 'Cum au fost lichidati "chiaburii" din Moldova', *Cugetul*, no. 5–6, 1991, pp. 58–63 and Mihai Gribincea, 'Deportarile staliniste din Basarabia', *Sub Povara granitei imperiale* (Bucharest: 1993), pp. 43–58.
21. Michael Bruchis, *One Step Back, Two Steps Forward* (Boulder: East European Monographs 1982), p. 71.
22. Reproduced after Nedelciuc (1992), p. 16. Cf. George I. Jewsbury, *The Russian Annexation of Bessarabia 1774–1828* (Boulder: East European Monographs 1976), p. 57 and Ion Nistor, *Istoria Basarabiei* (Bucharest: 1991), pp. 179, 197 and Stefan Ciobanu, *Basarabia. Populatia, istoria, cultura* (Bucharest and Chisinau: 1992), pp. 24–5.
23. Ibid., p. 9.
24. Vladimir Trebici, 'Basarabia si Bucovina – aspecte demografice', in *Sub povara granitei imperiale* (1993), pp. 83–4.
25. Ibid., p. 86.
26. For more details see Adrian Pop, 'Chestiunea basarabeana in politica de "independenta" a Romaniei', in *Sub povara granitei imperiale* (1993), pp. 96–115.
27. Cf. Pol Kolost, Andrei Edemsky and Natalya Kalashnikova, 'The Dniestr Conflict: Between Irredentism and Separatism', *Europe–Asia Studies*, vol. 45, no. 6, 1993, p. 979.
28. Anneli Ute Gabanyi, 'Moldova Between Russia, Romania and the Ukraine', *Aussenpolitik*, no.1, 1993, p. 105.
29. Ibid., p. 103.
30 Nedelciuc (1992), p. 49.
31. *Keesing's Record of World Events*, vol. 40, no. 3, 1993, p. 3. See also Charles King, 'Moldovan Identity and the Politics of Panromanianism', *Slavic Review*, vol. 33, no. 2, 1994, pp. 345-368.
32. Nedelciuc (1992), p.117.
33. Ibid., p. 30.
34. Chiril Levinta, 'Conducerea militara in razboiul pentru independenta Republicii Moldova.', *Cugetuil*, no. 3–4, 1992, p. 60.
35. Nedelciuc (1992), p. 117.
36. Victor Barsan, *Masacrul inocentilor. Razboiul din Moldova, 1 martie–29 iulie 1992* (Bucharest: Fundatia Culturala Romana 1993), pp. 231–2.

37. The so-called Ilascu group was charged with murder, terrorism and diversion in the armed conflict between Moldova and the Dnestrian Republic. The requests of the Moldovan government that the defendants be handed over to Moldova and the protests of the Romanian officials and different international bodies had no result. *Supplement to the RFE/ RL Research Report*, vol. 2, no. 50, 1993, p. 18.
38. *Pamint si oameni*, no. 5, 27 March 1993.
39. Interview with General Lebed in *Izvestiya*, 26 February 1993 and Russian Television, 16 March 1993 quoted in Vladimir Socor, 'Russia's Army in Moldova: There to Stay', *RFE/ RL Research Report*, vol. 2, no. 25, 1993, p. 44.
40. Ibid., p. 42.
41. Adrian Karatnycky, 'The Ukrainian Factor', *Foreign Affairs*, vol. 71, no. 3, 1992, p. 105.
42. *Border of Territorial Disputes*, 1992, p. 154. Cf. Romain Yakemtchouk, *L'indépendance de l'Ukraine* (Bruxelles: 1993), p. 278.
43. Yakemtchouk (1993), p. 280.
44. Barsan (1993), pp. 138–9.
45. Gabanyi (1993), p. 105.
46. Kolost et al. (1993), p. 997.
47. Radu Dimitrescu, 'Realitati demografice in jurul pactului, Ribbentrop–Molotov', *Sfera politicii*, 5 April 1993.

7. Carpatho-Ukraine

Istvan Madi

Carpatho-Ukraine (named Subcarpathia by the Hungarians and Subcarpathian Rus by the Czechs) was created as a geopolitical unit after World War I. The area of this territory is 12,656 square kilometres. Between the wars it was part of Czechoslovakia and in the years 1939–44 part of Hungary. At present this territory is the Transcarpathian Oblast of the Republic of Ukraine. The majority of the territory's population consists of Slavic Ruthenians but Hungarians have traditionally been the largest minority group. Subcarpathia's Hungarian minority is concentrated in the major cities of the territory – Ungvár (Uzhgorod), the territory's capital; Munkács (Mukachevo); Nagyszöllös (Vinogradov); and Beregszász (Beregovo) – and they have preserved their absolute majority in the areas bordering with Hungary (see Map 7.1).[1]

1. THE HISTORY OF THE TERRITORY

For more than a thousand years the present territory of Carpatho-Ukraine was part of the North-Eastern Upper Region of the Kingdom of Hungary and it did not have a particular denomination. It received its name only after 1918. At the end of World War I the victorious Western powers decided to dissolve the ancient Hungarian State. The whole of Upper Hungary, including the territory of Subcarpathia, was ceded to the newly created Czechoslovakia.

The Peace Treaty of Saint-Germain-en-Laye stipulated the autonomy of the so-called Subcarpathian Rus. The League of Nations guaranteed this status in November 1920 and it was confirmed in the Constitution of the Czechoslovak Republic.[2] Nevertheless, in practice this autonomy was little more than a mere formality since centralism was the dominating principle in public administration.[3] The organization and frontiers of this

Map 7.1. Carpatho-Ukraine.

autonomous territory were completely incidental. It was also hard to integrate this remote province into the economic system of Czechoslovakia. A major setback was that this mountainous region was separated from its natural hinterland, the Great Hungarian Plain. The economic development of the territory slowed down and the number of emigrants who were fleeing poverty increased dramatically in the inter-war period.

From the ethnic point of view the new autonomous territory was not very satisfactory. Almost one-fourth of the Ruthenians living in the newly created Czechoslovak Republic were left outside the province. The southern part, i.e. approximately one-fifth of the territory, was populated by Hungarians whose proportion in those areas was over 90 per cent.[4] The reason for ignoring the right of self-determination for the Hungarians in favour of Czechoslovakia was that all the main roads and railway lines passed through the regions populated by Hungarians. Their possession was thus vitally important for maintaining the connection with the whole of the region.

By the end of the 1930s the internal weakness of the Czechoslovak state became quite clear. The non-Czech population was dissatisfied with Czech domination. As a result of a changed geopolitical situation the dissolution process began at the end of 1938. After the first Vienna Award the southern part of the territory, which was populated by Hungarians, including the major towns Ungvár, Munkács and Beregszász, was returned to Hungary. In the northern part that remained under the Czechoslovak rule concrete steps were taken in order to establish a real Ruthenian autonomy after the resignation of the Czechoslovak President Eduard Beneš. It was not viable from a political or economic point of view, however.

Following the Slovak declaration of independence, Hungary occupied the northern territories in March 1939. Hungarian politicians made plans about preserving the autonomy of the Slavic Ruthenians but the proximity of the Soviet Union after September 1939 made them more cautious. Fears grew at the beginning of 1940, when certain maps were published in Soviet newspapers indicating that the Ruthenian territories were part of the Soviet Union.[5]

The situation deteriorated dramatically after Germany occupied Hungary in March 1944. After that, harsh measures were instituted in Subcarpathia. The large Jewish community was transported to Nazi death camps. Food shortages became extremely serious and the approaching Soviet Army cast a dark shadow over Subcarpathia. In October 1944 the Soviet armed forces penetrated into Subcarpathia. There were no serious battles in the territory because Hungarian (and German) forces had withdrawn rather rapidly from Subcarpathia to prevent being encircled in the Great Hungarian Plain. The Red Army captured Ungvár on 27 October 1944 and on the next day the hostilities came to an end with the seizure of Csap (Chop).

The beginning of the Soviet rule was, for a considerable part of the population of Subcarpathia, even worse than the war. Within three weeks of the occupation of the territory the NKVD began its 'work'. All Hungarian males between the ages of 18 and 50, approximately 45,000 people, were rounded up and taken to Soviet labour camps. According to conservative estimates at least half of them perished.[6] The same happened to the Subcarpathian German community. These brutal acts were not merely one form of Soviet revenge or collective punishment but were effective tools for intimidating the 'unreliable' population of the territory.

The Soviet authorities created the Communist Party of Transcarpathian Ukraine under the leadership of Ivan Turjanica. At its statutory congress in Munkács on 19 November 1944 it was decided that the territory must be ceded to the Soviet Union as soon as possible. It was clear that the Soviet leadership wanted to prevent the reestablishment of a Czechoslovak administration. A week later, on 26 November, the so-called Congress of Local People's Councils declared the territory to belong to the Soviet Union 'in accordance with the will of the local population'. From that day onwards until January 1946 there was a rather strange administrative unit in Subcarpathia. It was called the Transcarpathian Ukrainian Republic and it had its own government and authorities. The real power, however, was in the hands of the NKVD.

All relations with the Czechoslovak administrative organizations were ordered to be broken off. Under these circumstances there was nothing for the Czechoslovak representatives to do but to leave the obviously lost territory in January 1945.[7] The *fait accompli* was formally recognized by the reestablished Czechoslovakia in June 1945 when a Soviet–Czechoslovak agreement about the annexation of Subcarpathia to the Soviet Union was signed.

The Transcarpathian Ukrainian Republic ceased to exist in January 1946. According to a decree of the Presidium of the Supreme Soviet of the Soviet Union the former Transcarpathian Ukrainian Republic became the Transcarpathian Oblast of the Ukrainian Socialist Soviet Republic. The territory was divided into thirteen districts.[8]

The other former possessor, Hungary, renounced her claim in respect of Subcarpathia. The Hungarian administration and a considerable part of the Hungarian population had fled from the territory in the autumn of 1944. In the armistice agreement of January 1945 Hungary was forced to abandon Subcarpathia by accepting the restoration of the border set up in the Trianon Peace Treaty in 1920. This was reaffirmed and sanctioned in the Peace Treaty of 1947.

2. THE CHARACTERISTICS OF THE TERRITORY

The ethnic makeup of Carpatho-Ukraine is still highly complex. Nowadays more than twenty different ethnic groups can be identified in Subcarpathia, several of which have been living side by side for centuries. The Hungarians have been living in the region for more than a thousand years and the presence of the Ruthenians can be traced back to the thirteenth century.[9]

The Hungarian census taken in 1941 found more than 850,000 people living in Subcarpathia. The Ruthenians were the majority and their share was 64 per cent. The percentage of Hungarians was 29 per cent. The ratio had been very similar in 1910.[10] However, World War II caused dramatic changes in Subcarpathia's ethnic makeup. The territory's Jewish and German communities practically ceased to exist and as a result of the large-scale escape from Soviet invaders and the Soviet genocide against the Hungarian male population the number of Hungarians at the end of the 1950s was only 60 per cent of the number of Hungarians twenty years earlier. Since then their number has been slightly but constantly increasing.

Because of the great strategic importance of Subcarpathia the new Transcarpathian Oblast of the Ukrainian SSR became one of the best-guarded and most isolated border regions in the Soviet Union. It was also one of the most conservative oblasts of Ukraine. In addition the population had to suffer from Sovietization and Russification. The names of more than one hundred Hungarian and Ruthenian villages were changed in 1946. The cultural organizations and educational network of the minorities were destroyed. The intelligentsia and national churches were persecuted. Local and national traditions were eliminated and replaced by 'superior' Soviet values. Centrally governed universal industrialization led to extensive economic dependence throughout the Soviet Union and there was large-scale settlement of Russians. Until the late 1980s Russian was the predominant language in Subcarpathia. On the other hand, in order to keep the Soviet Empire together the Russians were forced to give some concessions to the dominant nations in the republics. Thus people belonging to these semi-dominant nations enjoyed preferences in obtaining posts in the party and the state organizations.[11]

Since 1946 Ruthenians have not been recognized officially as a separate nationality and their language has been regarded as a Ukrainian dialect. Even the name Ruthenian was prohibited and replaced by the name Carpatho-Ukrainian. The Ruthenians had no organizations to represent their interests or to coordinate their cultural activities. In order to assimilate them large-scale Ukrainian settlement was initiated. In the party and state organizations Ruthenians were strongly underrepresented and they became second-class citizens in their homeland. If they wanted to be promoted they had to declare themselves Ukrainians.[12]

The situation of the Hungarian minority was even worse. In the Soviet period Hungarians were the most distrusted and discriminated group of the population of the territory. Only in the mid-1970s were Hungarian officials appointed as deputy chairman and party secretary in Beregszász Raion (district) although more than 80 per cent of its population were ethnic Hungarians. Even in the late 1980s only 7 per cent of the party members and 3 per cent of the staff of the public administration were Hungarians while their share of the total population of Subcarpathia has constantly been about 14–15 per cent.[13] After World War II no classes were taught in Hungarian until the year 1953. Until 1969 the Hungarians had no national organizations to represent their interests or to coordinate their cultural activities. Yet, Subcarpathian Hungarians preserved their identity and their forced assimilation was only partially successful in towns and failed completely in the countryside.[14] The Hungarians had to put up with their status as third-class citizens.

Within the framework of Sovietization (and Ukrainization) thousands of Russians and especially Ukrainians were settled in Subcarpathia after 1945. In 1989, when the most recent Soviet census was taken, Subcarpathia had 1.26 million inhabitants, half of them living in villages. There were 977,000 Ukrainians (78 per cent of the population), of whom 600,000 were estimated to be Ruthenians. However, Ruthenian sources claimed that the real number of Ruthenians would be higher. Hungarians made up 13 per cent but their share also, in reality, is larger. The differences between the official figures and the figures given by the ethnic minority group itself are explained by the fact that people were forced to renounce their nationality.[15] The share of Russians was officially 3 per cent but the real figure has been estimated to be closer to 8 per cent. There were also small Slovak, German and Romanian communities.[16]

Soviet policy treated non-Orthodox churches with extreme harshness. Under Soviet rule members of the Roman Catholic Church, Protestant Churches and the Greek Catholic Church were persecuted, many priests were arrested and deported and church buildings were closed or turned into warehouses or at best into museums. The Greek Catholic Church, which was the national church of the Ruthenians and which also had some Hungarian members, was forced to dissolve in 1949. Its churches and assets were completely confiscated and given to the Russian Orthodox Church.[17] Nevertheless, the churches did help to preserve the languages and national identities of the minorities.[18]

Subcarpathia's overall level of development has been much higher than the Soviet or Ukrainian average. Living conditions in Subcarpathia are much better than in other parts of Ukraine. Besides emotional elements this is the main reason why a growing proportion of the local population sympathize with the territory's greater independence. Subcarpathia has, at least by Soviet or Ukrainian standards, a well-developed infrastructure and productive agriculture. However, Gorbachev's campaign against alcoholism caused serious devastation to the territory's agriculture, since the flourishing grape plantations were completely destroyed in the name of anti-alcoholism.[19] This deprived peasants of their major source of revenue. As the Carpathian Mountains are covered with large forests, forestry plays a particularly important role in the territory's economic life. However, the intensive tree felling has begun to cause growing environmental problems. Subcarpathia's considerable industrial potential has been primarily based on local resources. The leading branches of Subcarpathian industry are wood processing, furniture, paper and pulp and food. The territory's capital, Ungvár (Uzhgorod), has a sizeable machine and engineering industry. Finally, it must be mentioned that Subcarpathia is very rich in sodium chloride (rock salt): Aknaszlatina (Szolotvin) is one of the biggest rock salt mines in Europe.

From the strategic point of view it can be said, without exaggeration, that Subcarpathia was an important component of Soviet military doctrine and policy towards Europe. This was also admitted by Stalin who after the capture of the territory declared in his general order that the Soviet Army had seized a very important bridgehead.[20] He was absolutely right, since by taking possession of Subcarpathia the Soviet Union not only won direct access to the Carpathian Basin but also became capable of exerting an even more decisive influence on the policy of the neighbouring countries. A straight line from the Carpathian Basin led to Southern Germany and Austria, not to mention the favourable access opportunities towards the Western Balkans and Northern Italy. Quite understandably, Subcarpathia has been full of military garrisons. The biggest ones were located in the neighbourhoods of Ungvár and Munkács. Subcarpathia has preserved its geopolitical significance after the dissolution of the Soviet Union. To a certain extent the territory means the same for Ukraine as the Baltic meant for Peter the Great at the beginning of the eighteenth century – an open door towards the Western countries.

3. THE ETHNIC REVIVAL OF HUNGARIANS AND OTHER SUBCARPATHIAN PEOPLES

Thanks to Gorbachev's *glasnost* and *perestroika* a genuine cultural and political reawakening began in Subcarpathia at the end of the 1980s. In April 1988 the Soviet President Andrei Gromyko visited Budapest, which marked the beginning of an increase and improvement of cultural and travelling opportunities for Subcarpathian Hungarians. In 1989 ecclesiastical contacts were established and support for Hungarian religious life in Subcarpathia became possible.[21]

Cultural links with Hungary have contributed to the fact that the Hungarians can be regarded as the most reform-oriented group in Subcarpathia. On the other hand the status of the Hungarians as third-ranked citizens gave them a strong motivation to initiate changes. The Hungarian Cultural Association of Subcarpathia (HCAS) was set up in Ungvár by five hundred founding members in February 1989. It was the first independent public organization representing the territory's Hungarian minority. The main objectives of the HCAS have been to preserve and foster the Hungarian minority's native language, education, culture, national symbols, traditions and identity. The HCAS is engaged in promoting a civil society and preparing the Hungarian minority for self-government and private entrepreneurship.[22] Within a year of its founding the HCAS was able to set up a well-organized network of 175 chapters, reaching into every Hungarian-populated settlement in Subcarpathia. With a membership of 30,000, the association became a strong political force second in size only to the Communist Party. In the 1990 local elections the HCAS was given the right to nominate candidates and it sent eleven deputies to the 124-member Transcarpathian Oblast Soviet. The HCAS candidates were also elected to village, district and city councils. Subcarpathia's capital, Ungvár, got its first Hungarian deputy mayor for more than four decades.[23]

The activities of the HCAS have also contributed to developments in the Hungarian educational system. Hungarian nursery schools numbered fifty-five in 1990 and the network of Hungarian elementary and secondary schools was significantly expanded. In addition, Hungarian history is once again being taught in all Hungarian schools, which is not the case in other countries bordering Hungary that have Hungarian minorities.[24] However, the state of higher education still leaves much to be desired because Subcarpathian Hungarian students have remained dependent on scholarships from Hungarian universities. In Subcarpathia bilingual (Ukrainian and Hungarian) place and street names have been introduced, streets and squares have been renamed, and memorial plates of monuments to famous Hungarians have been erected. The celebration of Hungarian national holidays has been authorized, as has the use of the Hungarian flag and national anthem and the name Subcarpathia.[25]

In the beginning of *perestroika* there was intensive cooperation between minorities in Subcarpathia, which was also a great asset for the Hungarian minority's activities. From 1989 onwards the Hungarians also cooperated with the Ukrainian democrats in the Ukrainian Popular Front (RUKH).

The Ruthenians were also able to set up their own organization in 1989. With the help of Subcarpathian Hungarians, the Society for Carpathian Ruthenians (SCR) was established to protect Ruthenian interests. In the first two years the Ruthenian political movement developed rather slowly. Only after Ukraine's declaration of independence did it begin to develop at a faster pace but its efficiency was undermined by poor organization.[26]

Within the framework of ethnic revival the territory's other minorities (Germans, Slovaks, Gypsies, Romanians and Jews) also established their own cultural associations. In their fight against the communist *nomenklatura* these groups often worked together, reinforcing each other. In January 1991 the National Roundtable, renamed the Democratic League of Nationalities in October 1991, was set up not only by Hungarians and Ruthenians but also by Germans, Slovaks and Gypsies. The Romanians and Russians joined later.[27]

In the Soviet era the Russians were the most privileged minority in Subcarpathia. They were strongly overrepresented in the territory's leading echelons. The collapse of the Soviet regime was a disaster for them but instead of sticking to the old regime they started to support national minorities' freedoms and became defenders of local interests.[28]

4. AFTER THE COLLAPSE OF THE SOVIET UNION

The dissolution of the Soviet Union brought about dramatic changes in the legal status of Subcarpathia. From 24 August 1991 the territory became part of the newly independent Ukrainian Republic. Soon afterwards Ruthenian and Hungarian political organizations, together with other smaller native minorities of Subcarpathia, raised the issue of autonomy. They were aiming to create an autonomous national republic divided into ethnic zones within a federal Ukraine. This issue of autonomy brought an end to the unity that had been achieved by the Hungarians, the RUKH and other democratic forces in the struggle against the power of the Communist Party apparatus.[29]

The Ukrainian nationalists reacted with distrust and anger to the initiative and branded it unconstitutional and a threat to Ukraine's territorial integrity. They made every effort to block the referendum on the issue. The RUKH and the new Ukrainian democratic bloc parties supported only cultural autonomy for the Hungarian minority. The reason for the reaction was their view that Subcarpathia was an integral part of Ukraine and Ruthenians were ethnic Ukrainians.

To clarify the situation a group of Ukrainian officials led by Leonid Kravchuk, at that time the Chairman of the Ukrainian Supreme Soviet, visited the region. During negotiations with local representatives a compromise solution was reached. The term autonomy was replaced on ballot sheets by that of a special self-governing administrative status within an independent Ukraine, a formula that meant that the territory would no longer be subordinate to the Ukrainian government, only to the Ukrainian parliament and head of state. Kravchuk also endorsed the call for the creation of a special economic zone. On 31 October 1991 the referendum on the autonomy issue together with the all-republican level referendum on Ukraine's independence was organized by the territorial soviet.[30]

In the referendum of 1 December 1991 the population of Subcarpathia not only endorsed the full independence of Ukraine but also voted in favour of granting the territory a special self-governing status within the independent Ukrainian Republic. Moreover, in Beregszász Raion (formerly Beregovo Raion) the ethnic Hungarians voted for the creation of a Hungarian national district.[31]

On the autonomy issue the Hungarians cooperated with the Ruthenians. Some cautiousness has been sensed, however, since the Hungarians are uncertain how they would fare in an autonomous Ruthenian republic. They also feared the emergence of aggressive Ukrainian nationalist sentiment. The anti-Hungarian Ukrainian nationalism was expressed in August 1991 when several Hungarian monuments were damaged. The Subcarpathian Hungarians have also been trying to avoid getting involved in the intensifying Ukrainian–Ruthenian conflict. The Hungarian Democratic Alliance of Ukraine (HDAU), which was founded in October 1991, made a declaration of its support for the Universal Declaration of Human Rights, the Helsinki Final Act, the Paris Charter for a United Europe, Ukraine's sovereignty and the May 1991 agreements between Ukraine and Hungary. It condemned all manifestations of nationalism and said that it intended to act as a bridge between Ukraine's various nationalities.[32]

Among the Hungarians there has also been one issue of serious controversy. It was related to the question of Hungarian autonomy in Subcarpathia, which was raised in September 1991 in Beregszász Raion, the only district in Subcarpathia with an absolute Hungarian majority and a region where the HCAS had been most active and independent. Beregszász Hungarians called for a referendum on the creation of a

Hungarian autonomous district which other Hungarian settlements would be free to join. This demand caused heated debates within the ranks of the Hungarians since the proposed autonomous district excluded some 70,000 members or one-third of the Hungarian minority together with its educational and cultural institutions in Ungvár and Munkács. Activists in Beregszász were accused of being selfish and dividing the minority.[33] As a result of conciliatory negotiations conflicting views were largely moderated and Hungarians have opted for the widest self-government of Subcarpathia, including also the autonomy of the territory. Yet the question of a Hungarian autonomous district has remained on the agenda.

In late January 1992 the territorial soviet elected a new chairman and approved the text of the draft constitutional amendment giving legal basis to Subcarpathia's special self-governing status. According to this draft Subcarpathia had a right to the status of a special self-governing administrative territory to be incorporated into the Ukrainian Constitution as a subject within an independent Ukraine and not as part of any other kind of administrative-territorial body. The draft was submitted to the Ukrainian parliament, however, and so far it has not been recognized and codified in law by that body. Thus the status of the territory within the newly independent Ukrainian state has remained ambiguous and this ambiguity has unfortunately been causing increasing tension in Subcarpathia.

It is worth mentioning that Russians living in Beregszáz Raion voted almost unanimously for the Hungarian national district in the referendum held on 1 December 1991.[34] The smaller minorities of Subcarpathia voted almost unanimously for the territory's autonomy. It seems that the fear that the national identity of the region's numerous ethnic groups will not be recognized adequately has prevailed, a factor that keeps the various minorities close to each other.[35]

5. THE OFFICIAL RELATIONS BETWEEN HUNGARY AND UKRAINE

There has been impressive development in the Hungarian–Ukrainian relationship. The government of Hungary and all major political forces have supported Ukraine's endeavour for independence and Hungary was among the first states to recognize Ukrainian independence. The Hungarian foreign policy has naturally also paid special attention to the situation of ethnic Hungarians in Subcarpathia.

The first visit by a foreign head of state to Subcarpathia was made by the President of the Republic of Hungary, Arpad Göncz, in September 1990. In the course of this presidential visit, during talks between Foreign Ministry secretaries of state, the idea of concluding a Hungarian–Ukrainian basic treaty was floated. The first Ukrainian draft was completed in the spring of 1991. The document did not cover the question of the borders of the two countries and did not refer to the Hungarian minority of Subcarpathia, however.

In May 1991 the Ukrainian President Leonid Kravchuk visited Hungary and this time the Hungarian Prime Minister Jozsef Antall emphasized the question of border-zone cooperation as well as the situation of the Hungarian minority. The Declaration on the Basic Principles of Cooperation between the Republic of Hungary and the Soviet Socialist Republic of Ukraine in Guaranteeing the Rights of National Minorities was signed and it has remained one of the most important bilateral documents concerning minority rights up until the present day. The attached protocol called for the setting up of a joint committee of experts and representatives from the national minority concerned.[36] In the course of further expert consultations – at Ukraine's request – the principle of the inviolability of borders was included in the second draft of the basic treaty. Following this, a decree on the equal usage of ethnic group languages with the official language was issued in Subcarpathia. The new law was supported by the Hungarians. The minority law was prepared quickly, and the situation of the Hungarian minority apparently improved.

The Hungarian–Ukrainian basic treaty was signed in Kiev in 6 December 1991. In Clause 2 the contracting parties mutually excluded territorial claims and Clause 17 was pertinent to the rights of the Subcarpathian Hungarian minority. This treaty was ratified in May 1993 by the Hungarian parliament. It is true that there were representatives protesting against the recognition of the existing border and the abandonment of territorial claims but they comprised only a small minority since more than 90 per cent of the representatives voted for the ratification of the treaty without any amendment.

There were two main reasons for this Hungarian acceptance. First of all it is an unquestionable fact that Ukraine with her territory of more than 600,000 square kilometres, a population over 50 million and a large army and considerable nuclear armament is a regional power in Central Eastern Europe. The second reason for the Hungarian willingness to maintain good relations with Ukraine is the fact that in the last two years the

Ukrainian state has taken concrete steps for the improvement of minority rights and the situation of Subcarpathian Hungarians has greatly improved, especially in comparison with the Hungarian minorities in Romania and Slovakia. Hungary resolutely supports efforts aimed at creating a special economic zone in Subcarpathia and does everything to facilitate this process. From the Hungarian point of view a special economic zone in Subcarpathia would be the best solution to the territory's economic difficulties. It would also be favourable for all neighbouring states. The Hungarians are convinced that the free movement of persons, goods and services, the large-scale development in social contacts and the common economic prosperity can eliminate ethnic conflicts and territorial disputes. The Hungarian standpoint also is that, since Ukraine was not a sovereign country before 1991 nor an actor from the point of view of international law, the present state of Ukraine cannot be blamed for its history and border changes.

6. FUTURE PROSPECTS

The official Ukrainian–Hungarian relations are friendly and there is a good understanding between the two states. There are, however, certain dark clouds over Subcarpathia. The first concern is the desperate economic situation.[37] The increasing poverty and uncertainty have precipitated the emigration of Subcarpathian Hungarians. The most regrettable phenomenon is the massive emigration of intellectuals.[38]

The other concern overshadowing the future is the potential aggressiveness of the Ukrainian and Ruthenian nationalism and the possibility of a Ukrainian–Ruthenian conflict. While the Ukrainians regard Ruthenians as Ukrainians who should have no special national rights, more and more Ruthenians have become convinced that the only solution to their problem is the secession from Ukraine and thus they demand independence for Subcarpathia. The other, more realistic secession-minded Ruthenians recognize that a sovereign Ruthenian republic would not be politically and economically viable, so they contemplate joining one of the neighbouring states. While many of them consider association with Hungary, there are people who would prefer to join Slovakia. So far consensus has not been achieved on this issue and confusion adversely affects the efficiency of the Ruthenian political movement.

Although Ruthenian nationalism has a strong anti-Russian and anti-Ukrainian character it appears to be prepared to take a tolerant, conciliatory attitude towards other native ethnic communities living in Subcarpathia. The Hungarian community has based its strategy on the premise that the state will not make concessions on minority issues unless the minorities themselves become more active. Since this strategy has paid off, the Hungarians are more confident about their future. It cannot be denied that the much more advanced Hungary exerts a strong attracting influence on the neighbouring Subcarpathian Hungarian minority. Nevertheless, the overwhelming majority of Subcarpathian Hungarians accept the existing realities.

One factor determining the future of Subcarpathia is the unpredictable Ukrainian–Russian relationship and the enormous economic difficulties of the Republic of Ukraine. These problems understandably create pressure on Ukrainian democracy. In this respect the question of whether democracy or nationalism will prove to be dominant in Ukraine will have significant impact on Subcarpathia.

NOTES

1. The Hungarians constitute an absolute majority in 85 settlements of the territory's 580 settlements including the City of Beregszász (Beregovo). In addition they have a considerable percentage in a further 15 settlements. See Gyula Balla, *There Are Changes in Subcarpathia as Well* (Budapest: Uj Ido Kiadó 1989), p. 14.
2. Ibid., p. 11.
3. *Világszövetség*, no. 3, 1992.
4. Census of 1910.
5. Gyula Juhász, *Documents of Hungarian Foreign Policy* (Budapest: Kossuth Kiadó 1988).
6. Jenö Nagy, *The Deportation of Subcarpathian Hungarian Males in Autumn 1944* (Ungvár and Budapest: Intermix Kiadó 1992), p. 12.
7. Jószef Bottlik and György Dupka, *This Is the Homeland. Facts, Data and Documents from the Life of Subcarpathian Hungarians* (Szeged: Universum Kiadó 1991), p. 52.
8. Balla (1989), p. 12.
9. Alfred A. Reisch, 'Transcarpathia's Hungarian Minority and the Autonomy Issue', *RFE/RL Research Report*, vol. 1, no. 6–7, 1992, pp. 17–23.
10. Census of 1941.
11. Alfred A. Reisch (1992), pp. 18–19 and Ljuba Siselina, 'The National Policy of the Soviet Union and the Subcarpathian Hungarian Minority', *Régió*, vol. 3, no. 5, 1992, p. 167.
12. *Kárpátalja*, 12 October 1990.
13. Siselina (1992), p. 169.
14. *Társadalmi Szemle*, May 1991, pp. 23–41.
15. *Kárpátalja*, 24 April 1990.
16. Reisch (1992), p. 18. (National composition of the population of the USSR according to the All-Union census of 1989 and *Vestnik Statistiki,* no. 10, 1990, pp. 76–7.) For the data of 1975 see also Balla (1989), p. 14.

17. *Hatodik síp*, June 1991.
18. Reisch (1992), p. 18.
19. Siselina (1992), p. 171.
20. Bottlik and Dupka (1991), p. 51.
21. Reisch (1992), pp. 19–23; *Reformátusok Lapja*, 28 April 1991 and *Uj ember*, 29 September 1991.
22. Public roundtable discussion held in Ungvár on 20 December 1990. Published under the title 'Subcarpathia', in *Társadalmi Szemle*, May 1991, pp. 23–41.
23. Ibid. and *Kárpátalja*, 24 November 1990.
24. Reisch (1992), p. 20 and *Magyar Nemzet*, 1 June 1992.
25. Reisch (1992), pp. 18–23.
26 Ibid.
27. Ibid.
28. Ibid.
29. Ibid.
30. *Pesti Hírlap*, 4 November 1991.
31. Ibid.
32. *Magyar Nemzet*, 12 October and 12 November 1991.
33. *Pesti Hírlap*, 4 November 1991.
34. *Pesti Hírlap*, 4 January 1991.
35. Reisch (1992), p. 22 and *Magyar Nemzet*, 3 September 1991.
36. *Magyar Nemzet*, 1 June 1992.
37. *Világszövetség*, no. 3, 1992.
38. Balla (1989), p. 14.

8. Eastern Poland

Wojciech Materski

In the light of comparative analysis of the territories annexed by the USSR during World War II, the case of Eastern Poland is not typical. The annexation resulting from the partition of Poland by Stalin and Hitler affected a vast territory of one of the biggest states in inter-war Europe and caused tremendous changes in the political map of Europe.

The territories that were annexed by the Soviet Union in 1939 and that remained parts of the Soviet Union after the post-war settlements were the following provinces of Poland in whole or in part: Vilnius (Wilno), Wolyn, Stanislawów and Tarnopol, Nowogród, Polesie, Bialystok and Lvov (Lwów/Lviv) (see Map 8.1). The total area of these territories is about 200,000 square kilometres – about half of the size of the whole area of the Second Republic of Poland (1918/21–39). Vilnius and its region (Wilenszczyzna), which were ceded to Lithuania, had an area of 6,700 square kilometres (1.7 per cent of the area of the Second Republic of Poland).[1] The territory that was ceded to the Soviet Socialist Republic of Belorussia and is now a part of the Republic of Belarus covered 103,000 square kilometres (26.5 per cent of the pre-war area) and the territory ceded to the Soviet Socialist Republic of Ukraine, which is now a part of the Republic of Ukraine, is 89,700 square kilometres in size (23 per cent of the pre-war area).[2]

1. THE ANNEXATION

The Second Republic of Poland achieved her independence in 1918. In the years 1919–20 a Russo-Polish war was waged over the possession of the borderlands. The Polish Army occupied large territories and in March 1921 the Russo-Polish frontier was established by the Treaty of Riga.

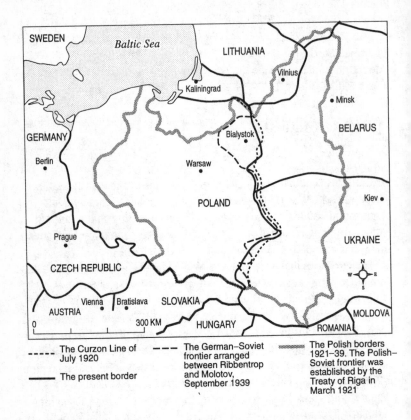

```
- - - -  The Curzon Line of          - - -  The German–Soviet        ═══  The Polish borders
         July 1920                           frontier arranged              1921–39. The Polish–
                                             between Ribbentrop             Soviet frontier was
─────    The present border                  and Molotov,                   established by the
                                             September 1939                 Treaty of Riga in
                                                                            March 1921
```

These borderlands were ethnically complex. East of the so-called Curzon Line, which had been negotiated in 1920 and which eventually became the Polish–Soviet frontier with minor changes in Yalta in 1945, Ukrainians numbered 37 per cent, Poles 36 per cent and Belarusians 9 per cent of the total population of 10.8 million (census of 1931). The rest of the population were Jews, Russians, Germans and Lithuanians. These peoples had come under Polish hegemony in the 16th century when the Polish–Lithuanian Commonwealth was established as a consequence of the marriage of Lithuania's Grand Duke Jogaila (Jagiello) to Poland's Queen Jadwiga in the 14th century.

On 1 September 1939 the German Army invaded Poland. Seventeen days later the Germans were supported on two fronts by the Red Army, which encroached upon the practically defenceless territories of Eastern

Poland. The foundation of this collaboration was a non-aggression pact known as the Molotov–Ribbentrop Pact, which was signed on 23 August 1939 in Moscow. The accompanying secret protocol was an agreement on the liquidation of the Polish state by Stalin and Hitler.[3]

In the preliminary Soviet–German resolution the partition of the Polish state was to go along the rivers San, Vistula (Wisla) and Narev (Narew). This settlement was changed in the course of the Moscow negotiations after the occupation of Poland. The negotiations culminated in the signing of the Treaty on Friendship and Borders between Germany and USSR on 28 September 1939. Moscow considered it more profitable to annex Lithuania, which had originally been assigned to Berlin, than her originally assigned territories in Central Poland. After this change, the line of demarcation and simultaneously the border of Soviet annexation of the Polish territories ran along the rivers Pisa, Narew, Bug and San.

The authorization of the first annexation started in October 1939 when Vilnius (Wilno) and its region (Wilenszczyzna), which were occupied by the Red Army, were ceded to Lithuania[4], which was independent and remained so for about a year. The rest of the annexed territories were ceded to the Ukrainian and Belorussian Soviet Socialist Republics. The commissariat of the Soviet authorities ordered plebiscites that legalized the incorporation of these territories to the USSR. Their results were prejudged like all such manifestations of the people's will in the territories annexed by the USSR. The rest of Poland was under German rule and the Polish Government led by General Wladyslaw Sikorski was in exile.

USSR citizenship was imposed upon all the citizens of Poland who found themselves in the territories annexed by the USSR at the beginning of November 1939. Whether they had been natives of Eastern Poland or refugees from Central and Western Poland made no difference. Several weeks later about 150,000 Poles were forcibly drafted into the Red Army.

Stalin's pact with Hitler resulting in the division of the Polish state was evidently incompatible with international law and agreements signed earlier by Berlin and Moscow. This was especially apparent in the case of Eastern Poland. This fact had been emphasized many times by the legal Polish authorities, among other occasions in the note dated 21 October 1939 which was addressed to the governments of all countries having diplomatic relations with Poland.[5]

When the German offensive against the USSR began in June 1941 the problem of the national status of the Eastern Territories of Poland returned to the international agenda. In July 1941 the Polish Government, which under pressure from the British Government, held negotiations with the representatives of the USSR in London. The Poles demanded that the formula of *status quo ante bellum* be applied, but they only managed to get a reassurance that 'the Soviet-German treaties from 1939 concerning territorial changes in Poland have lost their power'.[6] In practice this enigmatic wording meant that diplomatic relations between Poland and USSR were started anew and an amnesty of all Polish prisoners of war was proclaimed by the USSR.[7]

In December 1941 when the German Army was close to Moscow and the Soviet Government was in exile in Kuibyshev, Stalin offered the Poles the Curzon Line with certain modifications. It had already been mentioned in 1939 by the British minister Halifax and this made Stalin's suggestion look morally reasonable. The Curzon Line was east of the line of demarcation of the Molotov–Ribbentrop Pact which granted the regions of Przemysl and Bialystok with their Polish majority to Poland. The discovery of the bodies of thousands of Polish officers in the Katyn Forest[8] caused the breaking off of diplomatic relations between Poland and the Soviet Union in April 1943 and weakened the possibilities for the Poles to influence any future negotiations. Because of the toughness and strength of Stalin – the Red Army was again quickly moving westwards and the Western Allies needed to ensure that no coalition between Japan, Germany and the USSR would form – serious negotiations for a Polish borderline east of the Curzon Line were already impossible in practice. In 1943 at the meeting of Stalin, Churchill and Roosevelt in Teheran the question of compensation for the Poles in the west for the lost territories in the east was brought on to the agenda for the first time by Churchill.

In Yalta on 6 February 1945 the Curzon Line, with minor changes, was eventually legalized. A decision on the Oder–Neiße Line in the west was made in Potsdam on 2 August 1945.[9] A Polish–Soviet border agreement was signed on 16 August 1945.[10]

2. THE ETHNIC PICTURE

The Second Republic of Poland, reconstructed in 1918 on part of the territory of the First Republic of Poland, had been a multinational state. The national minorities had constituted more than one-third of the population. The Eastern Territories, especially, had diversified the ethnic picture.

In 1939 the ethnic picture of the territories of Eastern Poland which were ceded to the Soviet Union was the following:

1. Vilnius and its district (Wilenszczyzna) had a total population of 550,000 inhabitants. There were 322,000 Poles, 108,000 Jews, 75,000 Belarusians, 31,000 Lithuanians and 14,000 from other nationalities (Russians, Germans, Karaites, Armenians etc.).[11]
2. The territories of the Second Republic of Poland that now belong to Belarus had a population of 4.7 million inhabitants. There were 2.32 million Poles, 1.1 million Belarusians, 426,000 Jews, 90,000 Russians, 55,000 Ukrainians and 737,000 from other nationalities.[12]
3. The territories of the Second Republic of Poland that now belong to Ukraine had a population of nearly 8 million inhabitants. There were 4.47 million Ukrainians, 2.6 million Poles, 600,000 Jews, 80,000 Germans and 178,000 from other nationalities.[13]

During the war the Polish population experienced the terror of NKVD,[14] the deportations of the intelligentsia and losses from the war. As many as 1.24 million Eastern Poles were evacuated to Poland in July 1945. Together with those who had fled to the West in the war years the total number of Eastern Poles who left their homelands was a little over two million.

The Poles who remained in the Eastern Territories were afraid of revealing their origins and renounced their nationality and religion.[15] After World War II the persecution of the Poles continued. Despite the declared right of all the nations of the USSR to a free development of their own culture and education, the Poles were vigorously denationalized and deprived of jobs. Their access to culture and education in their mother tongue was limited. They were also deported to the Russian interior, accused of having earlier supported the Polish underground army. Especially severe persecutions were suffered by the Roman Catholic Church.[16]

Now the Poles in Belarus amount to 418,000 (according to statistics from the beginning of the 1980s they totalled 25 per cent of the inhabitants in the Grodno region). In Ukraine Poles officially number 219,000. According to the Lithuanian data Vilnius and its region have approximately 260,000 Poles.[17] After two generations the Polish inhabitants of the territories of former Eastern Poland are still almost exclusively uneducated and culturally backward in comparison with the Lithuanian,

Ukrainian or Belarusian populations. The Poles have the lowest qualifications of those employed in the state administration and military.

3. THE CHARACTERISTICS OF THE TERRITORY

The fortifications on the eastern border of Poland had no important strategic significance for the USSR. The majority of the fortifications were based on natural characteristics of the region and were facing east.

Strategically most important for Moscow was to secure control over access to the so-called Smolensk Gate. That was the name for the territory east of the River Bug, between the rivers Niemen and Pripet (Prypec). It was the shortest and the most convenient way of attacking Russia from the west. The Polish invasion threatening Moscow at the beginning of the 17th century came that way, as did Napoleon's offensive and that of the *Wehrmacht*. In 1939 this area became a part of the territory annexed by the Soviet Union but the frontier according to the Curzon Line left it on Poland's side. The Soviet Union in practice had a hold on the Smolensk Gate, though. This was achieved after the war as Poland became part of the Soviet Bloc.

Moreover the annexation of the territories of Southern and Eastern Poland facilitated the exertion of pressure on Romania and the Soviet annexation of Bessarabia and Northern Bukovina. It also provided the means for safeguarding Kiev and to counteract threats similar to that of 1920, when the Polish–Ukrainian army had taken the capital of Ukraine from Soviet troops in essentially one attack. Because of the weak infrastructure of roads in Belarus and Ukraine the railways of South-Eastern Poland were especially important from both the economic and the military point of view.

Economically the territories were of little value. In Boryslaw region near Lvov large quantities of crude oil, natural gas, ozocerite and hard coal were mined. The main centres of the chemical industry were in Lvov and Drohobycz. The food industry was in Grodno and Chodorow and the centres of the timber industry in Rudnik, Lvov, Stryj and Równe.

Despite the existence of two cultural and political centres, the university towns of Vilnius and Lvov, the territories annexed by the USSR were very poorly urbanized. The vast majority of the people, amounting to more than 80 per cent of all inhabitants, were agricultural workers.

4. THE PRESENT DAY

On the question of the legality of the present borders the policy of the Polish authorities and non-governmental organizations is consistent. It is based on the thesis that according to the Final Act of the CSCE in Helsinki on 1 August 1975 there is no problem concerning borders in Europe. Many times during various official occasions President Lech Walesa, Minister of Foreign Affairs Krzysztof Skubiszewski and other Polish officials have confirmed this view.[18] This attitude is also disseminated in the Polish press, radio and television.

This conciliatory Polish attitude is partly explained by the fact that in the post-war settlement Poland gained new territories in the west, and raising the question of the legality of the eastern border would sooner or later lead to a questioning of the western border as well. Another part of the explanation is that Poland's good relations with her newly independent neighbours Lithuania, Belarus and Ukraine are vital to all concerned. The instability of Russia and the fear that in the case of serious disputes Russia might be able to put pressure on the parties have led to a desire to avoid all tensions. Also the economic benefits of good relations, together with a certain willingness on the part of all the countries to look good in the eyes of the West, make efforts to maintain good relations worthwhile.

As a rule public opinion supports this reasoning, although among the older generation nostalgia for family territories in the east can be sensed. This is demonstrated in peaceful forms that have not caused tempers to rise. Regional societies have been created (of Lvov and of Vilnius) and numerous traditional accounts have been published (for example songs and sketches of the urban folklore of Lvov). There are no significant statements considering the change of the formel status of the annexed territories of Eastern Poland and their problems are treated as the internal concerns of Lithuania, Belarus and Ukraine.

The problems of the Polish population living in the territories that belonged to Poland before World War II are now broadly discussed. Some actions aimed at helping them in economic and health-related problems (for example, the results of the Chernobyl disaster) have been organized. Polish firms and societies are engaged in the renovation of Polish monuments, e.g. cemeteries and churches, that were devastated under the Soviet rule. The gathering of funds and assistance for the renovation of damaged monuments of a Polish character concerns not only the lost territories but also genuine Russian territories, for instance Moscow and

St. Petersburg. Organizations acting in this field, for instance the Committee for Polish Cultural Heritage in Ukraine, espouse very strongly the aim of rescuing the monuments of Polish culture. Their concern is preservation and they very firmly distance themselves from any kind of revisionist aims in relation to the existing border.[19]

The Polish authorities are trying to compensate for the many years of silence about the problems of the Poles in the territories annexed by the USSR. By means of official contacts they are endeavouring to ensure the well-being of the Polish population in Lithuania. In Belarus and Ukraine they have provided opportunities for cultural development and education in Polish, Roman Catholic church services, free access to Polish books and newspapers and in the borderlands a chance to view Polish television. From the Polish point of view the negotiations on this problem by the Polish Minister of Foreign Affairs in Minsk, Kiev and Vilnius and with the Lithuanian, Belarusian and Ukrainian politicians in Warsaw seem to be going well.

A special mission is the extension of support for the Roman Catholic church in the former territories of Eastern Poland. As a result of many years of atheistic and anti-Polish policy it lost all its real estate and also, with no place for worship, the possibility in practice of conducting religious services. In 1990 Ukraine repossessed forty-six Catholic churches that had been turned into museums of atheism, warehouses or machine centres by the Bolsheviks. The return of religious life does not always happen without friction, though, because in these multinational and multireligious regions the churches are often claimed by more than one owner.

5. LITHUANIA

The Poles in Lithuania number approximately 260,000 (about 7 per cent of the total population). Their specific situation arises from their very strong concentration in Vilnius District (67 per cent of the people, excluding the City of Vilnius) and in Salcininkai (Soletsniki, Soleozniki) District (82 per cent of the people).

When Lithuania was struggling for her independence Polish politicians supported these aims both in the international sphere and through bilateral contacts. However, the Polish minority in Lithuania found the changes threatening. The Poles, who had been living in the same regions for centuries, protested for example against legislation passed in January 1989 that required all state officials to acquire at least a rudimentary knowledge of Lithuanian within two years.

The Lithuanian Poles organized themselves politically in March 1989, and in 1989–91 they passed a series of autonomy resolutions. They also demanded approval for the slogan that for the Lithuanian Poles, Lithuania is the Fatherland and Poland is the Motherland.[20] Their three main postulates were national autonomy within an area more or less within the borders of Vilnius and Salcininkai districts, education in Polish (also for priests) and the return of closed churches to the Poles. These actions evoked sharp conflict because the Lithuanian Poles, when safeguarding their own rights, chose to prefer certain Soviet laws and practices to the laws and declarations of independent Lithuania.[21]

After the Moscow *coup d'état* in August 1991 two Polish district councils were dissolved and accused of standing in the way of Lithuanian independence. There has also been a project to extend the boundaries of the City of Vilnius to Vilnius District, which would mean that the Poles no longer have a majority in the district. Nor would they have a right to regain land through privatization measures as such measures do not apply within Vilnius City limits.

Still, despite the difficulties caused by the problems of the Lithuanian Poles and the fear of some Lithuanians that the question of borders has not yet been finally settled, official Polish–Lithuanian relations have turned out to be correct and friendly. These good relations were manifested with the signing of an interstate Polish–Lithuanian declaration in January 1992 by the Ministers of Foreign Affairs Krzysztof Skubiszewski and Algirdas Saudargas. An important article in this declaration concercs the inviolability of Poland's post-war borders.[22] The change of authorities in Lithuania after the last parliamentary elections has also helped to push the misunderstandings concerning the Lithuanian Poles' aspirations for autonomy into the background.

Eventually in April 1994 the Treaty of Friendly Relations and Good Neighbourly Cooperation Between the Republic of Lithuania and the Republic of Poland was signed. The treaty still needs to be ratified by the Lithuanian parliament. Among other things, the contracting parties mutually confirmed the integrity of the present territories of both states independently from the processes of the formation of their borders in the past.

6. BELARUS

In the Belorussian Soviet Socialist Republic the identification with the centre was always strong and national identity was not well developed. Before the *coup d'état* in Moscow in August 1991 Poland had very few opportunities to cultivate good relations with Belarus. Declarations of friendship and cooperation with Russia and Ukraine were signed in October 1990 but attempts to do so with Belarus failed. The real reason had to do with the republic's difficulty in extricating itself from Moscow's control. There was also distrust for Poland due to Soviet propaganda that Poland would seize Belarusian territory.

Relations between Poland and Belarus improved dramatically after Belarus declared independence on 25 August 1991. By October 1991 they had already signed an economic accord and a Declaration on Friendship and Cooperation. Among other things the two parties stated they had no territorial claims against each other and that the border could not be changed in the future. The Polish and Belarusian authorities also undertook to improve the conditions of the Belarusian minority in Poland (about 300,000 people, 0.7 per cent of the total population) and the Polish minority in Belarus (418,000 people, 4.0 per cent of the total population).

The main reason for these friendly relations is probably the liberal minority policies of both countries. In Belarus the national minorities have experienced no obstacles in acquiring citizenship and the government has encouraged the opening of Polish schools. Some tension has been caused, however, by the rapid rebuilding of Roman Catholic congregations, especially in the Grodno region. From the Belarus point of view the efforts in reconstructing the Catholic Church in Belarus are connected with a repolonization policy.[23]

7. UKRAINE

In October 1990 Poland and Ukraine signed the Declaration on the Foundations and Fundamental Directions in the Development of Polish–Ukrainian Relations where it was stated that the parties had no territorial claims against one another and that no claims would be raised in the future. This declaration was followed by several accords. In May 1992 the two countries signed the Treaty of Friendly Relations and Good Neighbourly Cooperation that also affirms the inviolability of borders.

Neither in the Ukrainian policy nor in the activities of Ukrainian non-governmental organizations is any fear for Polish territorial demands visible.

The minority question has also been the subject of much care and thought. The Ukrainian authorities have enabled the Polish population to cultivate their cultural life and pursue an education in their native language. Numerous churches have been revived and large-scale visits of people to Poland have been allowed – for instance – the mass pilgrimages during the visit of Pope John Paul II to Poland. The Declaration of the Rights of Nationalities in Ukraine was approved by the Ukrainian parliament in November 1991 and it guarantees a number of political, economic, social and cultural rights to all the minorities in Ukraine.

Despite their secured legal position the Poles in Ukraine constitute a passive population because of the denationalization process during decades of Soviet rule. Also some anti–Polish sentiment is in the air in Western Ukraine and the Ukrainian National Front RUKH has voiced demands for territorial revisions with Poland 'up to the River San'. The slogans are of minor significance, though, and on the whole Polish–Ukrainian relations seem set on a good course.[24]

8. PROSPECTS FOR THE FUTURE

The future developments of the territories that were annexed from Poland in 1939 are considered to be strictly the internal matter of the states that now rule them, i.e. Lithuania, Belarus and Ukraine. Nothing suggests that Poland would have exerted or would like to exert influence upon them. The only possibility that could arise is in connection with the tendency to create Euroregions like Euroregion Karpaty, which joins together the already economically connected borderlands of Southern and Eastern Poland, Ukraine, Slovakia and Hungary. I see no possibility that in the predictable future the Polish authorities would emphasize the fact that in the inter-war period these territories belonged to Poland.

In international relations the delicate question of ethnic minority rights can cause certain tensions. I do not foresee problems in Polish–Ukrainian relations which seem to be progressing favourably There may, however, be certain difficulties in Belarus connected with the very rapid repolonization process in the Grodno region which is being observed with concern by Minsk. Also, in Polish–Lithuanian relations some tensions are to be expected, mainly connected with the denationalization of land and the obstacles already created by the Lithuanian authorities for the Poles, who wish to regain farms that were nationalized in the 1940s. Most probably the problem of establishing a Polish autonomous district will return, as will the question of equality of the Polish language in Roman Catholic liturgy in Vilnius Cathedral and the bilinguality of higher education. It does not seem likely, however, that the Polish authorities will make official statements on these problems.

To conclude, the issue of Eastern Poland and its partition in accordance with the Stalin–Hitler pact is now a historical problem which will not return in the sense of a new geopolitical arrangement. Taking the stability of the borders for granted in their present configuration is necessary for joint Polish–Lithuanian, Polish–Belarusian, Polish–Ukrainian and also for Polish–Russian relations, in order to work out a historical interpretation of this problem that would enable a future to be built on the basis of a non-antagonistic background.

NOTES

1. *Vedomosti Verkhovnogo Soveta SSSR*, no. 37, 1939, p. 3. According to another source the figure is 8,300 square kilometres, i.e. 2.1 per cent of the area of the Second Republic of Poland. *Maly Rocznik Statystyczny Polski 1939–41* (London: Ministerstwo Informacji Polski 1941), p. 5.
2. Ibid.
3. *Documents on German Foreign Policy 1918–1945*, series D, vol. VII (London: US Government Printing Office 1956), pp. 246–7.
4. The return of Vilnius and its region (Wilenszczyzna) to Lithuania was a tactical gesture that helped make the Lithuanians sympathetic to the Soviet Union and made it easier to the RSFSR to annex the whole of Lithuania later on.
5. The note read: 'The Polish Government is in evidence that in the Polish territory temporarily occupied by the USSR a plebiscite was ordered about the annexation of those territories to the USSR as if in accordance with the will of the population. The Polish Government proclaims herewith that the ordering of this plebiscite in the territories under military occupation contradicts the regulations of the law of the nations.' *Documents on Polish–Soviet Relations 1939–1945*, vol. I (London: Heinemann 1961), pp. 19–20.
6. *Dziennik Polski* (London), no. 324, 31 July 1941.
7. *Izvestiya*, 13 August 1941.
8. Wojciech Materski (ed.), *Katyn. Documents of Genocide* (Warsaw: Institute of Political Polish Academy of Sciences 1993).
9. USSR returned to Poland about 10 per cent of the area of 200,000 square kilometres that was annexed in September 1939. These comprised a small part of Warsaw Province and six districts of Bialystok and a part of Lvov Province.
10. A treaty on a minor exchange of territories was signed in Febuary 1951. A territory of about 480 square kilometres close to the upper Bug was given to the Soviet Union and territory of the same size to the east of the upper San was given to Poland.

11. Leonas Sabaliunas, *Lithuania in Crisis. Nationalism to Communism 1939–1940* (Bloomington and London: Indiana University Press 1972), p. 277. According to another source the total population was 537,000; there were 371,000 Poles and 71,000 Jews. See *Maly Rocznik Statystyczny Polski* (1941), p. 9. There exist many contradicting statistics. The differences are partly explained by the fact that Lithuanians living in Polish territories were afraid of revealing their nationality.

12. Ibid.

13. Ibid. In these Belarusian and Ukrainian lands Poles made up the majority in the cities while the countryside was populated by Belarusians and Ukrainians.

14. Soviet People's Commissariat for Internal Affairs, *Natsionalnyi komissariat vnutrennykh del* (in Russian). An organ of the KGB that was renowned for organizing political purges.

15. See Jan Siedlecki, *Losy Polaków w ZSRR w latach 1939–86* (London: Instytut Historyczny im. gen. W. Sikorskiego 1987), pp. 43–6.

16. *Zhurnal Moskovskoi Patriarkhi*, no. 6, 1966, p. 19 and *Diyannia soboru greko-katolitskoi cerkvi u Lvivi 8–18 bereznya 1946* (Lvov: 1946), p. 10.

17. Piotr Lossowski, *Polska-Litwa. Ostatnie sto lat* (Warsaw: Oscar 1991), p. 97.

18. Cf. Jadwiga Staniszkis (ed.), *Polityka wschodnia Rzeczypospolitej Polskiej na progu lat dziewięćdziesiatych (szkice do prognozy)* (Warsaw: Institute of Political Studies Polish Academy of Sciences 1991).

19. *Przeglad Tygodniowy*, 21 April 1990 (an interview with the chairman of the Committee, Professor Alfred Jahn).

20. *Litwa. Biuletyn PAP* (Warsaw: Polish Press Agency 1992).

21. In May 1990, Salcininkai (Soletsniki, Soleczniki) District proclaimed itself a Polish National-Territorial District where the Constitution of the Lithuanian Soviet Socialist Republic was to remain in force. Also, after the Lithuanian parliament had prohibited it, Polish officials in Lithuania continued to allow ethnic Poles to be drafted into the Soviet Army. See Stephen R. Burant, 'International Relations in a Regional Context: Poland and Its Eastern Neighbours – Lithuania, Belarus, Ukraine', *Europe–Asia Studies*, vol. 45, no. 3, 1993, pp. 395–418.

22. *Rzeczpospolita*, 14 January 1992.

23. *Gazeta Wyborcza*, 1 January 1993 (an interview with R. Szporluk).

24. A good and informative survey on bilateral relations between Poland and her neighbours after the collapse of the Soviet Union and an important source for this chapter is Burant (1993).

9. The Northern Part of East Prussia

Peter Wörster

The present region of Königsberg (officially renamed Kaliningradskaya Oblast in 1946) is part of the historical territory of East Prussia, the eastern German province west of Lithuania and north of Poland (see Map 9.1). It also included the territory of Memel (today Lithuania) and the southern part of East Prussia, which was occupied by Poland in 1945. Thus we can say that East Prussia was divided into three parts in 1945: Polish in the south, Russian in the middle, and Lithuanian in the north. The present chapter deals with the Russian part, extending from a totally arbitrary and non-historical line of demarcation (from Braunsberg in the west to Goldap in the east) between the Polish and Soviet zone in the south to the Memel River in the north. This territory covers about 15,100 square kilometres. Its capital is the city of Königsberg, the former capital of East Prussia as a whole. The main river is the Pregel, which flows into the Baltic Sea near Königsberg.

1. THE HISTORY OF THE TERRITORY

East Prussia is part of the Prussian land,[1] to which the highest authorities of the Middle Ages, the Emperor and the Pope, sent the Teutonic Order to fight against the heathen Prussians, after the Poles in Mazovia had met with no success in previous efforts. The Teutonic Order took possession of this land in 1236. Here the Order built up one of the most modern states in the Middle Ages. About a hundred towns and thousands of villages were founded. German settlers came from the northern and western regions of Germany, and also from Silesia. Later, when the number of German settlers dwindled, the Order allowed people from Polish Mazovia (who later became the Masurians, the 'men from Mazovia') and from

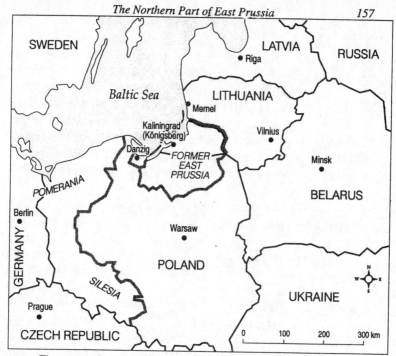

—— The present borders

————— The borders of Germany before World War II

Map 9. 1. The northern part of East Prussia.

Lithuania to come to Prussia and settle in the southern, northern and eastern parts of the land.

The pre-German population, the Baltic Prussians (Prußen), were gradually assimilated by the German people in a centuries-long process. The core of the Prussian language resisted for more than 400 years, until the 17th century, when it finally died out. In the 19th and 20th centuries, the majority of the Prussian Lithuanians and Slavic Masurians also became Germans as the result of long-term social processes. In the 20th century, Prussian Lithuanians and Masurians wanted to dissociate themselves from Polish and Lithuanian pretensions, and this attitude accelerated the process of assimilation.

The Teutonic Order dominated the area until 1454–66, when the powerful German cities in the western part of Prussia (e.g. Danzig, Thorn and Elbing) withdrew from the Order and elected the King of Poland as their protector to guarantee the rights of the towns and the special status of this part of Prussia. The Order had to acknowledge this change in its position, and remained only in the eastern part of Prussia. Here, its situation steadily worsened, owing to the fact that it received no further support from the German Reich – neither additional settlers nor military help nor diplomatic aid in its conflict with Poland. In 1525 the last Grand Master of the Order, Albrecht of Hohenzollern, changed the state of the Teutonic Order into a secular duchy and established himself as the first duke in Prussia. He was converted to Lutheran Protestantism after a visit to Wittenberg, and the eastern part of Prussia became one of the earliest German Protestant countries. This was connected with the acknowledgement of the supremacy of the King of Poland, who defended this political transformation against the opposition of the Catholic Church and the Emperor.

In 1544 Albrecht founded the University of Königsberg, which became the main centre of learning and academic culture in the entire region and remained so for more than two and a half centuries. The Hohenzollern dynasty in Mark Brandenburg inherited the duchy from their Prussian relatives. They succeeded in shaking off first the Polish and then the Swedish domination in Prussia in the Thirty Years' War, and thus attained sovereignty over Prussia. Here, since Prussia was not part of the German Reich, it was possible to transform the duchy into a kingdom in 1701.

During the Seven Years' War (1756–63) East Prussia was occupied by the Russians from 1758 to 1763. For most of the inhabitants, it was a very peaceful occupation without any real hardships. Afterwards the land was given back to the King of Prussia.

In 1772, when Poland first had to surrender territories (the so-called First Polish Partition), Frederick the Great succeeded in gaining the main part of the territory later called West Prussia, which made it possible to establish a land bridge – the Hohenzollern provinces of Pomerania and (East) Prussia. The two parts of the former state of the Teutonic Order were now reunified. During the 18th century the various parts of the Hohenzollern dynasty merged, so that we can finally speak of the Kingdom of Prussia as a whole.

In the time of the Napoleonic Wars, Prussia had to renounce all of its provinces west of the Elbe River, but still kept Brandenburg, Pomerania, Silesia, and East and West Prussia. East Prussia became the backbone of the resistance against the French, and thus of the renewal of the entire Prussian state.

In cultural history, the time of Immanuel Kant, Johann Gottfried Herder and Johann Georg Hamman was of extreme importance, not only for Germany, but for the Baltic provinces and Russia as well.

In the first month of World War I, Russian divisions occupied a large part of East Prussia, and stopped only a few kilometres away from the capital, Königsberg. The Russian First Army under Rennenkampf approached from the north, and the Russian Second Army under Samsonov from the southeast. The situation became very dangerous for the Germans. The Prussian general staff succeeded in fighting separately against the two Russian armies. Of decisive importance for the military situation in the east and also for the morale of the East Prussian population was the German victory at the Battle of Tannenberg under the command of Paul von Hindenburg at the end of August 1914. The Russians under Samsonov were defeated, and Samsonov committed suicide. By 1915 the whole of East Prussia had been liberated.

A dangerous situation arose after the war: the Treaty of Versailles demanded the renunciation of the East Prussian region north of the Memel River (the Memel territory, which was annexed by Lithuania in 1923) and a plebiscite in the southern region of East Prussia (Masuria and a part of Ermland) notwithstanding the fact that East Prussia as a whole was geographically separated from the Reich by the so-called Polish Corridor, and thus became an exclave. In the plebiscite under Allied control, more than 95 per cent voted for remaining with Germany. This was a good example of self-determination in regard to peoples and regions, and it was a grave mistake on the part of the 'peace-makers' at Versailles, St. Germain and Trianon not to apply this concept everywhere to settle territorial conflicts after World War I. Twenty years later, these problems led to World War II.

In March 1939 the Memel territory was reunified with East Prussia by a treaty with Lithuania. The historical borders of the province had remained stable and unchanged for 500 years, from 1422 to 1920. The National Socialist government in Germany ignored this after September 1939, when the new artificially created district of Zichenau (Ciechanów) and the small district of Suwalki, both in occupied Poland, were added to the province of East Prussia.

At the end of August 1944 the city of Königsberg was bombed twice by the Royal Air Force. Only the old parts of the city (Altstadt, Löbenicht, Kneiphof, Speicherviertel and adjacent areas) were destroyed. Militarily speaking, this operation was senseless. In October 1944 the Red Army entered East Prussia and occupied the eastern parts of the province.[2] The German Army was able to repulse the Soviet force for about two months. The latter committed atrocities against the defenceless German population, most of them women, children and old people. Cruelties in the little village of Nemmersdorf, in the district of Gumbinnen, were particulary notorious. The inhabitants, feeling themselves threatened and fearing to fall into the hands of the Red Army, tried to flee. This was in the middle of a severe winter, with insufficient preparation and without any able-bodied men, since these were serving as soldiers.

On 9 April, General Otto Lasch, the last German commander of Königsberg, capitulated to the superior force of the Red Army (35,000 German soldiers against 250,000 Soviet soldiers), in order to save the lives of about 110,000 civilians remaining in the capital and an indeterminate number of people in the outlying districts who were unable to flee.

The fate of these people was uncertain. From 10 April to 12 April, the Soviet soldiers were allowed to plunder the city. Atrocities were committed during this time, and also later. The reports of surviving victims are frightening even today. The Germans, especially the women, were subjected to all kinds of wanton violence. The German soldiers were taken prisoner and deported to Russia, either directly or via camps near Königsberg or elsewhere in East Prussia. About 150,000 civilians were also deported to Russia for hard labour. Only a few came back to Germany. The remaining civilian population was expelled from their homes and driven into the surrounding countryside on forced marches, during which they were subjected to further humiliation and violence. Many of them died during these deportation marches. Among them was Karl Heinrich Meyer (1890–1945), an invalid veteran of World War I who was professor of Slavic languages at the University of Königsberg and whose lectures on Dostoyevsky were the last ones given at the University. He died near the town of Cranz. The only aid given these refugees came from the German doctors, nurses and clergymen who had remained in Königsberg after it had fallen to the Soviet Union.

The German population in the city dropped from about 110,000 in April 1945 to about 73,000 the following June, and to only 25,000 to 30,000 in the summer of 1947, when the evacuation and expulsion of Germans from Königsberg began. About three-quarters of the Germans who had fallen into the hands of the Red Army in April 1945 died in Königsberg or were deported to Russia, where many of them later died. About 65,000 Germans were expelled from the rural districts of the Königsberg region.

There are four aspects of the Soviet policy towards the Germans in Königsberg that seem quite incomprehensible:

1. *German Administration.* The Soviets appointed German communists as mayors in several quarters of the city. They had no staff and no authority, but served only to transmit Soviet directives to the German population.

2. *Antifascist Club (later German Club).* The Soviets tried to influence the remaining German intellectuals by subjecting them to communist indoctrination. Under the harrowing circumstances that prevailed, this attempt was doomed to failure.

3. *The Press.* In June 1947 (a remarkably late date) the Soviets began to publish a German-language newspaper: *Neue Zeit.* It appeared twice a week until October 1948. There was no German on the editorial staff. Only in its earliest issues did the newspaper deal with certain problems of the Germans in Königsberg, but only from the official Soviet point of view. Soviet propaganda predominated completely.

4. *A Protestant Bishop.* One of the best-known Protestant clergymen in Königsberg at that time was Hugo Linck. He became the unofficial spokesman for the Germans, who had no kind of official representation. The Soviets asked Linck to become the Protestant bishop of East Prussia. It is still unclear what the Soviets' motive was, what they expected, and what purpose a Protestant bishop could serve in East Prussia. Linck declared that only a general assembly of all German Protestant clergymen in the province was entitled to elect a Protestant bishop. Thereupon the plan was dropped, and never mentioned again.

One might suppose that these Soviet steps were taken in an effort to improve the Germans' situation, but there is no indication that this was their true purpose. Rather, they were only short-lived tactical attempts to pacify the Germans and force them to accept Soviet rule. Within the whole context of Soviet policy towards the Germans at that time, especially in the Königsberg area, these efforts seem to be quite unrealistic. It is difficult to see any long-term plan to maintain a German population in the city.

The further fate of East Prussia was a very important question at the wartime conferences of the Allies: in Teheran (28 November–1 December 1943), Yalta (4–11 February 1945) and Potsdam (11 July–2 August 1945). The Western powers were willing to accept most of the Soviet claims.

At first, the whole of East Prussia was to be given to Poland. Stalin seemed to respect this solution as a kind of compensation for Poland, which had suffered loss of territories in the east (the Soviet annexation of 1939). Roosevelt supported these plans, and added a proposal to expel all Germans from East Prussia, just as the Turks had expelled the Greeks from Turkey after World War I. However, Roosevelt knew nothing about the true situation in this province; he always spoke of the German minority in East Prussia, and ignored the fact that he had helped Stalin maintain the annexations resulting from the Hitler–Stalin Pact of 1939. At the same time, Stalin used the Polish claims to German territories as a means of putting pressure on Poland.

At Teheran, Stalin for the first time demanded the northern part of East Prussia for the Soviet Union, leaving only the southern part for Poland. He argued that the Soviet Union needed an ice-free port, and moreover claimed that East Prussia was originally a Slavic territory. Both 'arguments' were untrue: 1) The annexation of the Baltic states had already given the Soviet Union an ice-free port in Libau (Liepaja, Latvia); 2) East Prussia was never a Slavic territory. This was a typical example of imperialist policy: Stalin wanted to establish a firm Soviet–Russian outpost on the Baltic Sea in order to keep both the Poles and the Baltic peoples in check, and 'to come to the throat of Germany', as Churchill characterized the Soviet leader's motive.

There is still an open question: why did the USA and England not reject the Soviet demands?

Both the Soviet and the Polish claims to East Prussia were based only on the desire to expand at the expense of defeated Germany. The Polish government-in-exile in London tried to fight against the Soviet plans in East Prussia, since the Poles wanted to acquire the province as a whole. But they failed, since Churchill had agreed to the incorporation of the northern part of East Prussia into the Soviet Union, so that this province had to be divided between the Soviet Union and Poland.

At Yalta no one opposed Stalin's plan to annex the northern part of East Prussia. Later, in the Potsdam Agreement (in which there was no German participation) the Allies agreed that the German territories east of the Oder–Neiße Line (i.e. one-quarter of Germany's total territory),[3] which had already been transferred to Polish administration by the Red Army, should remain under Polish control until the western border of Poland could be definitively established by a peace conference. As to the northern part of East Prussia, the Potsdam Agreement defined the Soviet sphere as running from the Baltic Sea, north of the towns of Braunsberg and Goldap, to the point where the borders of East Prussia, Lithuania and Poland meet. At Potsdam, the US and British leaders declared their readiness to support Soviet claims at the forthcoming peace conference. For the Allies at Potsdam, Germany undoubtedly continued to exist according to the borders of 1937.

Regarding the expulsion of Germans, the Potsdam Agreement spoke cynically of a 'transfer of population in a humane manner', although forcible expulsion had already begun. The Agreement mentioned only the Germans in Poland, Czechoslovakia and Hungary, where they indeed were minorities (although there were more than 3 million of them in Czechoslovakia). The text of the Potsdam Agreement said nothing about the populations of the German provinces in the east, such as Silesia, Pomerania, Danzig and East Prussia. Likewise, nothing was said in particular about the Germans in the northern part of East Prussia that was now under Soviet control.

The Soviet Union annexed the territory of Königsberg in October 1945, six months after it had been conquered by the Red Army.

2. THE STATUS OF THE TERRITORY UNDER SOVIET RULE

After it was officially annexed, the territory was still ruled only by the staffs of the Red Army and the Soviet secret service. It was not until April 1946 that a special administrative unit was set up: Kenigsbergskaya Oblast, which was then incorporated into the Russian Socialist Federal Soviet Republic (RSFSR). Despite the fact that the Red Army remained the dominant institution in the territory of Königsberg for several decades, it is possible to date the establishment of some kind of formal civilian administration as beginning in the spring of 1946.

Mikhail Kalinin, one of Stalin's intimates and the Chairman of the Supreme Soviet Presidium in Moscow, i.e. at that time the official head of the state, died in June 1946. In honour of this Bolshevik leader, who was responsible for many wartime atrocities (e.g. Katyn), the venerable city of Königsberg was renamed 'Kaliningrad' in July 1946. This new name stands as a symbol of the total Russification and Sovietization of the northern part of East Prussia. All reminders of the German past were to be expunged: not only was the name of the capital changed, but also the names of all the towns, villages and rivers.

Since April 1946 the region of Königsberg has been part of the RSFSR. It was integrated into the military and economic northwest region of the Soviet Union, to which the Baltic states and the Leningrad Oblast also belonged. The territory of Memel had been given to Lithuania early in 1945, long before the conference at Potsdam, where the fate of this territory was no longer a topic of discussion. The fate of the Germans still remaining in the Memel territory under Lithuanian rule was not so harsh as that of those living in the Königsberg territory under direct Soviet rule. The question of the Memel territory was topical in 1990 and 1991, when the Russians pointed to the fact that the Lithuanians had received Memel only as a result of the Soviet victory over Germany, and if the Lithuanians intended to leave the Soviet Union, the question of the future status of the Memel territory would have to be discussed anew.

The internal administrative organization of the Königsberg region varied. At first, the German districts were abolished in favour of many very small units (*raiony* in Russian). This new organization proved to be impracticable, so instead a few very large units were set up. They suffered a similar fate: they too were abolished, and new units resembling the former German districts were established.

The policy of the Soviet Union towards the northern part of East Prussia was based mainly on military interests, and on the desire to have a harbour as far to the west as possible. Königsberg, the city and the harbour, with all its geographical, maritime and administrative potentialities, became the most important base for all Soviet activities in the North Sea and the Atlantic (military, trade, science, propaganda and aid to the Sovietophile states in Africa and Latin America). Compared with the importance of the city of Königsberg, the rest of occupied East Prussia was not of any particular importance for the Soviet Union, nor is it for Russia today.[4]

As a consequence of the end of the Cold War and of the independence of the Baltic states and Belarus, the position of Königsberg has radically changed. The region is now an isolated enclave that belongs to Russia but has no direct land connection with her.

3. THE CHARACTERISTICS OF THE TERRITORY

As explained above, Stalin claimed the territory of Königsberg in order to set up a Soviet–Russian outpost between Poles and Balts, on the shore of the Baltic Sea. As a result, the largest ethnic group consists of Russians, but all in all, 59 nationalities are represented there. The precise percentages for the main groups are:

	1959	1970	1979
Russians	77.6 %	77.1 %	78.3 %
Belarusians	9.4 %	9.4 %	9.0 %
Ukrainians	5.8 %	6.6 %	6.8 %
Lithuanians	3.5 %	3.2 %	2.4 %

There are also less than 1 per cent Jews, Poles, Mordovians, Tatars, Chuvashes and others. In 1970 there were said to be about 10,000 persons of 'other nationalities', including some one to two thousand Germans who had remained in East Prussia after the war. The number of Germans settling in East Prussia from Central Asia is not known, but could amount to around 20,000 persons.[5]

It is very difficult to say how many Germans lived in the present-day territory of Königsberg, because this territory did not exist before the war and therefore there are no statistics for the region in regard to its post-war borders. It can be estimated that approximately 1.1 to 1.2 million people lived in the territory before 1939. The population in recent years – about 900,000 persons – does not approach the size of the pre-war population. Furthermore, it must be realized that about 50 per cent of the population lives in the capital, and about 80 per cent in all the towns together. The other districts have fewer than 10 to 15 persons per square kilometre.

The geopolitical and military situation has already been described. The region of Königsberg became a Soviet outpost to keep the Poles and Balts in check. One of the most important bases of the Red-Banner Fleet is still located in Pillau (Baltiisk). The headquarters of important staffs of the Soviet (now Russian) Army are still located in Königsberg and Insterburg (Chernyakhovsk). In the Samland region (west of Königsberg) the Soviets set up bases for rockets that could reach all of the NATO and neutral states in Central and Southern Europe. As a result of Russian troop withdrawal from Germany, East Central Europe and the Baltic states, the Russian military presence in the region of Königsberg is increasing today: estimates range between 100,000 and 250,000 military persons, i.e. between 10 and 25 per cent of the inhabitants of the territory. 'Kaliningrad became the focus for a major programme of military entrenchment and housed a wide range of land, sea and air forces. With its defence industries and military service centres, the region increasingly acquired the character of a garrison state.'[6]

The economy of the region had two important elements: 1) dockyards and the fishing industry, 2) the manufacture of special kinds of paper (cellulose industry). Both were already in existence before the annexation, and now, in the new circumstances, both are faced with serious problems. Recently, the region has been declared a 'free-trade zone' (*Yantar,* meaning amber) with the aim of building a northern Hong Kong, but at present it is impossible to visualize the consequences of the declaration since so far it has not taken on any concrete legal form.

A hindrance to the economic development of the Königsberg region is its rather useless infrastructure. French Telecom is, however, rebuilding the telephone connections. Moreover, the electricity necessary for the territory depends totally (about 80 per cent) on the nuclear power station Ignalina in Lithuania with all the possibilities for Lithuania to take advantage of this fact.

There is only one major cooperative project at present between Russians and Germans in the region: rebuilding the old Königsberg–Elbing Autobahn (Kaliningrad–Berlin Autobahn, as the Russians call it), which at present runs only from Königsberg to the Russian–Polish border. Only about 10 per cent of the exports from the region go to Germany which lags behind Sweden, Poland and Spain in this respect.

4. THE ATTITUDE OF THE FORMER POSSESSOR TOWARDS THE QUESTION OF EAST PRUSSIA

The former German Democratic Republic acknowledged the post-war boundaries as legal borders in the Treaty of Görlitz with Poland in 1950. The question of the northern part of East Prussia was not specifically mentioned. From then on, in the GDR there was no discussion about questions connected with the German provinces in the east. At the same time, research into historical and other aspects of the question was suppressed.

In the Federal Republic of Germany there was widespread feeling (both in political circles and among the general public) that the status established in 1945 was illegal and unjust: the annexation of territories as a whole, the expulsion and total expropriation of the native population, acts of violence against the German population permitted by the Soviet, Polish and Czech authorities and, last but not least, the repression of the small groups of Germans who had remained. The Potsdam Agreement was made without any kind of German participation, and is therefore, according to international law, not binding on the Germans. Nevertheless, everyone accepted the fact that Germany could exist only in its boundaries of 1937 (as the Allies had declared in Potsdam), and could not include the areas taken over by Hitler. Final answers regarding the borders of Germany and the territorial claims of Poland could be given only at a necessary future peace conference. For these reasons, the territory of Königsberg was still considered to be part of Germany as a whole. Chancellor Konrad Adenauer attained consent regarding this view in the German Treaty (*Deutschlandvertrag*) of 1952–54 with the Western Allies. This was the general opinion of all political parties, with the natural exception of the communists.[7]

A fundamental change appeared at the end of the 1960s. The treaties with the Warsaw Pact states (*Ostverträge*) drawn up by the Brandt administration in 1970–72 were interpreted in the sense of a definitive determination and acknowledgement of Germany's post-war borders, but according to the legal system of the Federal Republic, especially the Constitution (*Grundgesetz*), these treaties could not be a substitute for a peace conference leading to a regular peace treaty. The question of borders would have to remain open and be discussed in the '2 + 4' negotiations in 1990 that led to the reunification of the two German states. In connection with these negotiations, both German parliaments, the *Deutscher Bundestag* in Bonn and the first democratically elected *Volkskammer* in Berlin, acknowledged the final status of the Oder–Neiße Line as the border (including the city of Stettin west of the Oder River) in several declarations. The special status of the territory of Königsberg was not mentioned in any of these declarations and treaties of 1990.[8]

Neither official policy nor political parties nor public attitudes consider the possibility of returning the region of Königsberg to Germany. The collapse of the Soviet Union and the unnatural situation inside and outside the Russian enclave of Königsberg make the issue of the further fate of that region an urgent question in European politics, that should not be disregarded in German foreign policy. However, the German government and German political parties seem to be most unwilling to deal with this problem. But in the meantime, the problem is growing. Many of the Russian Germans from Central Asian republics want to settle in the northern part of East Prussia if it is not possible for them to go to the Federal Republic directly, where there are likewise many social and economic problems. Moreover, there remains the general question of the future of the Königsberg region. It already seems necessary to take steps to check the potential danger to peace and stability in Central Europe in order to prevent the northern part of East Prussia from becoming a bone of contention among various competing states.

For these reasons, German policy-makers and the general public should spend some time considering this issue. The Germans should have a feeling of special historically-based responsibility for this poor devastated country of East Prussia. Yet, it would apparently be better if the European Union rather than the German government dealt with the future status of the Königsberg region and tried to find a 'European solution'.

So far the European Union has not done much on the issue. Yet, at the beginning of 1994 an EU Commission visited Königsberg and considered that the region of Königsberg is that part of Russia through which this country can join the EU as soon as possible.[9]

Some of the German lands (such as Bremen, Mecklenburg-Vorpommern and Brandenburg) already have their own representatives in Königsberg.[10] But there is no German Consulate General. Poland[11] had already established her own Consulate at the beginning of 1993 under Consul General Dr Jerzy Bahr, an expert in the history of Königsberg and East Prussia. Lithuania is soon to establish her Consulate in Königsberg. However, the question of a German Consulate General is a more complicated political issue. In summer 1994, Yeltsin stopped the plan for a German Consulate because he had to pay attention to the strong opposition in the parliament to which the Russian Foreign Minister Kozyrev was listening – in this special case.[12]

Another attitude is taken by the victims of post-war European policy: the German people of East Prussia, who were humiliated, expelled and dispossessed after the war. Most of these people are still members of the *Landsmannschaft Ostpreußen*, with headquarters in Hamburg. They wish to preserve their rights, which are among the general human rights being discussed currently in an attempt to make the world aware of what happened after the war in the eastern German provinces, and to make it clear that we cannot accept such deeds without encouraging other states and their leaders to act in a similar manner (cf. events in former Yugoslavia). The German population of East Prussia is trying to help their hereditary homeland in cooperation with today's Russian population in order to stop the process of further deterioration in a traditional German region. They are organizing humanitarian aid for both Russians and Germans in the region of Königsberg. There are already numerous examples of practical cooperation between German East Prussians and Russians, including local Russian authorities.

The German East Prussians do not have any long-term objectives concerning the future status of the region. But it is a fact that the German East Prussians can support Russian efforts to develope a separate regional consciousness and follow their own inclinations to do something for their own future and for the future of the region, without waiting for solutions from Moscow.

5. THE LOCAL ATTITUDE

After the breakup of the Soviet Union, there is a very uncertain situation inside and outside the region of Königsberg. There are many questions and imponderable points in Moscow's policy, and in the attitudes of Poland and Lithuania towards the problem of Königsberg. As a result, there is no consensus among the population and the decision-makers in the territory. It is not only a political question *per se*, but also a problem of age groups. Here, as elsewhere, the younger generation does not have the same orientation problems as the older generation. Thus, there are many different points of view regarding the main issues in the territory of Königsberg.

We can see the beginnings of sociological and political research in Königsberg, e.g. the Kaliningrad Sociological Centre, a commercial institute headed by Boris A. Tregubov. He and his staff have been working since September 1991. They questioned a representative group of around 1,000 persons at the end of 1992. The findings in this poll were as follows (if we can trust the results):

1. Forty to forty-five per cent wish to restore the historical name of the city to Königsberg (tendency: rising). Russian colleagues have told me that about 70–80 per cent in the generation up to the age of 40 are in favour of the name Königsberg. The older generation, some veterans of the war, many leading members of the military staff, and unskilled workers are against a return to the historical name.

2. Seventy per cent are afraid of the new situation in the territory of Königsberg as an exclave after the independence of Lithuania and Belarus. Sixty-eight per cent are especially afraid of Lithuanian claims; 30 per cent are afraid of Germany; 40 per cent are ready to accept an independent Balto-Russian state as a part of the European Union, or under the latter's protection. This model could also be imagined as a German-Russian condominium under the EU. Given recent circumstances, it is remarkable that a minority of about 6 per cent wanted this territory returned to Germany, since they thought that this would be the only way to stabilize the economic and political situation in the long run. This minority opinion is very interesting, since it seems to be quite unrealistic in the context of recent European policies.

3. About 60 per cent of the population are in favour of privatizing the entire economy, and are willing to be employers themselves. But there is a tremendous lack of money, and therefore about 30 per cent would be willing to work in Western countries (mainly in Germany) in order to earn the money necessary for founding new businesses of their own in the region of Königsberg.

4. Forty-two per cent favoured the settlement of Russian Germans from Central Asia (tendency: rising). The Russian population hopes to improve the economic situation in this manner, because the Russian Germans are known to be good workers, and since the Russians hope for more support from Germany if there is a larger number of Germans in the region – especially people who can speak both German and Russian. Thus the younger generation, the urban population and the intellectuals in general are in favour of the settlement of Russian Germans in the region. By contrast, the older generation, the generation that is still passionate about the Soviet defeat of Germany in World War II, farm labourers, and people of low educational level, are afraid of an influx of Germans from the Central Asian republics. In the last election to the State Duma the

party of Zhirinovsky won about 30 per cent in the area of Königsberg. During his visit to Königsberg in May 1994 Zhirinovsky rejected categorically any kind of return of the area to Germany, whereas he had earlier expressed some views to this end.[13]

Today, living conditions in the region (e.g. inflation, unemployment, crime, the general availability of goods) are worse than in Lithuania or Poland.

There are indications that many Russians intend to leave the region, and other indications that other people – and not only soldiers or Russian Germans – are moving into the region. There is the administration of the region under Yuri Matochkin (an intimate friend of Boris Yeltsin), who favours a further development of the *Yantar* free-trade zone. He also seems to be in favour of close Russian–German cooperation in the region, since he often criticizes the lack of German interest and activity.

The local administration seems to favour a more independent status for the Königsberg region, so that at the end of a period of transition Königsberg will be part of the Russian state, will stay under Russian sovereignty, but will be able to decide all questions of local and regional interest on its own without directions from Moscow – above all in regard to currency, taxes, economy, trade, and relations with the countries around the Baltic Sea. Within the local administration there already exists an office of international affairs.

President Yeltsin's decree On the Free Economic Zone was already published in 1991, but at the time of writing there is still no law on the implementing regulations. The Russian Security Council is recommending a normal 'treaty' between Königsberg and Moscow, but there are many political hesitations. The party of Zhirinovsky is not the only group to be afraid of the possibility that other republics and regions of the Russian Federation could emulate the Königsberg-Russian claims for autonomy and self-determination.[14]

There are clubs, societies and circles with varying interests and orientation, but all are faithful to the German past of Königsberg, and East Prussia in general. Here, there is increasingly close cooperation between Germans and Russians. For the past four or five years, the regional group of the Soviet (now Russian) Cultural Foundation (*fond kultury*) has become well known for its impressive work. Its chairman, Yuri Ivanov, is also a member of the regional parliament. Another well-known organization is the Kant Society under its chairman Leonard Kalinnikov from the Russian University in Königsberg, which was founded in 1967. The Immanuel Kant Museum was established in Königsberg in 1974. There is also a (Russian!) East-Prussian Club. Even in communist times, the Kant Museum was the unofficial centre of regional history, maintaining the cultural heritage of 700 years as far as was possible in those days.

In 1994 Germans and Russians are organized a joint celebration in honour of the 450th anniversary of the Albertus University which was founded by Duke Albrecht in 1544.

Several Russian newspapers were founded beginning in 1946, of which the daily *Kaliningradskaya pravda* has the largest circulation. There was also the remarkable publication *Kenigsbergskii kurer*, with a subtitle in German: *Königsberger Kurier*. It began in 1991, before the coup in Moscow, and appeared about once a month, with a circulation of around 5,000 copies, and was particulary influential among the decision-makers in the region. It was devoted to the past of Königsberg and its importance for German and general European culture, and especially to the history of German–Russian relations over the past centuries. Its articles were published in Russian, with a German summary of the more important ones on the last page. This journal ceased publication in the first half of 1994.

In 1992 the new quarterly *Zapad Rossii* (The West of Russia) started. The journal is devoted to literature, art, history of the territory, current affairs, ecology etc. It is open not only to Russian authors but also to Germans, Lithuanians and Poles. All articles are in Russian; even poetry is translated into Russian.

In March 1993 a new paper, *Königsberger Express*, began publication. As its editors claim, it is the first German-language newspaper of Kaliningrad. It is intended as a bridge between the present city and territory of Königsberg/Kaliningrad, on the one hand, and Germany, on the other, in regard to cultural, intellectual and economic questions. This publication was obviously sponsored financially by Germans at first, but the editorial staff is exclusively Russian. It began with a circulation of 10,000 copies.

6. FUTURE PROSPECTS

The future of the region is quite uncertain: there is the uncertain political situation in Moscow; there are conflicting attitudes and demands in

Poland and Lithuania; there is the still unclear role that could be played by Germany and/or the European Union; there is still a question as to what the population of the region wish and hope for, assuming that they could decide for themselves.

Thus it is very difficult to speak of future prospects. Instead of trying to be a prophet, I would like to come back to certain essential points that should be taken into consideration in further discussions and decisions regarding the northern part of East Prussia. In summary, the future of this territory must be based on a restoration of law, human rights and historical awareness, which were disrupted after the war, not only in regard to East Prussia, but also to the Baltic states, where history, 50 years later, has finally corrected itself.

The present instability in and around Königsberg, this challenge to Russian, German and overall European policy, is a result of the unjust treatment of East Prussia and the other pre-war German eastern provinces. This European challenge is being taken up by other countries, which are trying to find ways and means of coping with it, but this does not include Germany itself. Little can be clearly stated regarding the intentions of the Russian population in the territory, or the feelings and wishes of the expelled Germans. Now, as to the essentials I mentioned earlier:

1. Events during the decades following 1945 have to be recognized, as well as their historical context. If this is not accomplished, there will be little chance for a long-term, firmly-founded and viable new status.

2. The Russian population that is now predominant in the region has needs and rights that must be respected and fulfilled.

3. The rights of the original German inhabitants, who were expelled and dispossessed, must be recognized as far as possible today. This can be achieved only if Europe as a whole can return to the principles of law and justice instead of power and violence. The great philosopher Immanuel Kant explained in his famous book *Zum ewigen Frieden* (On Perpetual Peace), published in Königsberg in 1795,[15] that the condition for establishing peace between peoples and states is the acknowledgement of law and justice. Unjust solutions resulting from power and violence cannot establish a long-term, orderly and effective basis for relations between peoples and states; they

cannot bring about 'peace'. For this reason I have mentioned the rights of the original German population.

4. The possibilities of German–Russian cooperation in the region of Königsberg should also open the door for the return of the Russian Germans to Königsberg, not primarily to the towns, but to the countryside, where there is a tremendous need for additional inhabitants. Of course it would not be possible for all of the approximately two million Germans living in Russia and Central Asia to come to the region of Königsberg, but it should be possible for a considerable number of them. They would have a good chance to form a bridge between Russia and Germany, culturally and economically. This problem of the Russian Germans is one of the most complicated and urgent issues in German–Russian relations today. As a result of recent developments in the Central Asian republics of the former Soviet Union, the Germans there (like the Russians) are being more and more repressed by radical Islamic groups.

5. We must accept the fact that this territory is part of Russia. As a Russian enclave between Poland and Lithuania, it would seem to have a very complicated geopolitical position, so that further arrangements will have to be made with these neighbouring states. The region of Königsberg should not be annexed by or divided between these neighbours, as certain groups (but obviously not the official governments) in Poland and Lithuania would like to do.[16]

6. Another question concerns the kind of military presence that Russia will be able to maintain in this area south of the Baltic Sea, and how a military balance can be set up that will not pose a threat to any of the states around the Baltic Sea, but will enable Russia to defend the territorial status quo against the surrounding neighbours. The Russian Minister of Defence General Grachev on his visit to Königsberg in March 1994 created the new slogan 'Kaliningrad – the special zone of defence' and referred in this way to the 'special zone of trade' which should already years ago have determined the new place of the region in Russian policy. It is still unclear what Grachev's slogan means in concrete terms.

    It is a matter of fact that a high concentration of troops and military equipment in the region today cannot be maintained if the economy and trade are to be developed and if the region of Königsberg is to become a prosperous territory where people of all the states around the Baltic Sea can meet together.[17]

7. Except for the detailed political and economic questions the main problems of the territory's future seem to be:

    a) What kind of autonomy or even self-determination is the territory of Königsberg able to gain from Moscow? How can the local Russian administration achieve more scope if the party of Zhirinovsky continues to reject any special status and will not allow more regional rights, pretending that this would weaken the unity of the Russian Federation?

    b) What kind of support can the EU and especially Germany give – in the words of the English journalist Peter Johnson: 'Is it possible that some kind of Re-Germanization would be in the interest of the territory and its present inhabitants?'. Johnson does not accept the propaganda-slogan of 'Re-Germanization' against any kind of German engagement but he points to the fact that Germany is the natural partner of the region of Königsberg – of course without any discussion of borders.[18]

8. The fact also has to be recognized that the region of Königsberg is part of a 700-year-old German province, and that the Germans thus should have some kind of historically-based interest in the well-being of this area more than any other European country can have.

9. In this way Königsberg could become a key for a new era in German–Russian relations, as a bridge for cooperation between the two countries. Königsberg would thus have a chance to regain its position as a 'cornerstone of Europe', as the German historian Walther Hubatsch has entitled one of his books about East Prussia:[19] a cornerstone of European policies and economies, and, last but not least, a cornerstone of European security. In this way we can try to stabilize the situation in order to prevent future conflicts in the area.[20]

In conclusion: the Russians who are now in Königsberg, and the Germans who have a special relationship with it, should work together there in the spirit of Immanuel Kant to preserve peace, now and in the future. This is much more than a question of mere finances or economics or military presence.[21]

NOTES

1. About the history of East and West Prussia as a whole cf. Bruno Schumacher, *Geschichte Ost- und Westpreussens* (Würzburg: Holzner Verlag 1977), XIV. The latest comprehensive volume is Hartmut Boockmann, 'Ost- und Westpreussen', in *Deutsche Geschichte im Osten* (Berlin: Siedler Verlag 1992). About the history of the City of Königsberg cf. Fritz Gause, *Die Geschichte der Stadt Königsberg in Preussen* (Köln and Graz: Böhlan Verlag 1965–71). The latest publication about the city is Gerhard von Glinski and Peter Wörster, *Königsberg – die ostpreussiche Hauptstadt in Geschichte und Gegenwart* (Berlin and Bonn: Westkreuz Verlag 1992).

2. The latest article about the end of the war in the East, especially in East Prussia, is Hans-Werner Rautenberg, 'Der Zusammenbruch der deutschen Stellung im Osten und das Ende Königsbergs. Flucht und Vertreibung als europäisches Problem', in Bernhard Jähnig and Silke Spieler (eds.), *Das Königsberger Gebiet im Schnittpunkt deutscher Geschichte und in seinen europäischen Bezügen* (Bonn: Verlag Kulturstiftung der Vertriebenen 1993). Comprehensive information about the fate of the German population remaining in the city and area of Königsberg may be found in the recently published book of Eberhard Beckherrn and Alexej Dubatow, *Die Königsberg-Papiere. Neue Dokumente aus russischen Archiven. Schicksal einer deutschen Stadt* (München: Langen Müller Verlag 1994).

3. Comprehensive basic information about the German Eastern territories in general is available in English in Goettingen Research Committee (ed.), *Eastern Germany. A Handbook. Law, History, Economy* (Wuerzburg: Holzner Verlag 1960–63).

4. About the fate of the northern part of East Prussia, the Königsberg region, see Peter Wörster, 'Das nördliche Ostpreußen nach 1945', in *Dokumentation Ostmitteleuropa* (Marburg/Lahn: Verlag des Herder-Instituts 1978–80); Peter Wörster, 'From Germany's East Prussia to the Soviet Union's Kaliningrad Oblast: A Case of Sequent Occupance', *Soviet Geography*, April 1986, pp. 233–47 and Hubertus Neuschäffer, *Das 'Königsberger Gebiet'* (Plön: 1991).

5. About the resettlement cf. Peter Wörster, 'Die Besiedlung des Königsberger Gebietes nach 1945 – Bilanz eines sowjetischen Experiments', in Jähnig and Spieler (1993).

6. Mark Galeotti, 'Kaliningrad: A Fortress Without a State', *IBRU Boundary and Security Bulletin*, July 1993, pp. 56–9 and Andrew Nagorski, 'Free-Trade Zone or Fortress? Kaliningrad: The Baltic Outpost's Identity Crisis', *Newsweek*, 23 May 1994.

7. Cf. Dieter Blumenwitz, *What is Germany? Exploring Germany's Status After World War II* (Bonn: Verlag der Kulturstiftung der deutschen Vertriebenen 1989).

8. The latest article about the legal status of the Königsberg region is Gilberg Gornig, 'Der Rechtsstatus des nördlichen Ostpreußen', in Jähnig and Spieler (1993).

9. Cf. European Parliament (ed.), *Entschließungsantrag zur Lage in der Region Kaliningrad*, 15 January 1992. Cf. *Königsberger Express*, no. 2, 1994.

10. Cf. *Königsberger Express*, no. 6, 1994.

11. On Polish attempts cf. Karl Hartmann, 'Polens Interesse an Königsberg', *Osteuropa*, vol. 43, no. 7, 1993, pp. A 363–80.

12. Cf. *Welt am Sonntag*, 19 June 1994.

13. Cf. *Königsberger Express*, no. 6, 1994.

14. Cf. *Frankfurter Allgemeine Zeitung*, 16 June 1994. About the present state of planning and discussing the Free Economic Zone cf. the comprehensive study of Heike Dörrenbächer, 'Die Sonderwirtschaftszone Jantar' von Kaliningrad/Königsberg. Bilanz und Perspektiven', *Arbeitspapiere zur Internationalen Politik*, no. 81 (Bonn: 1994).

15. The first edition in English language appeared as early as 1798–99. One of the latest editions is Immanuel Kant, *Perpetual Peace and Other Essays* (Indianapolis: Hackett 1983).

16. Cf. Wilfried Böhm and Ansgar Graw, *Königsberg morgen. Luxemburg an der Ostsee* (Asendorf: MUT-Verlag 1993).

17. On this question see Philip A. and Shane C. Petersen, *The Security Implications of and Alternative Futures for the Kaliningrad Region* (McLean, Virginia: The Potomac Foundation 1992); Peer Lange, 'Militarisierung oder Demilitarisierung des Gebiets

Kaliningrad – Das sicherheitspolitische Schlüsselproblem in der Ostseeregion.', in Jähnig and Spieler (1993); Christian Wellmann, 'Friedenspolitik und wirtschaftliche Entwicklung: Das Beispiel Kaliningrad', in Christoph Butterwegge and Martin Grundmann (eds), *Zivilmacht Europa. Friedenspolitik und Rüstungskonversion in Ost und West* (Köln: Bund-Verlag 1994). The book will be published soon. I have to thank Dr Wellmann for allowing me to read his excellent analytic study before publishing. See also Annemarie Grosse-Jütte, 'Die Region Kaliningrad/Königsberg: Chance oder Gefahrenherd im Ostseeraum?', in *Aus Politik und Zeitgeschichte. Beilage zur Wochenzeitung Das Parlament*, series B, no. 18–19, 1994, 6 May 1994.

18. Peter Johnson, 'Das Gebiet ist ein Unikum', *Königsberger Express*, no. 1, 1994, p. 8.
19. Walther Hubatsch, *Eckpfeiler Europas. Probleme Preußenlandes in geschichtlicher Sicht* (Heidelberg: Quelle und Meyer Verlag 1953), p. 141.
20. The situation of Königsberg after the war and its future in a rapidly changing world has been the subject of many publications in recent years with often similar considerations. A selection of the most important studies includes: Gerhard Gnauck, 'Kaliningrad', in Sven Gustavsson and Ingvar Svanberg (eds), *Gamla folk och nya stater. Det upplösta sovjetimperiet* (Stockholm: Gidlunds Bokfölag 1992); Bo Huldt (ed.), 'Kaliningrad as a Regional and Global Power', 'Kaliningrad as a Centre of Baltic Cooperation', Papers presented to a seminar organized by the Polish and Swedish Institutes of International Affairs [held at Svetlogorsk (Rauschen) in Kaliningrad Oblast on 27–30 May 1992]. *Conference Papers*, no. 14, 1992; Raymond A. Smith, 'The Kaliningrad Region: Civic and Ethnic Models of Nationalism', *Journal of Baltic Studies*, vol. 24, no. 3, 1993, p. 233–46; Die Zukunft des Gebietes Kaliningrad (Königsberg). Ergebnisse einer internationalen Studiengruppe. *Sonderveröffentlichung des Bundesinstituts für ostwissenschaftliche und internationale Studien*, July 1993. The publication includes good surveys about the different points of view: Kaliningrad, Russia, Lithuania, Poland and Germany; Dieter Bingen, Das Gebiet Kaliningrad (Königsberg): Bestandsaufnahme und Perspektiven. Deutsche Ansichten, nos. I–II [both with English summaries]. *Mitteilungen des Bundesinstituts für ostwissenschaftliche und internationale Studien*, nos. 21 and 25, 1993 and Magdalene Hoff and Heinz Timmermann, 'Kaliningrad (Königsberg): Eine russische Exklave in der baltischen Region. Stand und Perspektiven aus europäischer Sicht', *Mitteilungen des Bundesinstituts für ostwissenschaftliche und internationale Studien*, no. 17, 1993 [with English summary].
21. This idea is impressively advocated by Wladimir Gilmanow, the young professor of German literature at the Kaliningrad University. Cf. his article, 'Zur gegenwärtigen Situation im Königsberger Gebiet – Bestandsaufnahme und Perspektiven. Eine russische Stimme aus dem nördlichen Ostpreußen 1993', *Deutsche Ostkunde*, vol. 39, no. 4, 1993, pp. 83–7. I am convinced that Gilmanow's views on the cultural history of East Prussia would help to stimulate the economic and spiritual renewal of the region of Königsberg.

10. Abrene

Bonifacijs Dauksts and Arturs Puga

The town of Abrene (Pytalovo) and its rural districts are the subject of a border dispute between the Republic of Latvia and the Russian Federation. In the years 1920–40(44) the town of Abrene and the rural districts of Kaceni, Upmale, Linava, Purvmale, Augspils and Gauri were part of the Republic of Latvia. According to the administrative division of tsarist Russia and in the Soviet Union from 1944 onwards, the town of Abrene was called Pytalovo and its rural districts were Vishgorod, Kachanovo and Tolkovo. The area of this disputed territory is 1,294 square kilometres (see Map 10.1).

The issue stems from the fact that according to a firm Latvian attitude the independence of Latvia which was proclaimed on 18 November 1918 has *de jure* never ceased to exist. In August 1991 the Latvian Constitution, dating from 1922, was restored fully by the Supreme Council of Latvia and the world community recognized the legal continuation of the Republic of Latvia of 1918. Latvians think that when the Soviet occupation alter if it has already ended, the legitimacy of the state borders, which were stipulated in the 1920 Peace Treaty between Russia and the Republic of Latvia according to the Latvian Constitution and international law, should be recognized.

1. INDEPENDENCE OF LATVIA AND THE REGION OF ABRENE

Centuries ago Baltic tribes lived in vast territories much further to the east than today. In the 12th and 13th centuries when the Baltic tribes were united to create state-like entities, the eastern part of present-day Latvia, including Abrene, was inhabited by the Baltic Letgallians. The region of Abrene bordered Talava, one of the most important Letgallian state-like

Territories of the Republic of Estonia 1920–44 annexed by the Russian Soviet Federated Republic in 1944.

Territory of the Republic of Latvia 1920–44 annexed by the Russian Soviet Federated Republic in 1944.

Map 10.1. Abrene (Latvia), Ivangorod and Petserimaa (Estonia).

groups and for this reason Abrene was also called Pietalava (Near-Talava). This ancient Latvian name was adopted by the Russians and changed into Pytalovo.[1]

Since the first half of the 13th century the territories of the Letgallians and some other Baltic tribes were ruled by German feudal lords. In the wars of the 15th century the region of present-day Abrene was seized by the joint forces of the dukes of Novgorod, Pskov and Muscovy. A slow process of Russification and adoption of Russian Orthodox Christianity started and lasted until the beginning of the 20th century. The rest of the territories populated by Latvian people were under Polish and Swedish rule and in the 18th century they all became part of the Russian Empire. In 1914 the territories populated by ethnic Latvians were Kurland Province, the southern part of Livland Province, a part of Vitebsk

Province and some fringes of Pskov Province where Abrene/Pytalovo was situated. During the years of World War I Latvian land was occupied by Germany.

After the Compiègne Armistice on 18 November 1918 Latvia was declared independent by the Latvian National Council. Then the Latvian war of independence was fought against Soviet Russian as well as German troops in 1918–20. The hostilities were stopped at the beginning of February 1920 when the eastern borders of the ethnic Latvian population were reached by the Latvian Army. The Peace Treaty between Latvia and Russia was signed in Riga on 11 August 1920. During the next two years the independent Republic of Latvia gained international recognition and membership in the League of the Nations. The Latvian Constitution came into force in November 1922. According to articles 3 and 77 the parliament of Latvia does not have juridical power to change borders stipulated by international treaties without a referendum.

In 1920 when Latvia and Soviet Russia had reached a border settlement, the borderlands were inhabited by both ethnic Russians and Latvians and no distinct ethnographical boundary divided their territories. It was thus inevitable that some ethnic Latvians were left on the Russian side of the state border and correspondingly ethnic Russians were left inside the Latvian border. A joint Latvian–Russian commission worked on the establishment of state borders for two years and in April 1923 its members endorsed the final description of the 352 kilometre-long border drawn on twenty-five maps. Abrene (Pytalovo) and its rural districts were recognized by Russia to be the eternal territory of Latvia.[2]

The figures of the census of 1935 reveal that the population of the said region was 44,600 people, i.e. about 2.3 per cent of the total population of the Republic of Latvia. Russians made up 85.9 per cent while the share of Latvians was 12.5 per cent. There was only one town – Abrene – which grew quickly in the 1920s and acquired official status as a town in 1933. In 1935 it had about 1,200 inhabitants (39 per cent Latvians, 52 per cent Russians)[3] and its railway junction connected two Latvian railway lines (Rezekne–Abrene and Gulbene–Abrene), and was thus significant from a strategic point of view. The majority of the population of Abrene District was rural. There was no large-scale industry but the number of small enterprises – mills, sawmills, dairies, etc. – reached 120 in the years 1935–37 and the number of shops and other commercial undertakings was relatively large. Also agricultural development reached the median level of Latvia as a whole and was in some cases even higher. Given the comparatively low development of industry and commerce, the wealth per capita in Abrene District was about half that of the general Latvian standard, but the median level of development could be compared with Latgale in Eastern Latvia.

2. WORLD WAR II AND THE ANNEXATION OF ABRENE

It has often been noted that the Soviet authorities never considered the peace treaties with the Baltic states to be legally binding and respectable documents of inter-state relations. Already in the 1920s, not to mention in the 1930s, the Bolsheviks were preparing a seizure and annexation of Latvia, Lithuania and Estonia. In the inter-war period the Kremlin regarded the possession of Abrene by the territories of Latvia as a temporary phenomenon. Likewise, the lifetime of the 'bourgeois Latvia' was anticipated to be short and the return of Latvia to Soviet Russia was considered to be only a matter of time.

In 1939 the treaties between Nazi Germany and the USSR divided Eastern Europe into spheres of influence between the two dictators Hitler and Stalin. Yielding to the ultimate claims and threats of the Soviet Union, Latvia signed a treaty of mutual assistance with the Kremlin which provided an opportunity to bring in Soviet troops and to build military bases on Latvian soil. Soon after, on 16 June 1940, Vyacheslav Molotov presented a new ultimatum demanding the establishment of a pro-Soviet regime and the admittance of more Soviet troops into Latvia. The following day Latvia was completely occupied by the Red Army. The establishment of a left-wing government did not save the formal independence of Latvia. Lithuania and Estonia suffered the same fate. After an undemocratic election farce that was identical in all three Baltic countries and the declaration of Soviet power in July, these states were annexed by the USSR in early August 1940.[4]

The German–Soviet war and the invasion of Latvia by the German Army was to follow. While World War II lasted the future of the Baltic states remained uncertain. American and British leaders did ask their ally Stalin about the destiny of the Balts, but in the end the West did not deem it wise to insist on putting the Baltic case on to the agenda of the post-war settlement.[5] In the summer of 1944 the Red Army returned to the territories of the Baltic states. Even if they were still to a large extent occupied by Germany it seemed to be necessary to the Kremlin to show the world who was 'the Lord of the Baltics'. The borders of the Latvian and Estonian Soviet Socialist Republics were shifted and parts of their territories were annexed by the Russian SFSR.

The USSR Supreme Soviet Presidium decree On the Formation of the Pskov Oblast Within the Territory of the RSFSR was issued on 23 August 1944. Referring to the appeal of the Latvian SSR Supreme Soviet Presidium it changed the Latvian–Russian border and incorporated the town of Abrene and the six rural districts of Abrene District into the territory of the Russian SFSR. Despite the fact that these decrees were officially prompted by pleas of local – mainly Russian – inhabitants, documents and memoirs testify that the inhabitants, including regional communist functionaries, learned about the transfer of the region to Russia only after August 1944. Even the members of the Presidium of the Supreme Soviet of the Latvian SSR in Moscow were expected simply to ratify the demand concerning the handing over of Abrene to the Russian Federation.[6]

3. THE DESTINY OF THE LOCAL RESIDENTS

In the mid-1940s there were about 50,000 residents in the Abrene region. The ratio of different ethnic groups had not substantially changed since the 1930s. Russians formed a majority of 85.5 per cent, the share of Latvians was 12.5 per cent and other nationalities made up 2.0 per cent.[7]

After the annexation some peasants and representatives of the rural intelligentsia left Pskov Oblast for the Latvian SSR but it is difficult to obtain accurate data about their number and nationalities. Up to now these former inhabitants of the Abrene region, currently living in other parts of Latvia, have sent approximately 3,000 claims to the Latvian parliament in the hope of receiving compensation for land and other property that was lost as a result of the annexation of Abrene.[8] At present the *Abrene* society has approximately 150 members. It has appealed for the return of the annexed territories and lost property asn also for an immediate settlement of such problems as access to graveyards in the Abrene region. The majority of the former inhabitants, who since 1988–89 have participated in the activities for the return of Abrene, are ethnic Russians. Considering their proportion of the pre-war residents of the territory this is no surprise.[9]

Appeals for the return of the annexed territories were also sent to the Presidium of the Supreme Soviet of the USSR in the 1940s and 1960s by the people who remained in the Abrene region. Their wish was motivated by the necessity to be closer to rural and cultural centres and access to better infrastructure. Some delegations arrived in Riga in order to express analogous requests, but every appeal was ignored.[10] However, the absolute majority of Russian residents of Abrene adapted to new Soviet realities in Pskov Oblast and became loyal citizens of the RSFSR. Their children were taught at school that this land had belonged to Russia from ancient times and that only because of the weakness of the newly formed state and the pressure from the imperialist world was socialist Russia temporarily forced to renounce the Baltic countries. In publications on the history of Pytalovo and in exhibitions of local folklore the materials dating from the era of the Republic of Latvia were often taboo.[11]

Since the 1950s, as a part of the socialistic industrialization process and planned mass migration, people from different parts of the Soviet Union were settled in the town of Pytalovo and its region. As a consequence, according to some estimates only about 5 per cent of the present population of this area are citizens or descendants of the citizens of pre-war Latvia.[12]

The development of agriculture in the Pytalovo region has been poor since the war but the town has preserved its significance as an important railway junction. Some industrial enterprises were built in the 1960s and 1970s. According to the Soviet census the number of residents of the town of Pytalovo was 7,100 in 1989 and there were 9,000 inhabitants in the rural areas of Pytalovo District.[13] In addition, a few thousand people are residents of the rural territory of the annexed Abrene region belonging in the 1980 and 1990s to the Pechory and Palkino Districts of Pskov Oblast.

4. THE ISSUE OF ABRENE IN LATVIAN–RUSSIAN RELATIONS IN 1990–94

In the years 1990–91, before the collapse of the USSR, negotiations between the Republic of Latvia and the Russian SFSR and also negotiations between the Republic of Estonia and the Russian SFSR were conducted in order to conclude interstate agreements. These documents were signed in January 1991 but the question of the annexed Baltic territories remained unsettled and open for future discussions between parliaments and state delegations. After the breakdown of communism in the autumn of that year the possibility of a condominium in the Abrene region was discussed by the official representatives of Latvia and Russia and at that time some high-ranking Latvians expressed a belief that after two or three years Abrene would be returned to Latvia.[14]

Political understanding between the leaders and politicians of Russia and Latvia ceased to exist, however, when the Russian Federation replaced the USSR and suddenly turned into a great power at the end of 1991. Both Latvia and Estonia were flooded with accusations of alleged discrimination against their ethnic Russian and Slavic populations and of deliberately straining relations with Russia. It seems that since 1992 influential Russian parliamentary and governmental circles have taken a political course aimed at reintegrating the Baltic states into the sphere of influence of neoimperialist Russia. Wishing to prolong its military presence as well as its political and economic control over the Baltic region, the Kremlin consistently spread worldwide disinformation about events in the Baltics, misinterpreting the essence of decisions taken by Baltic politicians. The problem of Abrene/Pytalovo was used for this purpose as well.

The Supreme Council of the Republic of Latvia released a decree on 22 January 1992 On the Nonrecognition of the Annexation of the Town of Abrene and the Districts of Abrene. It requires the delegation of the Republic of Latvia 'to resolve the Abrene issue during interstate negotiations with the Russian Federation, including the procedures for the determination of the amount of and the compensation for the material losses caused to the still-existing property of the State of Latvia and of the citizens of the Republic of Latvia in the town of Abrene and the six rural districts of Abrene District.'[15] According to this document the annexation of the town of Abrene and the six rural districts of Abrene District was carried out during the occupation of Latvia and violated the Peace Treaty of 1920 and the Latvian–Soviet Nonaggression Treaty of 1932. The USSR Supreme Soviet Presidium decree On the Formation of the Pskov Oblast Within the Territory of the RSFSR dated 23 August of 1944 was declared anti-constitutional and invalid from the moment of its adoption as was the case with other decisions concerning Abrene which were issued in Moscow and Riga during the years 1944–46. According to this resolution the border between the Republic of Latvia and the Russian Federation is still legally defined by Article 3 of the Latvian–Russian Peace Treaty of 1920.[16] This resolution, however, did not insist upon the return of the Abrene region to Latvia but just recognized the illegitimacy of its annexation.

In the domestic politics of Latvia the border issue has been given a relatively low priority. During the election campaign in the first free elections of Latvia the major ruling political forces, the Latvian Way and the Latvian Farmers' Union, did not stress the Abrene problem, understanding its complexity and vulnerability. In Latvian–Russian talks the troop withdrawals have been the main issue and Latvia has made a conscious effort to prevent other issues diverting attention from it. It is believed that the majority of political parties and Latvian citizens consider that a settlement of the dispute on Abrene will have to be founded on a compromise, after Russia recognizes the illegal annexation. Latvian authorities refer to the fact that the basic principles of the OSCE do not object to changes of post-war borders, provided that an agreement is reached through peaceful negotiations.

Until recently, the official Russian stand has been that the resolution of the Supreme Council of Latvia dating from January 1992 constitutes a territorial claim against Russia, which is unsubstantiated from both historical and legal points of view.[17] According to the Ministry of Foreign Affairs of the Russian Federation, the Latvian parliament has violated its own ratification of the Treaty on Guidelines on Interstate Relations with Russia of 14 January 1991 whereby both Latvia and Russia agreed to observe the territorial integrity of the other parties of the Helsinki Process in concordance with the documents of the CSCE. Simultaneously Russia has accused Latvia of being the first country in the new Europe to question the principle of inviolability of borders.[18] The Peace Treaty of 1920 has been regarded as a historical relic that should be declared null and void. It seems that, in the midst of a Russian constitutional crisis, Russian politicians have often lacked flexibility to discuss and seek ways for the normalization of relations with Latvia and Estonia.

However, in 1993 the first steps to normalize relations were taken in the talks between Latvian and Russian local authorities. Both parties expressed their own interests and an agreement was reached on some issues concerning economic and humanitarian issues as well as issues concerning customs regulations. It is important to stress that now as before ordinary people are living peacefully without frontier incidents on the Abrene/Pytalovo land between Latvia and Russia.[19]

The end of April 1994 saw a possibility of substantial improvement in Latvian–Russian relations as the Russian Federation and the Republic of Latvia signed a state treaty about the pullout of Russian troops from

Latvia. President Yeltsin officially condemned the Stalinist regime's illegal actions against the Latvian people in 1940–49.[20]

It may be hoped that this newly achieved basis for Latvian–Russian relations could help to solve those practical issues that are still unresolved. It would be preferable to settle the Russian–Latvian and Russian–Estonian problems in negotiations in which observers and experts from such international organizations as the OSCE and the Council of Europe would participate. Moreover, the border dispute can be discussed in the context of the Pact for Stability initiated by the EU. It is evident that a formula satisfying all parties involved should be found and that it should provide international legal evaluation of the border changes of 1944–46 between Russia and the Baltic states. From the Latvian point of view the property claims of Latvian citizens, the use of the Abrene/Pytalovo railway junction, and the present ethnic reality as well as the legal interests of both parties should be taken into account. International support could enable Russia and Latvia to start talks on the Abrene/Pytalovo question. Therefore, it would be very important to obtain ideas about a possible solution from independent experts and organizations as soon as possible. Riga has intimated that the Latvian party is ready to consider all possibilities as regards improving relations with Russia and strengthening peace and security in Europe. The interests of democratic Russia should obviously be analogous.

NOTES

1. Karlis Vanags, *Celvedis pa dzimto zemi* (Riga: S. L. min. izd. 1937), pp. 299–302 and Edgar Anderson, 'How Narva, Petseri, and Abrene Came to Be in the RSFSR', in Dietrich André Loeber (ed.), *Regional Identity Under Soviet Rule: the Case of the Baltic States* (Hackettstown: The University of Kiel 1990), p. 405.
2. The Treaty of Peace Between Latvia and Russia of 11 August 1920. *League of Nations Treaties Series*, no. 67, 1920–21, pp. 213–31.
3. Oskars Gerts, 'Abrenes atgriezums', *Neatkariga Cina*, 5 December 1991.
4. About the process of Latvia's occupation see the address of A. Gorbunovs, Chairman of the Supreme Council of the Republic of Latvia, to the 47th Session of the General Assembly of the United Nations on 25 September 1992 and the address of G. Andrejevs, the Latvian Foreign Minister, to the 47th Session of the Commission on Human Rights of the United Nations on 15 February 1993 and also A. Rumpeters, *Soviet Aggression Against the Baltic States* (New York: World Federation of Free Latvians 1974).
5. See Vilnis V. Sveics, *How Stalin Got the Baltic States* (New Jersey: Jersey City State College 1991).
6. An interview with Academician Aleksandr Nikonov, First Secretary of the Communist Party for Abrene District in 1944–45, in *Neatkariga Cina*, 5 December 1991.
7. Anderson (1990), p. 405.

8. An interview with Aleksandrs Kirsteins, Chairman of the Commission of Foreign Affairs of the Latvian *Saeima,* on Latvian Television, 23 August 1993.
9. *Latvijas Jaunatne*, 24 August 1993.
10. Anderson (1990), p. 404.
11. Juris Cibulis, 'Vai uzlasisim latvietibas drumslas', *Izglitiba*, 14 February 1990 and Viktor Vasiljev, *Pytalovo* (Leningrad: Lenizdat 1978).
12. *Records of the Session of the Supreme Council of the Republic of Latvia*, 22 January, 1992.
13. *Chislennost naseleniya RSFSR: Po dannym Vsesoyuznoi perepisi naseleniya 1989 goda*, (Moscow: Respublikanskii informatsionno-izdatelskii tsentr 1990), p. 119.
14. *Baltiiskoe vremya*, 24 October 1991.
15. The materials prepared by the Latvian Association of Scientists for the Council of Ministers of the Republic of Latvia suggest that the share of national wealth of the annexed territories would amount to 200 billion Russian roubles at February 1993 price levels. In the opinion of the Latvian parliamentarians, the total losses of Latvia following the region's annexation are estimated to be US$ 5 billion. See R. Rikards in *Jurmala*, no. 4, 1992.
16. Resolution of the Supreme Council of Latvia On the Nonrecognition of the Annexation of the Town of Abrene and the Six Rural Districts of the Abrene District, 22 January 1992 in *Latvijas Republikas Augstakas Padomes un Valdibas Zinotajs*, no. 6–7, 1992, pp. 175–6.
17. See for instance, an interview with Sergei Zotov, Chairman of the Russian delegation for negotiations with Latvia in *SM – Segodnya*, 26 September 1992.
18. 'Rossiya otvergaet territorialnye pretenzii Latvii', *Izvestiya,* 21 March 1992.
19. Dzintra Bungs, 'Seeking Solutions to Baltic–Russian Border Issues', *RFE/RL Research Report*, vol. 3, no. 13, 1994, pp. 25–32.
20. *Latvijas Vestnesis*, 5 May 1994.

11. East of Narva and Petserimaa

Indrek Jääts

This chapter discusses two territories that belonged to the Estonian Republic and were ceded to the RSFSR (Russian Soviet Federated Socialist Republic) in 1944. These are the eastern bank of the River Narva and the Petseri area (in Estonian Petserimaa or Setumaa). Both of these areas are small: the territory to the east of Narva is 1,198 square kilometres and the annexed territory of Petseri district is 1,135 square kilometres. In connection with the re-establishment of the independence of the Estonian Republic a question has arisen about the ownership of these territories (see Map 10.1).

1. THE HISTORY OF THE NARVA AREA AND PETSERIMAA UP TO THE YEAR 1917

Narva area

The area east of Narva belongs to the historical-geographical region called Ingermanland or Ingria whose inhabitants have traditionally been Finno-Ugric Izhorians (also called Ingrians) and Votians. From the 12th century it belonged to the lands of Novgorod and after the German–Danish feudal lords had conquered the lands of present-day Estonia in the 13th century, the River Narva became the border between Novgorod and the Livonian Branch of the Teutonic Knights.

When Novgorod was united with the rising Muscovite State in the 15th century Ivan III built a stronghold on the eastern bank of the River Narva, Ivangorod (Jaanilinn in Estonian). After many wars, as a result of which Ingermanland belonged in turn to Sweden and Russia, all of Estonia and

Ingermanland came under Swedish rule at the beginning of the 17th century. Under Russian rule Narva and Ivangorod were separated from the Estonian territories by a provincial border and from the 18th century Narva and Ivangorod belonged to St. Petersburg Province. From another point of view the 17th century marked the administrative unification of Narva with Ivangorod, which originally had been the Russian fortification opposing Narva. The organic unity of these twin towns lasted for three hundred years until 1944.

Culturally the Izhorians and Votians, the Finno-Ugric inhabitants of Ingermanland, were close to Russians as they had been Orthodox since the times of the Novgorodian conquest. The Orthodox were expelled from the territories that were ruled by Sweden and those areas were settled by Lutheran Finns from the Karelian Isthmus and Savo region (the so-called Ingermanland Finns). As a result of the Russian conquest the Orthodox Finno-Ugric nations were again extensively Russified. The process was intensified during the second half of the 19th century.

Petserimaa

Petserimaa was also inhabited mainly by Finno-Ugric tribes. In the 13th century the boundary between the possessions of the German feudal lords and Novgorod ran along the River Mädajogi and the upper reaches of the River Piusa. Petserimaa thus remained on the eastern side of this border. This boundary was to become the dividing line between states, provinces and religious denominations for centuries. After the decline of Novgorod, Petserimaa was incorporated into the Muscovite lands as part of Pskov Province. Over the following centuries the rivers Mädajogi and Piusa remained the western border of Russia, and when Russia conquered the rest of the territories of ethnic Estonians in the 18th century the state border disappeared, but the provincial border, and also the division between Orthodox and Lutheran Churches, remained.

The inhabitants of Petserimaa were Setus, ethnically Estonian and Orthodox by religion. They remained under the influence of Russian culture and the Orthodox Church but elements of Estonian traditions were kept alive among them. An important foothold for Russian religious and military policy was Petseri Monastery (Pskov *Pecherskaya lavra*) which was founded in the 15th century.

2. ESTONIAN INDEPENDENCE AND THE BORDERS

The territories populated by Estonians remained under Russian rule until February 1918. During World War I, on 24 February 1918, only a day after the Bolsheviks had retreated and a day before the Germans started occupying the Estonian territories, the leaders of the national movement declared Estonia independent, within her 'historical and ethnographic borders'. The main territory consisted of Estland Province together with the northern part of Livland Province which was populated by Estonians. They had already been united a year earlier by the Provisional Government of Russia which, according to Toivo Raun, had given birth to the political entity called Estonia.[1]

Narva and Petseri were also declared to be parts of independent Estonia. Six months before the declaration of independence the Setus had already submitted a petition to the National Council of Estonia about the unification of Petserimaa with the newly formed administrative unity of Estonia, and work upon a draft law had started.[2] In the town of Narva a referendum had been held about uniting the territory of Narva with Estonia. In the referendum 80 per cent of the town's inhabitants had supported the unification and in December 1917 Narva and Ivangorod had been declared united with Estonia.[3]

The declaration of independence of Estonia only had a symbolic meaning, though, as Germany had occupied her territories. The Soviet Union and Germany signed a Peace Treaty in Brest-Litovsk in March 1918 and the Soviet–German border was to run along the River Narva while Petserimaa was to belong to the German side together with the rest of the Estonian territories. This borderline was not to last. After the collapse of Germany, Soviet Russia took the offensive in the west and the Estonian war of independence began. At first Soviet troops reached far into Estonian territories but the situation changed in January 1919 when the Estonians started a counterattack. The last major Russian attacks were repelled in November and December 1919.

When the hostilities ended on 31 December 1919 the Estonian Republic controlled all the ethnic Estonian territories and also some territories with a Russian majority. According to the temporary Constitution accepted by the Estonian Constituent Assembly in June 1919 the territories of Estonia included the whole of Petserimaa and the territories on the eastern bank of the River Narva.[4]

The border between Estonia and Soviet Russia was confirmed in the Peace Treaty signed in Tartu in February 1920. In the treaty the Russian SFSR recognized the independence of the Estonian Republic. According to the treaty the eastern border of Estonia began from the coast of the Gulf of Narva 14 kilometres east of the mouth of the River Narva and ran almost parallel 7–12 kilometres to the east of the river. This frontier did not completely follow ethnic borders but was drawn instead more or less along the front-line of 31 December 1919.[5] This was undoubtedly one of the reasons why the leaders of Bolshevik Russia regarded the Tartu Peace Treaty and territorial concessions to Estonia as temporary. In his speech of January 1920 Vladimir Lenin predicted a quick change of regime for Estonia and a more favourable treaty for Russia.[6]

3. THE IVANGOROD AND PETSERI AREAS IN THE INTER-WAR YEARS

The borderlands of Ivangorod and Petseri were strategically important for Estonia. The areas served as a security zone that was important in preventing unexpected attacks against the main defensive line, by clarifying the strength and direction of the enemy's attack so that defence could be organized.[7]

In the Ivangorod region oil-shale was the most important mineral resource. In all about 40 million tons of oil-shale was found in the lands of Piiri and Raja rural districts, the best deposits near the riverbank.[8] However, the main source of livelihood was agriculture and along the River Narva and the Gulf of Narva fishing also was important. The communal ownership of land that had hindered the development of production was abolishd in 1925 and the lands were divided into private farms. Still the prevailing part of the population remained relatively poor.

According to the 1934 census more than three-quarters of the population in the territories to the east of Narva were Russians. The remaining population were either Estonians, Ingermanland Finns or aborginal Orthodox Izhorians who lived in the northern part of the area. In 1922 the share of Russians had been somewhat higher. The local population did not have frequent contacts with the inhabitants of other Estonian regions. Many people living to the east of Narva also had relatives behind the eastern border but contacts with them were rare as the Russian frontier was closed.

In the Estonian Constitution cultural autonomy was guaranteed to minorities of more than 3,000 people. Russians who lived closely together in compact settlements also had the possibility of local self-government. For Ingermanland Finns and Izhorians education in Finnish was provided. Still, the Narva area stood out for its low level of education, especially in the rural districts inhabited by Russians.

In Petserimaa the population was denser than in the Narva area and the natural conditions were better. There was gypsum, sand for glass, building materials and peat. The main source of livelihood was agriculture although as a result of the relatively high birthrate and communal ownership of land there was a constant shortage of land. Small farms could not provide enough food for the people. As a consequence the standard of living of the inhabitants of Petserimaa was below the Estonian average.

The total population of Petserimaa was approximately 65,000 in 1934. The Russians made up two-thirds and Estonians and Setus one-third of the population. The ratio had changed only slightly between the years 1922 and 1934. However in Petseri town the share of Estonians grew as the Estonian Republic favoured the growth of their own ethnic groups. Most of the Estonian newcomers were state employees. In 1922 Russians had amounted to 63 per cent of the town's inhabitants but in 1934 their share had fallen to 41 per cent while Estonians and Setus already made up 55 per cent. The Russians lived in the east. In the five easternmost rural districts of Petserimaa, Estonians and Setus amounted to less than 10 per cent of the population.[9]

4. THE ANNEXATION OF PETSERI AND IVANGOROD BY THE SOVIET UNION IN 1944

After the Soviet invasion of Estonia in 1940 and the German occupation in 1941, the Soviet occupation began in the summer of 1944. In August the Presidium of the Supreme Soviet of the Estonian Soviet Socialist Republic, which had been appointed by Moscow, sent a petition to Moscow asking for the unification of nine of the eleven districts of Petserimaa with the Russian SFSR.[10] The petition referred to the repeated requests of the local population as an argument for the unification. However, no such requests are known to have existed.[11] The districts of Petserimaa were united with the newly formed Pskov Oblast the following day.[12] All this had happened even before the occupation of the capital Tallinn in September. In October the leaders of the Estonian SSR sent a letter to Stalin asking for a more exact delinication of the ethnic border and the request was taken into consideration. A joint committee with Estonian members signed a document on dividing Petserimaa anew in November. The territory eventually ceded to Pskov Oblast was 1,135 square kilometres in size (i.e. about 70 per cent of the total area of Petserimaa) and it had a population of nearly 41,000 people, of which the number of Setus was about 6,000.[13]

The same pattern of annexation was used when the rural districts behind the River Narva were ceded to Russia. A petition to the leaders in Moscow about uniting the territories on the eastern bank of the River Narva with the Russian SFSR was submitted in November 1944 and in December a joint committee signed an act of annexation. The border between the Estonian SSR and Leningrad Oblast followed the River Narva, leaving the majority of the river islands to the Estonian Soviet Socialist Republic.[14] Until February 1945 Estonians in the region were allowed to move to the Estonian SSR and Russians who had been evacuated to Estonia were asked to return to their homes.

The border between the Estonian SSR and the Russian SFSR was legalized with the decree of the Presidium of the Supreme Soviet of the Estonian SSR on 3 October 1946.[15] In 1957 minor territorial exchanges on the Estonian–Russian border took place in the Räpina region. As a result of all these border changes Estonia lost about 5 per cent of its pre-war territory (2,333 square kilometres) and about 6 per cent of its inhabitants (75,000 people).[16]

Why did the leaders of the USSR undertake such redivisions? The desire to join the regions populated mainly by Russians to the Russian SFSR is understandable although the ethnic boundary was not fully followed. But why were the redivisions carried out in such a hurry? It can be assumed that the Soviet Union, fearing the possible opposition of the Western states to the reoccupation of the Baltic area and the claims for independence of the Baltic states, wished to secure for herself at least the small but strategically important border territories.[17]

5. THE EASTERN BANK OF THE NARVA RIVER AND PETSERIMAA AFTER WORLD WAR II

Narva

After the administrative redivisions the Narva Municipality of the Estonian SSR turned to the government of the Soviet Union and to the

Cases

Communist Party of the Soviet Union requesting the reunification of
Ivangorod with Narva. The requests produced no response, though, and
Ivangorod remained united with Leningrad Oblast and became an independent town. However, the border was not closed as it was only
administrative. Neither did the border hinder the use of the economic
potential of the River Narva. In the 1950s Narva hydroelectric power-
station was built in Ivangorod. The river was blocked with a dam and a
200-square-kilometre water reservoir was constructed. It flooded several
villages in Piiri Rural District and the well-known Narva Waterfall dried
up.

Ivangorod had been badly damaged in the war and many Estonians who
had lived there did not return home when the war was over. Neither did
the Ingermanland Finns, who had been evacuated to Finland, return to
their villages. Although they were later forced to return to the Soviet
Union they were settled elsewhere. The Izhorians and Russians did not
oppose the change of border as Russia was not culturally alien to them.
In spite of this they also were often considered untrustworthy and were
forced to move away. The present population consists mainly of recent
immigrants from other regions of the Soviet Union. According to the data
from 1989 the town of Ivangorod had 12,300 inhabitants, among them
only a few Estonians.[18] Now the villages in the countryside are empty and
there are fewer than thirty Izhorians left.

Petseri

As with the area east of Narva, a large number of people who were
evacuated from Petserimaa to other regions of Estonia during the war did
not return to their homes. Younger people especially saw their future
brighter in the Estonian SSR and therefore the remaining ethnic Estonians
were mainly of the older generation. Estonians were not allowed to
manage their own affairs but eventually in the 1950s an Estonian
secondary school was reopened in Petseri, although it is foreseen that it
could be closed down soon due to the lack of pupils.

During the post-war period several industrial enterprises were founded
in Petseri as a result of which labour from other parts of Russia moved to
the region. The number of immigrants now surpasses that of the native
inhabitants. According to the data of the *Petserimaa* association there are
26,000 inhabitants in the Petseri region at present, but only about one-
third of them were either citizens of the Estonian Republic or their

descendants.[19] According to the data from 1970 the number of ethnic Estonians in Pskov Oblast was not more than 4,746 and for some of them Russian was the native language. By and large, the attitudes towards the border issue correlate with the respondent's background. The local Estonians wish to reunite with Estonia, the former citizens of the Estonian Republic who are of Russian origin are passive and the recent immigrants oppose reunification.

6. THE PRESENT POLITICAL DISCUSSIONS OVER THE FUTURE OF THE PETSERIMAA AND NARVA AREAS

The national awakening that started in Estonia in 1988 brought the fate of Petserimaa and Ivangorod on to the list of topical issues. In March 1990 the Supreme Soviet of the Estonian SSR declared in a communiqué About the State Status of Estonia that the Estonian Republic proclaimed in 1918 was still a juridical reality although *de facto* occupied by the Soviet Union. This declaration pointed out that Soviet power in Estonia had been unlawful from the moment of its enactment.[20] On the basis of this thinking Estonia started to determine her future again on her own. A treaty on the fundamentals of Estonian–Russian relations was signed in January 1991 when Boris Yeltsin, the President of the Russian Federation, visited Tallinn. This treaty was partly based on the aforementioned communiqué but it did not mention the Tartu Peace Treaty as a basis for mutual relations.[21]

The Estonian Republic of 1918 was proclaimed re-established with the decree of the Supreme Council of the Estonian Republic About Independence of the State of Estonia at the time of the *coup d'état* in Moscow in August 1991. All decisions and decrees of the Supreme Soviet of the Estonian SSR about changing the Estonian borders during the period 1944–57 were declared legally invalid, and in conflict with the Tartu Peace Treaty and international law. It was decided that the problem of state borders would be solved during negotiations between the Estonian Republic and the Russian Federation.[22]

The Estonian–Russian discussions began in early February 1992 but so far no agreements have been reached on the common borders. The seventeenth round of bilateral talks ended in a stalemate in March 1994. In these negotiations all the issues causing tension between Estonia and

Russia have been simultaneously under discussion and inevitably linked with one another. However, from the very beginning the central question has been the pullout of the Russian troops from Estonia. The troop withdrawals have in turn been linked by the Russian delegation to the situation of ethnic Russians in Estonia. The Russian delegation claims that Estonia consistently violates the rights of the Russian-speaking minority who make up 30 to 35 per cent of the 1.6 million inhabitants of Estonia. As long as there is no mutual understanding about these two issues there are no high hopes for a smooth resolution of the border issue.

A broader question of principle connected with these intertwined problems is the status of the Tartu Peace Treaty. Estonians think that Russia's acknowledgement that the Tartu Treaty is the only juridically correct and internationally recognized document determining the Estonian–Russian border and thus that the treaty is still valid is a precondition for good mutual relations. In this connection Estonians also point out that in August 1991 most Western countries expressly re-established diplomatic recognition to Estonia and acknowledged the fact that Estonia had restored her statehood rather than declaring herself a newly independent state.[23]

From the Russian point of view the Estonian policy requiring the re-establishment of the Tartu Peace Treaty borders is not consistent with the Estonian–Russian State Treaty signed in January 1991 in which the borders were stipulated. According to the Russian view the attempts to refer to the Tartu Peace Treaty are unfounded, since those documents ceased to exist at the time when Estonia joined the USSR.[24] Another Russian argument in the legal controversy is that the currently disputed territories were not mentioned in the declaration of independence of 1918 to which Estonians also refer.

This dispute over a correct interpretation of international law – i.e. on the status of the Tartu Peace Treaty – is a matter of principle for both parties, but the practical consequences of Russia's recognition of the Tartu Treaty would also be considerable. At stake are citizenship rights, the property of the Estonian Republic and borders.

From an Estonian point of view the idea of state continuity is in practice most significant in connection with citizenship rights. To regard the present Estonian Republic as a legal continuation of the Estonian Republic of 1918 provides the possibility for ensuring that the granting of Estonian citizenship can be controlled. It is considered dangerous to grant citizenship automatically to all non-Estonians who have moved to Estonia after World War II. In that case Estonians would be threatened with becoming a minority in their homeland and of losing their national identity. The lost eastern territories act more as symbols of the state continuity and sovereignty than bearing importance as such. Given the development of arms technology the borderlands are relatively insignificant strategically although Petseri is still important to Estonia because of its railway junction.

The first formal initiative by Estonia in seeking the return of the annexed territories could be seen to be the statement of the Estonian government in July 1992 calling on Russia to pull her border guards back to the frontier set out by the Tartu Treaty.[25] Some days earlier the Russian Foreign Ministry had sent a note to Estonia accusing her of making territorial claims on Russia. It had been directed against Estonia's newly adopted Constitution which referred to Estonia's pre-war borders. Estonia was also threatened with economic sanctions by Russia.[26]

After one year of bilateral talks, which had not produced any solution to the border dispute, the present border, regarded by Estonia as a temporary administrative border, was fixed as the official state border of Russia by the Russian parliament in February 1993. Commenting on the move the then Foreign Minister of Estonia, Trivimi Velliste, called it a territorial claim by Russia.[27]

While the dispute has continued there have also been some incidents at the border. One example is from May 1993 when about 1,400 Estonian cyclists, demanding the return of the Petseri area to Estonia, were stopped by the Russian authorities at the border.[28] According to a Russian newspaper their aim had been to set up a signpost at the frontier fixed by the Tartu Treaty.[29] In June 1993 Russia started to erect new permanent checkpoints on its side of the present border[30] and in July the Russian Supreme Soviet approved a draft resolution renouncing the 1920 Peace Treaty. According to the weekly *The Baltic Independent,* an Estonian Foreign Ministry official pointed out that if Russia unilaterally annuls the treaties, it means, technically, that Estonia is at war with Russia.[31]

In February 1994 it was announced by a Russian Foreign Ministry official that Moscow might demarcate the border unilaterally if there continued to be no progress in the border dispute. Moscow stated that the current situation complicates border guarding and the work of customs officials. At this stage Estonia emphasized, what she has pointed out several times before, that once Moscow recognizes the Tartu Peace Treaty Estonia will take a more flexible stand and also take into account the interests of today.[32] At the end of April 1994 the President of Estonia, Lennart Meri, told a group of Russian journalists visiting Tallinn that the border dispute should be put on ice for five to ten years during which all other issues should be negotiated.[33] Finally in June 1994, President Yeltsin gave an order to demarcate the Russo–Estonia borders, without consulting Estonian representatives.[34]

The border issue is a delicate question in Estonian domestic politics, especially so because it has been linked with many other problematic issues. The extent to which the problems are eintertwined is illustrated by the fact that at the time when the border dispute became heated in the summer of 1993, a new aliens, law was passed by the Estonian parliament, drawing criticism from the Russian delegation and the Russian community in Estonia.[35] As a protest against it and other laws they regarded as discriminatory the city councils in Narva and neighbouring towns with a vast Russian majority organized referendums asking whether these towns should be declared autonomous territories within Estonia. The results were supportive of autonomy but according to the Estonian Constitution such referendums were illegal.[36]

None of the Estonian political parties can officially accept the present Estonian–Russian border without risking its popularity. It is a matter of authority and political pressure as other parties would not hesitate to make use of such a statement in their propaganda. For example, the official programme of the former ruling party *Isamaa* (Pro Patria) supports restoring the border fixed by the Tartu Peace Treaty. Many Estonians are however of the opinion that increasing the Russian population in Estonia with tens of thousands of Russians in the Narva and Petseri regions would strain ethnic tensions even more. For example Jaan Kaplinski, author and Member of Parliament, suggested that Estonia should give up the claim on borders fixed by the Tartu Peace Treaty. According to him it is more important for Estonia that the border is clearly marked than where it runs exactly.[37]

Public opinion is divided on the issue. An opinion poll conducted in December 1993 suggested that 53 per cent of Estonians support the restoration of the Tartu Treaty borders while 40 per cent are ready to accept a compromise. Non-Estonians were understandably more in favour of a compromise. Taking into account the views of both Estonian and non-Estonian residents the share of those willing to accept a compromise is 52 per cent and those supporting the restoration of the 1920 borders is 39 per cent.[38] It is also worth mentioning that according to the poll 66 per cent of Estonian politicians and 77 per cent of the Estonian elite were ready to accept a compromise. The responses differed also in relation to the Petseri and Ivangorod districts. Among the respondents there were those who were willing to let go of Ivangorod but not of Petseri while none of the respondents supported the return of Ivangorod alone.[39]

The most active organization in demanding the border of the Tartu Peace Treaty is the *Petserimaa union*, which was founded by Estonian citizens who have their roots in Petserimaa. It has organized different protests where the return of the lost Estonian territories has been demanded. It has also tried to draw attention to the violations of human rights in the Petseri region. The representatives of *Petserimaa* state that telephone calls in Estonian are being monitored and correspondence is being controlled in the Petseri region.[40] The Setu People's Congress, the first since World War II, was held in October 1993 in Estonian Petserimaa. The Congress demanded the restoration of Petseri County and free crossing of the administrative border for Setus.[41]

The Russo–Estonian border is also a matter of prestige also in Russian domestic politics. A clear reason for the prolonged dispute is the attitude of some old-style Russian politicians. Because it has been hard to get used to the independence of the Baltic states, the thought of relinquishing some land to them is considered even more impossible. The conservative forces of the Russian Supreme Soviet exerted pressure on the Russian delegation and the Supreme Soviet recommended that the delegation sould not negotiate changes frontier, without consulting it first. Also part of the Russian community in Estonia as well as some inhabitants in the disputed territories act as a pressure group. The Committee for Retaining Petserimaa for Russia that was formed at the end of 1991 has achieved wide support among local inhabitants of Russian origin.

It may be hoped, however, that despite all these numerous obstacles a mutually acceptable solution can be found. It naturally requires willingness to compromise from both parties. It is also important to take into account the situation of the local population in the borderlands: ethnic and cultural differences and borderlines, the fact that the present border divides villages and that the procedure of crossing the border is made both costly and tedious, which causes harm most of all to the local population. There are also some things which are of special importance to Estonians and Russians that are worth keeping in mind. Petseri Monastery is of great importance to the Russian Orthodox Church as well as to the Setu community. The Ivangorod stronghold, which was built during the reign of Ivan III, arouses patriotic feelings among Russians. From the Estonian point of view the question of the Petseri railway junction is especially problematic. It is also necessary to see that the well-being of all ethnic minorities – Estonians in Petseri as well as Russians in Narva and the neighbouring towns – are satisfactorily taken care of.

NOTES

1. Toivo Raun, *Estonia and the Estonians* (Stanford: Hoover Institution Press 1987), p. 100.
2. Edgar Mattisen, *Eesti Vene-piir* (Tallinn: Ilo 1993) pp. 23–5, 127–35.
3. Ibid., pp. 25–6.
4. The fate of the Narva region was also affected by the plans of independence of the Finno-Ugric peoples in Ingermanland. The main supporters of the idea were the Lutheran Ingermanland Finns. When the Ingermanland troops took part in the battles of the Estonian Independence War in Ingermanland, Estonians put forth a plan for an autonomous region of western Ingermanland, but the Ingrians did not agree because they were hoping to achieve autonomy for the whole of Ingermanland with the help of the Finns. These hopes, however, failed and Ingrians achieved neither independence nor autonomy.
5. In the negotiations Soviet Russia wished to neutralize both banks of the River Narva while Estonians demanded wide eastern territories because of strategic reasons. See Heinz von zur Mählen, 'Die Narva-Frage und die Grenze im Nordosten Estlands', *Zeitschrift für Ostforschung*, vol. 41, no. 2, 1992, pp. 248–57.
6. Mattisen (1993), pp. 70–71.
7. Arno Tiit, 'Riigipiir ja riigikaitse', *Päevaleht*, 26 November 1992.
8. Enno Reinsalu, 'Mis on Eesti Vabariigil Narva joe taga?', *Päevaleht*, 24 March 1990.
9. Census of 1934.
10. 'Dokumente Petseri- ja Virumaa jaotamise kohta', *Akadeemia*, vol. 3, no. 9, 1991, pp. 1949–50.
11. Mattisen (1993), p. 96.
12. The procedure that took place on 23 August 1944 was not affected by the fact that the original telegram of the Presidium of the Supreme Soviet of the Estonian SSR containing the petition got lost in the mail. It had to be sent again on 24 August. See Mattisen (1993), pp. 97, 158–9.
13. 'Dokumente Petseri- ja Virumaa jaotamise kohta', *Akadeemia*, vol. 3, no. 8, 1991, pp. 1753–8.
14. Ibid., pp. 1956–9.
15. Mattisen (1993), pp. 168–71.
16. Ibid., pp. 101, 122.
17. Edgar Anderson, 'Narva, Petseri ja Abrene sattuminen Vene NFSV koosseisu', *Akadeemia*, vol. 3, no. 7, 1991, pp. 1515–20. See also Edgar Anderson, 'How Narva, Petseri and Abrene Came to Be in the RSFSR', in Dietrich André Loeber (ed.), *Regional Identity Under Soviet Rule: The Case of the Baltic States* (Hacketstown: University of Kiel 1990).
18. Mattisen (1993), p. 118.
19. *Eesti Aeg*, 10 March 1993.
20. *Eesti Vabariigi Ülemnoukogu ja Valitsuse Teataja*, no. 12, vol. 25, 1990, p. 269.
21. Mattisen (1993), pp. 171–9.
22. *Riigi Teataja*, no. 32, 1991, p. 727.
23. *The Baltic Independent*, 9–15 July 1993.
24. See Ruslan Ignatyev in *Rossijskaya Gazeta*, 14 April 1994.
25. *Supplement to the RFE/RL Research Report*, vol. 1, no. 31, 1992, p. 75.
26. *The Baltic Independent*, 24–30 July 1992.

27. *The Baltic Independent*, 26 February–4 March 1993.
28. *The Monthly Survey of Baltic and Post-Soviet Politics*, June 1993.
29. *Krasnaya zvezda,* 20 May 1993.
30. *The Baltic Independent*, 18–24 June 1993.
31. *The Baltic Independent*, 16–22 July 1993.
32. *Supplement to the RFE/RL Research Report*, vol. 3, no. 9, 1994, p. 15.
33. *Rahva Hääl*, 30 April 1994.
34. *Rahva Hääl*, 22 June 1994 and *The Baltic Independent,* 1–7 July 1994.
35. *Supplement to the RFE/RL Research Report*, vol. 2, no. 27, 1993, p. 12.
36. *The Baltic Independent*, 16–22 July 1993 and *The Baltic Independent*, 23–29 July 1993.
37. Jaan Kaplinski, 'Töetund Vene-poliitikas', *Päevaleht*, 27 May 1994.
38. *Supplement to the RFE/RL Research Report*, vol. 1, no. 1, 1994, p. 20. See also *The Baltic Independent* 8–14 July 1994.
39. *The Monthly Survey of Baltic and Post-Soviet Politics*, January 1994, p. 34.
40. *Eesti Aeg*, 10 March 1993.
41. *The Monthly Survey of Baltic and Post-Soviet Politics*, October 1993, p. 7.

12. Karelia

Tuomas Forsberg

As a result of World War II Finland lost an area of 43,491 square kilometres – more than a tenth of her total area – to the Soviet Union. The ceded territory consisted of four parts: parts of Karelia (Karelian Isthmus, Ladoga Karelia, Border Karelia), parts of Salla and Kuusamo parishes, the Petchenga area (Petsamo), and four islands in the Gulf of Finland (see Map 12.1). From all the ceded areas the population, more than 400,000 altogether, migrated to other parts of Finland. Because the most valuable part symbolically, as well as in terms of area, population and economy was the lost parts of Karelia, the discussion on the lost areas in Finland has gone under the name of the Karelian question, although similar issues naturally concern all the ceded areas.

What makes the Karelian question more complicated than it otherwise would be is the terminology. Karelia is in a sense a northern Macedonia where battles are fought also over the names. When Finns refer to the Karelian question they usually have in mind only the ceded territories. What Russians understand by Karelia is the Republic of Karelia, which is in turn, in the older Finnish usage of the language, Eastern Karelia.[1]

1. THE PRE-HISTORY OF THE KARELIAN QUESTION

The areas that Finland ceded to Russia as a result of World War II resemble many other areas in Eastern Europe, where the borderline between adjacent nations has varied over the centuries. Moreover, the border between Finland (Sweden) and Russia (the Soviet Union) has been regarded as a border not only between two neighbouring states but also between two civilizations – Eastern and Western. Thus the origins of the Karelian question can be traced back to early history.

Map 12.1. Karelia and other ceded territories.

At the beginning of the second millennium the area from the White Sea to the Gulf of Finland was inhabited by Karelians whose language was close to Finnish, but who were nominally taxed by the Novgorodians. In the 13th century Sweden extended her area towards the east. The first peace treaty between Sweden and Novgorod was signed in 1323 in Nöteborg. It divided Karelia into two parts: the western part became Catholic (later Lutheran) and the eastern part Orthodox. In the 16th and 17th centuries Sweden expanded further to the east and annexed territories around the Gulf of Finland. In the Great Nordic War, however, Sweden lost her position as a Baltic great power and, under Tsar Peter the Great, Russia occupied Eastern Finland. In the Peace of Nystad of 1721 Russia received the area from the coast west of Vyborg up to Northern Karelia. In the next Peace Treaty of Åbo in 1743, a further area up to the River Kymi was ceded to Russia. Finally, in the Finnish War of 1808–9 the rest of Finland was annexed by Russia.

The next transfer of borders in Karelia was a peaceful technical arrangement. In 1811 those parts of Finland which had been annexed by Russia in the 18th century were reunited with the rest of Finland. This decision was motivated by ethnic and historical reasons, since all the returned areas were inhabited by Finns. In addition to that, the return was also regarded as a means to westernize the administrative system of the Russian Empire, because the Grand Duchy of Finland preserved its Swedish laws. The return of the old lands also aimed at stabilizing the political situation in Finland because it was assumed it would weaken her links with Sweden. Although some Russians regarded the ceded area as 'a part of Russia's living body' and although many parts of Karelia and areas near to St. Petersburg with a Finnish majority still remained a part of Russia, the location of the border did not cause notable border problems because it remained open.[2]

When Finland became independent in 1917, she received her 19th-century borders. As Finland defined herself as a nation-state, she was not content with her old borders which did not correspond to ethnic boundaries. Attempts to annex areas in Eastern Karelia by force did not succeed, however. Soviet Russia and Finland confirmed their borders in the 1920 Tartu Peace Treaty. Although the treaty was regarded as a 'shameful peace' on both sides, it was after all a negotiated compromise that caused only minor changes in the border. Finland had wished to receive areas from Eastern Karelia, where people had risen up and demanded unification with Finland and she urged at least an internationally recognized autonomy for these Karelian parishes. The Finns did not succeed in achieving this but they received what they regarded as economically more important, namely the region of Petchenga by the Arctic Ocean. Soviet Russia presented no territorial demands to Finland but was anxious because she received a foreign border close to Petrograd (Leningrad from 1924). The administrative border of the Grand Duchy of Finland had not created security problems but the new border was already, during the Russian Civil War, perceived as a security threat to Petrograd. The Russians later pointed out that they had to sign the treaty because of their temporary weakness.[3]

Growing international tension in the 1930s made the Soviet Union fear a German or British military threat via Finland. The border which was situated only 32 kilometres from Leningrad became more and more unacceptable and the Soviet leadership did not trust the Finnish policy of neutrality. This led the Soviet Union to demand part of the Karelian Isthmus, islands in the Gulf of Finland and a naval base of Porkkala west of Helsinki. In return they proposed an exchange of territory in Eastern Karelia. The Finns, however, did not agree with the proposed terms. On the one hand they underestimated the Soviet threat and on the other hand they feared that a cession of Finnish lands would lead to a Soviet occupation of the whole of Finland. Although some concessions were considered possible, the Finns were reluctant to negotiate over their territory even in terms of an exchange. The Molotov–Ribbentrop Pact of 1939 was not the cause of the dispute, but it gave the Soviet Union confirmation that Germany would not resist a forced change of borders or even a total annexation of Finland.

As the negotiations did not lead to a positive result, the Soviet Union attacked Finland and launched the Winter War in November 1939. The ultimate aim of the attack was to occupy the whole of Finland. When the war started, the Soviet Union refused to negotiate with representatives of the official Finnish government but, instead, recognized a puppet government of the 'People's Republic of Finland' formed in Terijoki (which was the first occupied Finnish parish on the Karelian Isthmus) and headed by an exiled Finnish communist, Otto-Wille Kuusinen. It is worth noting that in the peace treaty concluded with the Terijoki government large parts of Eastern Karelia were given to the new 'People's Republic of Finland' and only a small strip of land close to Leningrad was transferred to the Soviet Union. When the anticipated rapid victory failed to materialize, however, the Soviet Union was ready to make peace with Finland's legal government.[4]

In the Moscow Peace Treaty of 1940 Finland had to cede a territory much larger than what was originally demanded and even occupied in the war. The new border resembled, with minor exceptions, the border of 1721 drawn by Peter the Great. Thanks to the changes Leningrad was in a more secure position and the annexation of parts of Kuusamo and Salla parishes in the north safeguarded the Murmansk railway. However, the loss of Vyborg, the second largest town in Finland, made the Finns especially bitter and it was one of the main reasons why Finland so eagerly joined in the so-called Continuation War against the Soviet Union as an informal ally of Germany in 1941. In this war Finland not only reannexed the previously lost parts of Karelia but also occupied new areas in Eastern Karelia with the possible aim of building a Greater Finland.

The war between Finland and the Soviet Union ended in 1944. In the Interim Peace Treaty of Moscow, which, was confirmed in Paris in 1947, the borders of 1940 were reinstituted and Finland also had to cede her passage to the Arctic Ocean, the Petchenga region. As a consequence of the peace treaty, the Soviet Union also received a naval base on a fifty-year lease in Porkkala close to Helsinki. A few years later, a small peaceful border change between Finland and the Soviet Union occurred in Lapland: Finland sold the area around the Jäniskoski power plant, which was claimed by the Soviet Union, to repay the debt Finland owed to Germany.

To sum up, the motives for the annexation of the Karelian Isthmus and other territories were very clearly security-political, and the ethnic and historical background or economic value of the area played no decisive role. History was however used as a means to determine the new site of the border – because of Peter the Great the Soviet Union took more than it had originally demanded. Hence, history became a means of legitimating the annexation, but only after the Continuation War was the reason given for the annexation of Finnish Karelia, namely that it was ancient Russian land. Soviet historiography thereby ignored the Winter War and emphasized the role Finland played as an attacker and Nazi-Germany's ally. The mainstream Finnish historiography after World War II agreed on the guilt of Finland in the Continuation War and tried to point out the mistakes Finnish foreign policy decision-makers had made before the Winter War but it could not change the impression that the Winter War was initiated by the Soviet Union and that the Continuation War was its clear consequence.

2. CEDED KARELIA AFTER WORLD WAR II

After the war, the ceded Karelian area was at first incorporated into the Finnish–Karelian Soviet Republic, but a few years later the Karelian Isthmus was transferred to the Leningrad Region (Oblast). Because the annexed parts of Karelia were emptied of population, people from various parts of the Soviet Union, and especially from those parts that had suffered heavily from the war, moved to the area during the 1940s and 1950s. At that time also the place names and other symbols were Russified (that had not been done after the Winter War). Although the population was steadily increasing, the number of inhabitants remained somewhat lower than it had been before the war. It was estimated that some 250–300,000 inhabitants have made up the population in the former Finnish territories of Karelia.

Because the main interest of Russia in the area that had belonged to Finland was strategic, the territory was, from the Soviet point of view, a military buffer zone, and areas close to the border remained largely unpopulated. Administrative and military functions overshadowed the economic activity of the area, which rested mainly on forestry and agriculture. From the Finnish point of view new infrastructure was barely set up and towns, villages, roads and railways declined under Soviet rule.[5] In comparison to many other areas in the former Soviet Union cultural and societal life also remained limited. Because a local identity was difficult to develop in a centralized state anyway, it was particularly hard in these circumstances where there was no historical continuity for it. Although Vyborg was not entirely peripheral in the Soviet system, it lost its position as a trading centre. In some respects Vyborg benefited thanks to its position as a transit town and because of its closeness to Leningrad, but with the exception of some formal contacts such as the town partnership between Finland's Lappeenranta and Vyborg, the area remained quite isolated from the outside world.[6] The post-war histories of other former Finnish territories are roughly similar.

The position of the former Finnish Karelia as well as those of other other ceded territories changed with *perestroika* and *glasnost*. The power of Moscow over regions diminished, and the border was more often perceived as an opportunity than as a threat. At the beginning of the 1980s Vyborg was opened up to tourism and in the late 1980s even visits to the countryside were permitted, which considerably increased the number of eg. visitors, especially Finns. At that time Moscow also put forward plans for special economic zones and one of them dealt with the Vyborg region.[7] According to these plans Vyborg was intended to become an economic and scientific centre, and investments, especially from Finland, were expected. The plans for a free economic zone were however too ambitious. They did not succeed partly because the regulations and aims of the zone remained too vague and partly because of the recession in the Finnish economy, which cut down the latitude for Finnish enterprises. Anyway, in 1992 Finnish firms provided nearly 90 per cent of all foreign investments in the district of Vyborg. But large Finnish enterprises have not been interested in Vyborg, for their eye to future investments is mostly directed beyond Vyborg to St. Petersburg. With the exception of irregular and short-term small business, where profits can be made without investing, and the business associated with the growing Finnish day tourism, the economic basis of the area has not notably improved.[8]

When the border was opened, Vyborg moved rapidly from an isolated and silent to an active but disorganized town. The fact that Vyborg is the closest town in Russia to a Western country now shapes its daily life and gives the town its special character. Whilst Vyborg has been trying to rebuild its identity, the history of the town has been recognized as a resource. The Swedish and Finnish background has been acknowledged, and old town symbols have been restored.[9] In many respects Vyborg has found its own will. Vyborg is now clearly more than a mere transit town and a certain competition especially in economic matters between Vyborg and the Russian power centres, Moscow and St. Petersburg, has emerged. Besides many people in Vyborg, the town itself, which has been able to sell specific Vyborg cards for day-visitors, has benefited because of its situation close to the border and its history of having been a part of Finland. But not all people regard with pleasure the increased number of Finnish visitors who sometimes behave too arrogantly. The closeness of the border has also had some negative effects, because growing tourism has attracted hawkers and criminals, and raised prices.[10]

Vyborg, the old centre of Finnish Karelia, as well as the isthmus of Karelia, were hence separated from the Finnish-Karelian Soviet Republic that was downgraded and renamed the Autonomous Republic of Karelia in 1956. At that time Karelia became overwhelmingly Russian as regards its population. The share of the Finnish peoples (Finns, Karelians and Vepsys) has been declining and they make up only a little over 10 per cent of the total population. But Karelia preserved much of its own identity and declared sovereignty in November 1991 following similar acts by other autonomous areas that aimed at improving their position. The content of the sovereignty has been largely undefined, however. Karelia wanted to enhance its status but the declaration of sovereignty did not mean the same thing as independence. In the negotiations with Moscow in the spring 1992, rights to natural resources, taxation and currency incomes were established. Karelia also received the right to make treaties with third powers, if they were not in conflict with Russian law. Thus, the Karelian republic has been developing its own identity and autonomy in its own affairs since the collapse of Soviet rule.[11]

3. EVACUATED KARELIANS IN FINNISH SOCIETY

Almost all the Finns who had lived in the ceded areas left their homes voluntarily notwithstanding the fact that no real opportunity to stay was given to them. The 410,000 Karelians (10,000 of them from Petchenga, Salla and Kuusamo) were evacuated to Finland and, on the basis of a special law, settled all over Southern Finland with the exception of the territories with a Swedish-speaking majority.[12] The displacement caused some social problems, because many Karelians felt themselves isolated and especially those who were Orthodox were at first regarded by Western Finns as aliens and even as Russians. The social controversies died down fairly soon, however, and the Karelians were accepted as being part of their new local societies. The younger generations and children in particular adapted themselves relatively easily to the new environment.[13]

The Karelian evacuees organized themselves into various parish associations and into a wider Karelian Association. Karelians did not establish a party of their own but many of them, such as Johannes Virolainen of the Agrarian Party, became important politicians in the post-war society. Although the Karelians were mostly integrated into the mainstream politics of the traditional parties, they sometimes coordinated their policies over the Karelian question. The return of Karelia remained a central objective of the Karelian Association until the 1960s. On this issue it had regular contacts with the president, but it did not really try to work as a pressure group in public politics.[14]

The focus of the activity of the Karelian Association was not to be found in politics but in various cultural and social activities. Karelians preserved features of their culture and a certain affiliation to the lost area but already by the 1950s many of them no longer cherished hopes of a return to

Karelia. For cultural or identity reasons such a return was not regarded as necessary. For most evacuated Karelians, Karelia had become a paradise lost which existed more in their memories than in their plans for the future.

At the end of the 1980s a clear mood of Karelian nostalgia began in Finland. This nostalgia anticipated but did not directly relate to rising discussion about territorial changes. For example, a miniature of Vyborg was constructed in the Museum of Lappeenranta and the old phone book of Vyborg was republished. *Glasnost* in the Soviet Union also opened the border for 'home district travelling', an opportunity which was widely used. Various efforts have been made in recent years to restore cultural monuments, for example the old castle of Vyborg which was 700 years old in 1993. In addition to that, a few Finns, with a certain Karelian yearning, have even moved over and leased land for potato plantations on the Karelian Isthmus, so far with disappointing results, however.

4. THE KARELIAN QUESTION IN FINLAND AFTER WORLD WAR II

The Moscow Interim Peace Treaty of 1944 was regarded by the Finns as a heavy and unjust loss, as was the peace after the Winter War. However, Finland had practically no other choice than to accept the situation and to try to build sound relations with the Soviet Union. Before the Paris Peace Negotiations in 1947, the Finns still had some hopes that the border could be renegotiated. They thought that because the Soviet Union had won the war and relations between Finland and the Soviet Union had become amicable, there was no reason for the Soviet Union to keep strategic territory in Karelia. Both the government of Finland and specific Karelian delegations tried to change the minds of Soviet leaders by proposing various special arrangements. The Finns also tried to influence Western Powers, but in vain. The Finnish delegation in Paris set out the issue cautiously, but no chance to open the discussion of the border-line arose. Because this result was expected, the motive of the Finnish negotiators was rather to reserve for themselves the right for future adjustments and to satisfy domestic opinion.[15]

Although President J.K. Paasikivi (1946–56) was the main figure who established good relations between the Soviet Union and Finland, he was resolute that the Karelian question should not be forgotten. Because of the sensitivity of relations with the Soviet Union, however, he did not raise the issue publicly and was reluctant to demand it directly. He first tried to convince the Soviet Union of the economic and emotional value of Karelia to Finland and pointed out the common economic interests of the area for future Finnish–Soviet trade. Later he thought that the return of Karelia could be an appropriate price for continuing the Agreement on Friendship, Cooperation and Mutual Assistance, which was signed in 1948.[16] When this question was raised in 1955, the Soviet Union decided to return the naval base of Porkkala to Finland. No wonder then that the Karelian question was also discussed intensively in the Finnish press and demands for the return of Karelia were put forward. The Finnish Minister of Defence, Emil Skog, even suggested this privately to the Soviet Prime Minister, Nikolai Bulganin. Publicly it was hoped that the new Soviet leadership could make up, for the Finns, for the wrongdoings initiated by Stalin but the discussion ended when *Izvestiya* reacted negatively to it and Prime Minister Urho Kekkonen asked the press to soften their demands.[17]

Later, as President of Finland, Kekkonen (1956–81) also worked for the return of Karelia but mostly behind the scenes. Although Kekkonen was not Karelian, he had been elected to parliament from a Karelian electoral district. He saw the return of Karelia as one of his long-term dreams but his strategy on the issue was to regain Karelia step by step through collaboration. Kekkonen was known for his good personal contacts with the Moscow leadership and his ability to collaborate with it. He argued with Nikita Khrushchev that a return of Karelia would strengthen his position and make for good relations between the Soviet Union and Finland. On the basis of his efforts he succeeded in leasing the Saimaa Canal in the ceded territory in 1962. Kekkonen tried to extend this arrangment to the whole of lost Karelia but after Khrushchev had been deposed his chances to bring influence to bear on the Karelian question were weakened. All the time the Soviet military leadership was strongly against any border adjustments and Khrushchev had to 'thank' Kekkonen for understanding the necessity of retaining the status quo for general peace. Soviet diplomats had already warned, before the Porkkala negotiations, not to touch upon Karelia, and in the Brezhnev era the resistance of the Soviet Union stiffened.[18]

For domestic political reasons, Kekkonen changed his Karelian policy in the late 1960s and refused to receive the delegation of the Karelian Association. According to him the publicity had spoiled the opportunities for the return of Karelia.[19] After this incident the Karelian question vanished from Finnish politics for more than twenty years. The Karelians got the impression that Kekkonen had given up hope of resolving the Karelian question but obviously he did not bury the issue completely; he played with the idea that a Finnish recognition of the GDR would bring Vyborg back. Nevertheless, in its relations with the Soviet Union Finland rather retreated to a defensive position. The Karelian question also seemed not to cause any hesitation when Finland accepted the pledges of the CSCE document which denounced the right of making territorial claims. Public opinion was almost completely in favour of the CSCE process and the Karelian question was not even mentioned in the public discussion in this context.

5. THE KARELIAN QUESTION IN RUSSIAN–FINNISH RELATIONS

Since the dissolution of the Soviet Union, Finland has not raised the Karelian question at the interstate level. Neither have there been signs of attempts to demand special treatment for the former Finnish territories becoming part of the official Finnish policy towards its eastern neighbouring areas. The former Finnish lands are not perceived as being separate from other Russian lands. For example, the Finnish government does not see it inappropriate that Russia has built a military garrison base in Salla in the former Finnish territory. Officially, Finland seems to be more interested in taking care of ethnic Finns than former Finnish lands in Russia, but neither of the issues play a significant role in Finnish–Russian relations.

Russia has been concerned about the possible reopening of the Karelian question. She has therefore categorically denied the possibility of border changes and treated the former Finnish territories as wholly under her sovereignty. Yet, Russia has adopted a positive attitude towards policies regarding cooperation in the border region. On this basis, there has been limited but novel cooperation on many issues from agricultural projects to humanitarian assistance and restoration works.

Formally the status of the border was defined in the Basic Treaty Between Finland and Russia, which was signed in January 1992. In the preceding negotiations (between Finland and the Soviet Union) on the new basic treaty, the Soviet side tried to formulate a statement of the finality of the common border. The Finnish side in turn did not want to have any separate statement on borders. As a result the treaty includes an article on the border, but it is very vague. The article prescribes that Finland and Russia preserve their common border as a border of good neighbourhood according to the principles of the CSCE Final Act and respect each other's territorial integrity.[20] According to the Finnish interpretation this leaves open the possibility of changes to the border, whereas the Russians have interpreted it so that the treaty confirms the finality of the border.

When President Yeltsin visited Finland in the summer of 1992 and when President Ahtisaari visited Russia in the spring of 1994 the Karelian question was not – at least according to public knowledge – touched upon. The presidents have stressed that no border disputes between the countries exist but they have felt that the common border could be made more transparent.[21] The idea of the transparent border is, however, far from becoming reality. On this issue, especially, Finland has been very cautious because of fears of growing immigration and the spread of organized crime and Russia does not want to create a clear imbalance in the openness of the border.

6. THE DEBATE OVER THE KARELIAN QUESTION IN FINLAND AFTER THE END OF THE COLD WAR

In the course of the Cold War, Finnish society had learned to live, as a 'showcase of peaceful coexistence', with its eastern neighbour. At the end of the 1980s, the question of Karelia was publicly forgotten and consciously rejected, because its return seemed impossible in any case. The political culture of the 'Finlandization' era since the 1960s required criticism of the Soviet Union to be restrained, and the Karelian question was one of those issues which it was not thought appropriate to touch upon publicly. However, the debate over the ceded territories began again in Finland after the revolutions in Eastern Europe since they indicated a clear change in the Soviet attitude towards the post-war order and a general liberation from the Cold War atmosphere.

One of the first signs of the emerging question was an opinion poll published in spring 1990 according to which nearly half of those Finns questioned favoured an opening of negotiations over the return of Karelia.[22] However, the internal resistance to raising the issue was at that time still great. At the annual meeting of the Karelian Association, an attempt was made to open the discussion on the Karelian question, but it was not accepted. The association did not want to engage in discussion which it regarded as belonging to the foreign policy establishment. However, some individual politicians from a small, populistic Rural Party (SMP) and the small, separate Tartu Peace Movement proposed calling for negotiations over the return of Karelia and other lost territories. This launched the first public debate over Karelia in the media but the idea of initiating negotiations between Russia over the issue was rejected by all leading politicians. The debate itself was regarded as unnecessary and harmful.[23]

Only after the failed coup in Moscow and the regained independence of the Baltic states in August 1991, did the public debate over Karelia accelerate in Finland, at the same time as negotiations over a new treaty with Finland and the Soviet Union were initiated. Since then various proposals and arguments have been given both for and against the return of Karelia and other ceded territories. According to the polls in September 1991, a third of Finns supported negotiations with the Soviet Union over the return of Karelia.[24] This was less than a year before, but the support was now more clearly articulated. Demands for the return of Karelia were put forth in the press, and in parliament a member of the Rural Party (SMP) questioned the Finnish policy towards the Karelian question. The Karelian Association was also ready to prepare a proposal concerning future relations with Karelia, which was given to President Koivisto (1982–94) in January 1992. The association did not want to tie its hands with demands for the return of Karelia, but the idea was pushed forward by its chairman, Rauno Meriö, and by a separate people's delegation.

The claim of the pro-Karelian movement was that because of international justice and historical and cultural values, Karelia, according to the borders of 1939, should be returned to Finland. Chairman Meriö presented a plan according to which Finnish Karelia could receive an autonomous status similar to that of the Åland Islands. According to the model of Meriö and most other proposals, the Russian population could stay in the region although arrangements to facilitate their moving 'back' to Russia, on a voluntary basis, might be possible. It was suggested that negotiations and political and economic compensation could be the way to solve the issue; violence was absolutely rejected. The pro-Karelian movement also sharply focused the issue on the ceded parts of Karelia; a unification of the Republic of Karelia with Finland was not on their agenda. In this respect the Karelian question after World War II was far different from the Eastern Karelian question before the war. Furthermore, although the demands included all the ceded territories, many of the proponents held this position only as a starting point for discussions. There was no definitive all-or-nothing proposition, but the return of Vyborg was a kind of minimum objective.[25] Since the discussion was wide-ranging, various standpoints with different emphases were presented. In addition to Karelia it has been suggested also that other lost territories should be returned and it has been proposed that the question could be solved by leasing the former Finnish lands rather than by returning them directly.[26]

The Finnish Government and leading politicians did not show much enthusiasm for the return of Karelia. The dividing line in the attitudes towards the Karelian question did not seem to lie between different parties but between 'under-dogs' and 'top-dogs'. The higher one was in the political hierarchy, the less likely that one supported negotiations over the Karelian question.[27] In public, the reluctance of the 'top-dogs' was even more apparent. However, the attitudes of the political elite towards the discussion changed in the course of events. The leading politicians no longer insisted that the discussion should be banned in the name of good relations with the Soviet Union; instead they tried to convince people that the opening of the question was not a meaningful political objective at the moment.

The demands for initiating negotiations were targeted especially towards President Koivisto. He did not deny the right to discuss the issue but declared that the question had been resolved in three peace treaties.[28] Neither did he reject the loosely formulated proposal of the Karelian Association according to which connections to the ceded area should be developed.[29] But he argued that he had very different opinions on the issue from the representatives of the Tartu Peace Movement. President Martti Ahtisaari (1994–), in turn, who was born in Vyborg, has declared that he has not buried the issue finally, but he will not raise the subject because he does not wish to provoke difficulties in Finnish–Russian relations. Hence, according to him, there is a possibility that the issue might be discussed, but the initiative concerning the return of Karelia has to be launched by the Russian side.[30] Moreover, Ahtisaari has suspected that the majority of Finns are, after all, not interested in the return of Karelia.[31]

The popular approach of the leading politicians of the major parties on the Karelian question was to admit the moral injustice that had been done to Finland in the past but to insist that the Soviet Union was not ready to negotiate and therefore it was not worth opening the debate. This was, for example, the argument the Minister for Foreign Affairs, Paavo Väyrynen, used in parliament, and which was later adopted also by his successor, Heikki Haavisto.[32] This approach does not deny the possibility of the return of Karelia or see it as undesirable, but it leaves the question up to the Russians. The attitude implies that negotiations can be initiated if the circumstances change; in other words, if Russians are willing to discuss the issue.

Moreover, the idea of the return of Karelia was opposed for economic, political, social and strategic reasons. For many, the return of the ruined Karelia had no rationale and they regarded such hopes simply as reflections of atavistic and reactionary emotions. It was argued that the reconstruction of Karelia to the level achieved in Finland would be much too expensive.[33] When the Finnish economy went deeper into recession, the allocation of resources for such a big investment seemed to be out of the question, even if the reconstruction would create new jobs. Politically, the orientation towards Karelia was said to contradict the application for membership of the EU, because it would turn Finland's attention in the wrong direction and give false signals to Brussels. Furthermore, it was argued that the Russian minority who would become Finnish citizens would pose too many social, as well as possibly interstate, problems. The head of the general staff, General Gustav Hägglund, argued that for strategic reasons he would not take Karelia, 'even if it were served on a golden plate'. He emphasized the strategic value of the Karelian Isthmus to the Russians and the possible dangers of not understanding the logic of Russian strategic thinking.[34] Finally, it was also underlined that Finland should support the CSCE process. According to this view, to raise territorial claims would destabilize the international system in Europe.[35]

Among many politicians as well as other discussants there seemed to be a general consensus on an integrative approach to the Karelian question.[36] Accordingly, the border areas should be developed and integrated into Finland even if the borders themselves remained unchanged. Such measures would be more easily proposed than executed, however, because economic investments would be costly and insecure and opening the border, it was supposed, would create chaotic effects for Finland. It was therefore usually recognized that an open border could only be a long-term objective. What was hoped in practice was rather an 'osmotic' border that permits movement towards the east but not vice-versa.

The proponents of the return of Karelia tried, of course, to prove to the public that the economic costs had been exaggerated and that it would not be too expensive for Finland's economy. Yet, one of the main points of the pro-Karelia movement was that the return of Karelia was not a question of mere economic rationale but one of emotions based on history, culture and, principally, justice. They also tried to show that on strategic issues Finland and Russia could find compromises. Other named rationales for the return included the idea that for the development of the whole of Eastern Finland as an economically organic entity, Vyborg would be needed as a regional centre. Also environmental protection has been mentioned as a reason for the return of Karelia. Potential minority problems that would follow from its return were at first disregarded by the pro-Karelia movement. However, as a consequence of the Russian policy towards the 'near-abroad' which has stressed the rights of Russian minorities, many of those who have been in favour of the return of Karelia seem to have given up the idea that, in this eventuality, the Russian population could stay in the area. Instead they propose a payment that would help the Russians to move.[37]

In 1994, the high point of popular support for the return of Karelia seemed to have passed in Finland. Many hopes and expectations were targeted towards the CSCE meeting in Helsinki and the visit of President Yeltsin to Finland in 1992. Neither the meeting nor the visit fulfilled these hopes and after these events popular enthusiasm declined but did not vanish. In a poll conducted in September 1992 only 25 per cent of Finns supported negotiations over the border issue.[38] Since then the issue has lost its novelty but it continues to be alive and occasionally to evoke public discussion.

7. THE RUSSIAN RESPONSE

The representantives of the Soviet Union have categorically rejected any idea of border changes in Karelia and responded highly negatively even to the discussion of the Karelian question. The Russian standpoint has not changed noticeably and no leading politician has clearly backed the cession of Karelia to Finland.

Officially, there are small differences in the tone of response. Uppermost is the formal rejectionist view, according to which there is no Karelian question and no need for discussion. This line of argumentation has been adopted also by President Yeltsin. In an interview given before his visit to Finland in 1992 he explicitly denied the existence of the Karelian question. Yeltsin argued further that because every border adjustment is connected with wars, a border adjustment in Karelia would cause chaos in the whole of Europe.[39] In October 1991, the then chairman of the Supreme Soviet, Ruslan Khasbulatov, argued sharply that the Soviet Union would never negotiate over the issue. According to him the problem of territories was painful and he insisted that it must not be raised.[40] Some other representatives seemed to be more ready to admit the existence of the question and allow discussion over it. For example, the Russian Ambassador to Finland, Yuri Deryabin, stated that discussion of the border question is not in itself a hostile act, but he did not regard the return of Karelia as possible.[41] Instead of the border adjustments, many Russians, including Yeltsin, have felt that the border between Finland and Russia could be made more transparent and that cooperation in the area should be strengthened.[42]

So far the idea of the need for general stability has been the argument most often used to motivate the opposition to border changes on the Karelian question. All changes of borders are regarded as dangerous and therefore politically impossible to execute. Even if the injustice perpetrated in history resulting from the annexation of Finnish Karelia were admitted, Russians feel that all borders are arbitrary and therefore unjust. Some Russian discussants are also anxious about the possible mistreatment of the Russian population or their expulsion, if the territory were to be ceded. They stress that an injustice cannot be undone by creating another injustice. Others also point out that only a minority of Finns wish to return Karelia or that Karelians constitute a separate people from Finns. Moreover, opposition to border changes seems also to be rooted in concepts of territorial sovereignty, national honour, Russian land, the victory of the Great Patriotic War and so on, which are often indirectly used in the discussion.[43]

Some signs have indicated that Russia is ready to make symbolic concessions on the Karelian question even though talks on border shifts have been strictly avoided. Many Russians understand the natural wish of Finnish Karelians to discuss the issue, visit their homelands and raise cultural monuments there. Many Russians also share the view that the annexation of Karelia and the subsequent expulsion of Finns was morally wrong, but they may regard these acts as necessary at the time of World War II. Although Russia has not officially declared herself guilty of the Winter War, she no longer accuses Finland of starting it. As a sign of this changed attitude, in summer 1992, President Yeltsin laid a wreath at the monument dedicated to Finnish soldiers who had died in World War II. Furthermore, at the press conference during Ahtisaari's visit to Moscow in May 1994 Yeltsin for the first time clearly acknowledged that the annexation of Finnish Karelia was an aggressive act of Stalin's policy.[44] Moreover, Ambassador Deryabin has stated publicly that the decline of Vyborg was something Russia should be ashamed of.[45]

Although the existence of Finnish claims to Karelia are widely recognized in Russian political circles, the discussion of the issue has remained thin. The view of the Russian parliament, for example, is that the issue is solved and not a subject for continuing discussion.[46] One of the politicians who has many times touched upon the question of borders in Karelia is the leader of the nationalistic Liberal Democratic Party, Vladimir Zhirinovsky. He has warned Finns that if they continue the discussion of the Karelian question, it could be fatal.[47] Sometimes, he has threatened to incorporate the whole of Finland into Russia.[48] Recently, however, he has intimated that Vyborg would be returned to Finland.[49] Otherwise, only a few individual voices have publicly supported the ceding of Karelia to Finland. Even those who have supported the idea of returning the Kurile Islands to Japan have pointed out that the Kurile question is not comparable to the Karelian question because the latter has been confirmed by treaty. Some ideas have been circulated according to which the Finnish population in Russia, the Ingrians, who number around 20,000 persons, could receive an autonomous area on the Karelian Isthmus. Although they have been recently rehabilitated and received the right to move back to their home districts, the plans concerning their resettlement on the Karelian Isthmus have so far been unrealistic.

In comparison with the Karelian Isthmus, the idea of unification with Finland has had some popular support in the Republic of Karelia. According to some polls every third or fourth person questioned both among Russians and Finns (Karelians) supported the idea of joining Finland. Those who favoured the idea were mostly younger people who saw union with Finland as an economic opportunity. Opinions were divided, however, because older people still remember Finland as an enemy and many fear that Karelia would become only a backward periphery as a part of Finland.[50]

The President of the Republic of Karelia, Viktor Stepanov, has been eager to develop contacts with Finland, and the republic has put forward cooperative initiatives on different issue-areas to which the Finnish–Russian

Agreement on Cooperation in nearby areas gives a formal basis.[51] Stepanov has also suggested the possibility of leasing land to Finns. However, the possibility of a border change has been clearly denied. A small political movement of Finnish peoples and especially its radical faction notwithstanding, no political force in the Republic of Karelia has supported the idea of unification.[52]

8. FUTURE VISIONS

The Karelian question has not been on the agenda in relations between the Soviet Union and Finland since the mid-1950s. During the post-war years it became clear to Finland that she had much more to lose than to win by raising the issue publicly, since the position of the Soviet Union on the issue was rigid. The same line of thought has continued, and Finnish foreign policy leaders prefer good relations with Russia to disputes over lost territories even at the expense of domestic public opinion.

During the autumn of 1991 a lively debate on Karelia suddenly emerged in Finnish society. It seemed that most of the Finns shared the view that the transfer of Karelia to the Soviet Union was not morally right but only a few thought that the return of Karelia were a politically reasonable goal. Politicians who felt the conflict of pressures stressed that the initiation of negotiations had not been excluded but they would require better timing – i.e. when there was a more stable and democratic Russia. However, it is fairly unclear what the reactions of the Finnish citizens would be in reality, if the option was available. For many Finns the presence of a new Russian minority and the estimated economic burdens caused by unification would be hard to accept. Since the debate over the Karelian question was launched in Finland, public euphoria has decreased and it is doubtful whether public pressure will grow unless some major changes in Russia take place. Anyway, it seems that the foreign policy leadership of Finland will not raise the issue spontaneously unless Russian leaders are willing to discuss it.

Hence, the international status of the former Finnish Karelia and the other former Finnish territories seems to depend on Russia. As Russia's future seems to be fairly open, much can happen, but at present it seems obvious that Russia will not cede the territories voluntarily and the annexed areas themselves, though they wish to have more freedom than before, prefer to remain a part of Russia.

NOTES

1. There are also disagreements over who the Karelians are. Originally they were a Finnish tribe whose language was close to Finnish. When the tribe was divided and western Karelia became part of Finland (Sweden), their language was assimilated and became a dialect of Finnish whereas the Karelian language was preserved in a distinguishable form in the Russian part of Karelia. Therefore Russians often stress that Karelians are not really Finns. See Heikki Kirkinen, 'Karjalan kansan synty ja hajoaminen', [The origin and dispersion of the Karelian people], *Terra*, vol. 105, no. 4,1993, pp. 270–79, 1993.

2. See J.R. Danielson-Kalmari, *Viipurin läänin palauttaminen muun Suomen yhteyteen* (Porvoo: WSOY 1911).

3. See *Suomen ja Venäjän välisten Tartossa pidettyjen rauhanneuvottelujen pöytäkirjat* (Helsinki: Ulkoasiainministeriön julkaisuja 1923).

4. See Max Jakobson, *Diplomacy of the Winter War: An Account of the Russo-Finnish War 1939–40* (Cambridge: Harvard University Press 1961) and Osmo Jussila, *Terijoen hallitus 1939–40* (Juva: WSOY 1985).

5. It is worth noting that this very prevalent view in Finland is equivalent to the somewhat mythical view according to which the 'Old Finland' was treated as a backward province when it was a part of Russia in the 18th century.

6. The post-war history of the lost Finnish territories is by and large unwritten. For a Russian view on the history of the architecture of Vyborg see Jevgeni Kepp, *Vyborg* (Vyborg: Fantakt 1993) and for a Finnish view see Juha Lankinen, 'Menetetty Viipuri', in Jouni Kallioniemi (ed.), *Viipurin seitsemän vuosisataa* (Turku: Kirjaveteraanit 1993).

7. See e.g. Heike Dörrenbächer,' Sonderwirtschaftszonen – Ein Beitrag zur wirtschaflichen Entwicklung der UdSSR', *Osteuropa Wirtschaft*, vol. 36, no. 2, 1991, and Riitta Kosonen, 'The Filling of the Economic Space of Viborg Due to the Plans for Special Economic Zone – The Case of 'Imsveto'-Project', *Working Papers*, series F, no. 267, 1991 (Helsinki: Helsinki School of Economics 1991).

8. See Riitta Kosonen, 'Viipurin 700 vuotta: alueellinen keskus talousjärjestelmien muutospaineessa', *Terra*, vol. 105, no. 4, 1993, pp. 324–33, and Kari Liuhto, 'Viipuri – Pietarin talousalueen länsiportti: Suomalaisyritysten kokemuksia ja koettelumuksia nyky-Viipurissa', *Research Reports*, series B, no. 5, 1993 (Turku: Turku School of Economics and Business Administration. Research Centre and Institute for East–West Trade 1993).

9. See Riitta Kosonen, 'Approaching the Cultural Evolution of a Frontier Town: Institutions and Indigenous Development in Vyborg', *Working Papers*, series W, no. 89, 1994 (Helsinki: Helsinki School of Economics 1994).

10. See e.g. Inna Rogatshi, 'Viipurin uusi keskiaika', *Suomen kuvalehti*, 17 July 1992.

11. See Eira Varis, *Karjalan tasavalta tänään* (Ilomantsi: Joensuun yliopisto, Mekrijärven tutkimusasema 1993); Heikki Eskelinen, Jukka Oksa and Daniel Austin, *Russian Karelia in Search for a New Role* (Joensuu: Karelian Institute 1994).

12. See Silvo Hietanen, *Siirtoväen Pika-asutuslaki 1940* (Helsinki: Suomen Historiallinen seura 1982).

13. On Karelians, their adaptation to Finnish society and their culture see Heikki Waris, *Siirtoväen sopeutuminen. Tutkimus Suomen karjalaisen siirtoväen sosiaalisesta sopeutumisesta* (Helsinki: Otava 1952) and Pirkko-Liisa Sallinen-Gimpl, *Siirtokarjalaisten identiteetti ja kulttuurien kohtaaminen* (Helsinki: Suomen muinaismuistoyhdistys 1994).

14. See Jouko Teperi, *Karjalan liiton taisteluvuodet 1940–60* (Helsinki: Wiipurin suomalainen kirjallisuusseura 1994).

15. See J.K. Paasikivi, *Paasikiven päiväkirjat I* (Porvoo: WSOY 1985), p. 574 and Tuomo Polvinen, *Between East and West. Finland in International Politics 1944–47* (Porvoo: WSOY 1986).

16. See J.K. Paasikivi *Paasikiven päiväkirjat II* (Helsinki: WSOY 1986), pp. 565–74 and 968–70.

17. See e.g. Roy Allison, *Finland's Relations with the Soviet Union 1944–84* (London: Macmillan 1985), pp. 40–42.

18. See Juhani Suomi, *Kriisien aika. Urho Kekkonen 1956–62* (Helsinki: Otava 1992) and *Presidentti. Urho Kekkonen 1962–68* (Helsinki: Otava 1994).

19. See Esko Salminen, 'Väärä julkisuus esti Kekkosen Karjala-hankkeet', *Helsingin Sanomat*, 6 October 1991.

20. Jaakko Blomberg, 'Finland and Russia', *Yearbook of Finnish Foreign Policy* 1992 (Helsinki: The Finnish Institute of International Affairs 1992).

21. See *Helsingin Sanomat*, 12 July 1992 and 19 May 1994.

22. *Suomen kuvalehti*, 23 March 1990.

23. See e.g. the interview with Foreign Minister Pertti Paasio in *Karjalainen*, 25 November 1990.

24. See *Seura*, September 1991.

25. See *Helsingin Sanomat*, 28 December 1991 and *Karjala*, 30 January 1992 and 13 February 1992.

26. See e.g. *Turun Sanomat*, 6 June 1992 and *Iltalehti*, 8 April 1993.

27. According to an elite opinion survey conducted in 1993, only a little more than a tenth of the respondents were in favour of initiating negotiations with Russia over the Karelian question. See Weijo Pitkänen, 'Finland and Russia in a Changing Europe. Perceptions of the Finnish Political Elite', *Yearbook of Finnish Foreign Policy* 1993 (Helsinki: The Finnish Institute of International Affairs 1993).

28. An interview with President Koivisto in *Uusi Suomi*, 16 September 1991.

29. See *Helsingin Sanomat*, 3 March 1992.

30. See *Demari*, 24 January 1994 and *Ilta-Sanomat*, 9 April 1994.

31. See *Ilta-Sanomat*, 20 May 1994.

32. The answer of Minister Väyrynen to question no. 83 of MP Mäkelä concerning the opening of negotiations on the return of Karelia, *Press Bulletin of Foreign Ministry*, no. 340, 11 October 1991. See also the statement of Minister Haavisto, *Helsingin Sanomat*, 28 July 1994.

33. An estimated amount was reckoned to be more than $ 20 billion. See *Helsingin Sanomat*, 15 September 1991.

34. An interview with General Gustav Hägglund in *Keskisuomalainen*, 29 March 1992.

35. See Max Jacobson, 'Pitäisikö Karjala palauttaa?', *Helsingin Sanomat*, 15 September 1991.

36. See for example the speech of the President of the Parliament Ilkka Suominen, 3 June 1992, in Kauhava.

37. See e.g. 'How to Abolish the Remaining Half of the Consequences of the Molotov–Ribbentrop Pact – Now that the Baltic States Have Regained Their Independence?' 'Denial of the Finnish People's Homestead Continuity – One Form of Violation of Human Rights'. These were the themes of the press conference held by the *Tartu's Peace Movement* within the CSCE in Helsinki 30 March 1992; Yrjö Pessi and Reino Auvinen, *Suomen v. 1944 pakkoluovuttamien alueiden kehittäminen Suomen hallinnassa* (Lahti: Palonvara 1992); Rauno Meriö, 'Karjalako turvallisuusriski?', *Keskisuomalainen*, 5 April 1992 and Pentti Virrankoski, *Karjala takaisin- Suhteet Venäjään terveiksi* (Lappeenranta: Karjala-kirja 1994). See also Martti Valkonen, 'The Ceded Finnish Territories and the Karelian Question', *The Finnish Defence Review* 1993.

38. See Jyrki Iivonen, 'The Attitude of Finns Towards Current Developments in Russia and Finnish–Russian Relations', *Yearbook of Finnish Foreign Policy* 1992 (Helsinki: The Finnish Institute of International Affairs 1992).

39. See e.g. *Aamulehti*, 5 July 1992.

40. See *Federal News Service*, 3 October 1991 and *Helsingin Sanomat*, 18 February 1993.

41. See the interviews with Ambassador Yuri Deryabin in *Helsingin Sanomat*, 4 March 1992; in *Suomen Kuvalehti* March 1992 and in *Savon Sanomat*, 26 June 1992.

42. See e.g. the interview with Gennadi Burbulis in *Helsingin Sanomat*, 14 January 1992.

43. On the Russian views on the Karelian question see e.g. *Izvestiya*, 1 October 1991; *Izvestiya*, 19 October 1991; *Novoye vremya*, 11 February 1992; *Literaturnaya Rossiya*, 15 May 1992. See also Leonid Ignatov, 'Kysymys Karjalan palauttamisesta muistuttaa Krimin tilannetta',

Helsingin Sanomat, 16 June 1994 and Vyacheslav Tsushnin, '"Rajoistamme emme keskustele" – Karjala-kysymys Kremlin näkökulmasta', Lecture given at a seminar of the *46th Karelian Summer Festival* in Tampere, 17 June 1994.

44. See *Helsingin Sanomat*, 19 May 1994.
45. Interview with Ambassador Yuri Deryabin in *Helsingin Sanomat*, 4 March 1992.
46. See e.g. *Helsingin Sanomat*, 30 May 1994.
47. See e.g. *Turun Sanomat*, 19 February 1992.
48. See e.g. *KU Viikkolehti*, 8 May 1992 and *Die Welt*, 31 January 1994.
49. See Vladimir Zhirinovsky, *Poslednii brosok na yug* (Moscow: TOO Pisatel, IK Bukvitsa 1993) and *Helsingin Sanomat*, 5 January 1994.
50. See *Karjalan Sanomat*, January 1992 and *Kansan Uutiset*, 7 May 1992.
51. See e.g. *Kaleva*, 2 October 1991 and *Helsingin Sanomat*, 29 November 1992. On the policy of the Karelian Republic on this issue see also 'Karjala luo yhteistyötä yli rajojen'. An interview with Valeri Shljamin in *Carelia*, no. 8, 1993, pp. 75–86 and Y. Fokin and V. Semyonov, 'Russia-Finland: Regional Cooperation', *International Affairs* (Moscow), no. 3, 1994, pp. 12–16.
52. See *Helsingin Sanomat*, 14 May 1992 and *The Economist*, 9 January 1993.

13. The Northern Territories

Toshiyasu Ishiwatari

The Northern Territories, in Japan also commonly called the Four Northern Islands, viz. Habomai, Shikotan, Kunashiri and Etorofu, have been a subject of controversy between Japan and Russia or the Soviet Union for more than two centuries now. The designation of the Kurile Islands or the Kuriles is very often used in foreign reports.[1] The Northern Territories (5,000 km^2) are currently under the control of Russia. Japan has been insisting for more than forty years that Russia/the Soviet Union should return the Northern Territories to Japan.

From the official Japanese point of view, the group of islands which exists between Kamchatka and Hokkaido can be classified into two groups: one group of islands consisting of the islands from Shumushu to Uruppu, and the other group of islands consisting of Habomai, Shikotan, Kunashiri and Etorofu.[2] The former are the Kuriles in the true sense of the word, and thus the latter are not included in the Kuriles.[3] According to Russian usage, the Kuriles comprise all the islands between Kamchatka and Hokkaido (see Map 13.1).

1. THE HISTORY OF THE NORTHERN TERRITORIES

The original inhabitants of these islands, the Ainus, did not constitute any state. Because of their remote location, the islands were not discovered until comparatively recent times. Around the beginning of the 18th century, Russians began to make expeditions to the Kuriles but they could not extend their power to the Four Northern Islands.[4] The Japanese exploration of Etorofu and Kunashiri was carried out several times on a large scale by the shoguns' patrolmen. In 1798, they erected signposts on

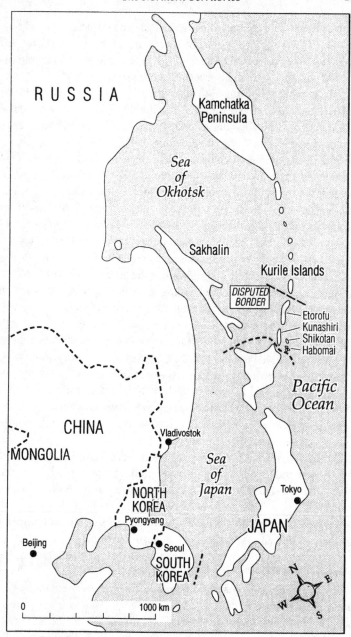

RUSSIA

Kamchatka
Peninsula

*Sea
of
Okhotsk*

Sakhalin

Kurile Islands

DISPUTED
BORDER

Etorofu
Kunashiri
Shikotan
Habomai

*Pacific
Ocean*

CHINA

Vladivostok

MONGOLIA

*Sea
of
Japan*

Tokyo

NORTH
KOREA

Pyongyang

JAPAN

Beijing

Seoul

SOUTH
KOREA

0   1000 km

N
E
W
S

Map 13.1. The Northern Territories.

Kunashiri and Etorofu, by which Japan declared territorial rights over the islands.[5] The Tokugawa Shogunate kept the islands under its rule. In 1807, Sakhalin was also placed under the shogun's rule.[6] At that time, the national boundary passed between Etorofu and Uruppu.

In 1855, after the termination of the isolation policy, Japan and Russia entered into diplomatic relations by concluding the Treaty of Friendship, Commerce and Navigation, also known as the Treaty of Shimoda, in February 1855. The Treaty of Shimoda included a territorial clause in Article 2, which read as follows: '*Henceforth the boundaries between Russia and Japan will pass between the islands Etorofu and Uruppu.* ... As regards the Karafuto (Sakhalin), it remains unpartitioned between Russia and Japan, as has been the case up to this time.' (My italics and omissions.) By this, the national border was, for the first time, legally fixed between Etorofu and Uruppu. Sakhalin was put under joint sovereignty.[7]

By the Kuriles–Sakhalin Exchange Treaty of St. Petersburg of 7 May 1875, Japan gained territorial rights over the group of the Kurile Islands in exchange for Sakhalin. According to Article 2 of the treaty, 'The Emperor of Russia cedes to the Emperor of Japan the group of the Kurile Islands which he possesses at present, ... this group comprises the eighteen islands from Shumushu to Uruppu, so that the boundary between the two states shall pass through the Strait between Cape Lopatka of the Peninsula of Kamchatka and the Island of Shumushu.'[8] This national boundary continued to exist until 1945. The Russo-Japanese War of 1904–5 ended with the conclusion of the Treaty of Portsmouth on 5 September 1905, by which Japan gained territorial rights to the southern part of Sakhalin (south of 50 degrees NL).

During World War II, on 13 April 1941, Japan concluded the Neutrality Treaty with the Soviet Union. The two parties promised to respect each other's territorial integrity, and that if either party were involved in a war with a third power, the other party would maintain neutrality during the war. The term of validity of the treaty would be five years, and if neither of the parties had given notice of its termination one year before the expiration of the given period, the treaty was to be regarded as having been automatically extended for the next five years.

At the meeting in Yalta on 11 February 1945, the Soviet Union, USA and Great Britain agreed to the Yalta Agreement: 'The leaders of the three great powers have agreed that the Soviet Union shall enter the war against Japan on the side of the Allies on condition that: ... 2. The former rights of Russia violated by the treacherous attack of Japan in 1904 shall be restored, viz.: a. The Southern part of Sakhalin as well as all islands adjacent to it shall be returned to the Soviet Union. ... 3. *The Kurile Islands shall be handed over to the Soviet Union.*' (My omissions and italics.)

On 5 April 1945 the Soviet Union notified Japan of the termination of the Neutrality Treaty, which meant that the treaty was supposed to lose its validity no earlier than April 1946. On 8 August 1945, although the treaty remained in force, the Soviet Union declared war upon Japan, and accepted the terms of the Cairo Declaration of 27 November 1943 and the Potsdam Declaration of 26 July 1945. The Soviet Union then invaded the southern part of Sakhalin.

On 14 August 1945, Japan accepted the Potsdam Declaration, which included the following territorial clause: 'The terms of the Cairo Declaration shall be carried out and Japanese sovereignty shall be limited to the islands of Honshu, Hokkaido, Kyushu, and Shikoku, and *such minor islands as we determine.*' (Italics mine.) The central terms of the Cairo Declaration of 27 November 1943 referred to above were as follows: 'The three Great Allies are fighting this war to restrain and punish the aggression of Japan. They covet no gain for themselves and have no thought of territorial expansion. It is their purpose that *Japan shall be stripped of all the islands in the Pacific which she has seized or occupied since the beginning of the First World War in 1914,* ... Japan will also be expelled from all the other territories which she has taken by violence and greed'. (My italics and omissions.)

Shortly after the end of the Pacific War with Japan's unconditional surrender on 15 August 1945, the Soviet Union made a surprise attack on Shumushu, and occupied at first all the Kuriles from Shumushu to Uruppu, and successively the Northern Territories by 3 September 1945.

2. THE STATUS OF THE NORTHERN TERRITORIES UNDER SOVIET RULE

At the time of occupation, there were about 10,000 Japanese military personnel and 17,167 civilians on the four islands: 5,262 on Habomai, 1,030 on Shikotan, 7,347 on Kunashiri and 3,528 on Etorofu. There were six villages.[9] Many of the Japanese succeeded in escaping to Hokkaido. After the occupation, the islands were immediately put under Soviet military administration. The Soviets sent settlers to the islands and introduced the Soviet currency.[10]

The annexation of the four islands to the Soviet Union was carried out according to the following procedures. On 3 February 1946, the Russian Soviet Federated Socialist Republic proclaimed that the Kurile Islands and southern part of Sakhalin belonged to Khabarovsk Oblast. The Presidium of the Supreme Soviet of the Soviet Union affirmed this and gave it a retroactive effect from 20 September 1945. From the same day, all local property on the islands including business concerns was proclaimed confiscated and to be the property of the Soviet Union.

On 2 January 1947, the government of the Soviet Union established Sakhalin Province, which comprised all of Sakhalin and the Kurile Islands. On 3 February 1947, the Supreme Soviet of the Soviet Union amended the country's Constitution to include the Kurile Islands in the Russian Soviet Federated Socialist Republic and a year later the Supreme Soviet of the Russian Soviet Federated Socialist Republic amended the Constitution so as to apply also to the newly annexed areas. Through these two constitutional amendments, the Kurile Islands and the southern part of Sakhalin were finally incorporated into Sakhalin Province.[11]

As no Japanese inhabitants wanted to stay on the islands or wished to be naturalized as Russians, the Soviet Union issued a compulsory deportation order on 22 July 1947 and took them to Sakhalin from where they were sent back to Japan. The properties of the expelled were totally confiscated. From that time, there were no Japanese inhabitants left in the Northern Territories.[12]

The recent dissolution of the Soviet Union did not bring any substantial changes to the legal status of the Northern Territories. Today the Northern Territories are part of the Russian Federation. There has been some talk of creating a North Pacific nuclear-free zone and also a special economic zone which would include the Northern Territories.[13] It is not clear, however, whether such plans would affect the legal status of the disputed territories. Nevertheless, the plan of a special economic zone is worth discussing, because it would undoubtedly vitalize the economic life of the islanders.

3. CHARACTERISTICS OF THE NORTHERN TERRITORIES

Today the residents of the Northern Territories are Russians, Ukrainians, Tatars and so on. They are citizens of the Russian Federation or citizens of the former Soviet Union. This is in contrast with some other territories annexed by the Soviet Union as a result of World War II that are for the most part coinhabited areas.[14]

The population of the four islands totals 23,000 excluding troops; 7,800 on Kunashiri (1,500 km²), 8,700 on Etorofu (3,100 km²), 6,500 on Shikotan (255 km²) and only frontier guards on Habomai (102 km²). Settlement was very restricted because of the geographical isolation of the islands. The average age of residents on Etorofu is 26 years, and that of the residents on the other two islands is similar.[15]

As regards economic activities, most of the industries are concerned with running fisheries and processing marine products.[16] There are also agricultural and mineral activities, but development of these is very restricted because of the severe climate and lack of manpower. The biggest canning factory is on Shikotan. It has over 1,200 employees, which also makes it the biggest in the entire Russian Federation. Every year it produces around two billion tons of different varieties of canned fish. The next canning factory in size is on Etorofu, with 620 employees. There are, altogether, five such factories with more than 80 employees in Shikotan and Etorofu. On Etorofu, there is the biggest hatchery in the Russian Federation. This hatching factory, which has 50 employees, annually discharges one billion hatched trout and salmon into the sea.[17] The waters around the Northern Territories are good fishing grounds rich in salmon, cod and shark. In 1977 the Soviet Union unilaterally brought into effect an exclusive fishing zone of two hundred nautical miles around the Northern Territories.[18]

From a strategic point of view, the Northern Territories are a matter of great concern for the Russians, as they were for the former Soviet Union. The Russian Pacific Fleet might be able to control the territory from Vladivostok and Nakhodka south to the Pacific Ocean, and the Tsushima Strait can be closed in case of conflicts. The sea route through the Soya Strait between Sakhalin and Hokkaido and the Nemuro Strait between Kunashiri and Hokkaido affords safer access to the Pacific Ocean. This why Russia holds on to the Northern Territories. Ground forces are deployed in the Northern Territories, except on Habomai. The size of the ground forces are estimated to be a division. Besides tanks, armour, anti-aircraft missiles and attack helicopters, ground forces are equipped with 152 mm long-range artillery, which an ordinary Russian division does not possess. About 40 MiG-23 fighters have been deployed on Kunashiri for the last ten years. The Russian Federation deploys nuclear-powered submarines equipped with SLBM in the Sea of Okhotsk, from where the USA is within range.[19]

At the Russo-Japanese summit held in April 1991 in Tokyo President Mikhail Gorbachev proposed to reduce the Russian force of arms stationed in the Northern Territories.[20] In March 1992, the Foreign Minister of Russia said that the force of arms had already been reduced from 10 000 to 7000.[21] And two months later in the same year, President Yeltsin expressed his intention to withdraw Russian forces from the Northern Territories in the near future, leaving only frontier guards. The withdrawal has not been reported clearly yet.

4. JAPANESE AND RUSSIAN ATTITUDES TOWARDS THE ISSUE

After her surrender at the end of World War II Japan was put under the control of the General Headquarters of the Allied Forces (GHQ), which existed until 1952. As early as December 1945 a written petition, asking to put the Northern Territories under the protective occupation of the US Armed Forces, was presented by the Mayor of Nemuro City in Hokkaido to General MacArthur, the then Supreme Commander for the Allied Forces. Though not expressed explicitly, this was the first request from the Japanese side for the return of the Northern Territories.

The most important thing for post-war Japan was to enter into a peace treaty with the victorious countries. It was concluded on 8 September 1951. The territorial issues were laid down in Article 2 (c) of the treaty, which reads as follows: 'Japan renounces all right, title and claim to the Kurile Islands and to that portion of Sakhalin and the islands adjacent to it over which Japan acquired sovereignty as a consequence of the Treaty of Portsmouth of 5 September 1905.'

The Soviet Union refused to sign the treaty. In the course of the negotiations in San Francisco about the conclusion of the peace treaty, the Soviet delegation proposed the demilitarization of the Japanese coast. The proposal was rejected because it would have given the Soviet naval forces an exclusive right of use of the Japanese straits.[22] The peace treaty became effective on 28 April 1952.

Although no peace treaty has ever been made between Japan and the Soviet Union, the relations between the two states were finally normalized, in a rather irregular way,[23] with the Japan–Soviet Joint Declaration of October 1956. Item 9 of this joint declaration reads as follows: 'The Union of Soviet Socialist Republics and Japan agree to continue, after the restoration of normal diplomatic relations between the Union of Soviet Socialist Republics and Japan, negotiations for the conclusion of a peace treaty. In this connection, *the Union of Soviet Republics*, desiring to meet the wishes of Japan and taking into consideration the interests of the Japanese state, *agrees to transfer to Japan the Habomai Islands and Shikoton [sic], the actual transfer of these islands to Japan to take place after the conclusion of a peace treaty between the Union of Soviet Republics and Japan.*' (Italics mine.)

In the negotiations for Soviet–Japanese normalization in 1955–56, the Northern Territories were a central theme for dispute. The different standpoints of the two states on this matter became clear in the course of the negotiations.

Japan's standpoint regarding the Northern Territories in contrast to the directly contrary Soviet/Russian standpoint can be summarized as follows:[24]

1. **Are the Northern Islands Japan's inherent territories?**

    Japan: The Four Northern Islands are originally Japan's proper territories. Moreover, Shikotan and Habomai, regarded from time immemorial as part of Ezo, are also administratively an integrated part of Hokkaido. As regards Kunashiri and Etorofu, Russia confirmed by the Treaty of Shimoda of 1854 that these islands belonged to Japan. The Four Northern Islands are not included in the islands of the Pacific which Japan seized or occupied since the beginning of World War I, nor in the other territories Japan had taken by violence and greed as laid down in the Cairo Declaration.

    Japan does not claim any territorial rights over Sakhalin. To sum up the history of Sakhalin: the Tokugawa Shogunate placed Sakhalin under its control (1807); Sakhalin became a condominium of both states (the Treaty of Shimoda, 1855); Japan lost territorial rights to the whole of Sakhalin (the Kuriles–Sakhalin Exchange Treaty, 1875); Japan occupied the whole of Sakhalin during the Russo-Japanese War (1905); Japan gained legitimately the southern part of Sakhalin (the Treaty of Portsmouth, 1905); the Soviet Union occupied the Japanese part of Sakhalin (1945); Japan renounced that portion of Sakhalin gained by the Treaty of Portsmouth. In contrast to the Four Northern Islands, Sakhalin ceased to be a part of Japan in 1875. From the viewpoint of international law, Japan cannot pre-date the issue to 1807 or 1855. This is why Japan is not interested in Sakhalin.

The Soviet Union/Russia: Historically, the Kurile Islands were discovered by Russians, and were from the beginning Russian territories. As a result of the Russo-Japanese War, Japan took the southern part of Sakhalin away from Russia by force. Japan violated, by this unlawful act, both the Treaty of Shimoda and the Kuriles–Sakhalin Exchange Treaty. Therefore Japan has no qualification for quoting these treaties to assert her territorial rights to the Kuriles.[25]

2.   The definition of the Kurile Islands

Japan: The Kurile Islands, which Japan renounced in the Peace Treaty of 1951, means only the islands enumerated in the Kuriles-Sakhalin Exchange Treaty of 1875, viz. the eighteen islands from Shumushu to Uruppu, not including the four islands.

The Soviet Union/Russia: The Kurile Islands means all the islands from Shumushu to Kunashiri.

3.   The binding effect of the Yalta Agreement

Japan: The Soviet Union/Russian Federation grounds her right to the Four Northern Islands on the Yalta Agreement. However, the Yalta Agreement was signed by three heads of states, and is binding on only these three states. According to the axiom that *Pacta tertiis nec nocent nec prosunt*, the Yalta Agreement does not bind Japan.

The Soviet Union/Russia: Japan accepted all the terms, which the Allies had decided, and surrendered without reservation. The decisions of the Allies had been based on the different agreements between them. As the Yalta Agreement was also included in these agreements, Japan is not exempt from the Yalta Agreement.

4.   Which state is the recipient of the renounced Kuriles?

Japan: Japan renounced the Kurile Islands under the 1951 Peace Treaty. However, the peace treaty did not decide to which state the Kuriles should be transferred, still less to the Soviet Union. As no recipient state of Japan's renunciation was explicitly named in the treaty, it is logical to reason either that the Kuriles were presumed to be transferred to all the signatories of the peace treaty or that they should become *terra nullius*. In any case, the Soviet Union, which had not signed the peace treaty, cannot have any territorial right to the Kurile Islands.

> The Soviet Union/Russia: The General Order no. 1 of 2 September 1945, issued by General MacArthur (then Supreme Commander for the Allied Powers), provided for the Japanese surrender of the Kurile Islands to the Soviet forces. By the Soviet acceptance of this order, the Kurile Islands were removed from Japan's sovereignty, and these islands reverted to the Soviet Union. This was confirmed in the Directive no. 667 issued on 29 January 1946 by the Supreme Commander for the Allied Powers, which ordered in Paragraph 1 that the Japanese Government cease exercising, or attempting to exercise, governmental or administrative authority over any area outside Japan. The Kurile Islands are included in these areas outside Japan.

Even today, after diplomatic controversies over the Northern Territories have continued for more than thirty years, the points of difference are exactly the same. In 1960, after the revision of the US–Japan Security Treaty, the Soviet Union stiffened her attitude and asserted that Habomai and Shikotan would be held until all US forces had been withdrawn from Japan.[26] In the Russo-Japanese Joint Communiqué of 10 October 1973, both states recognized the importance of concluding a peace treaty for resolving the as yet unresolved problems remaining since World War II. Japan interpreted this equivocal phrasing 'the yet unresolved problems' as referring to the Northern Territories issue, whereas the Soviet Union took it to refer to the issue of fishing in the waters surrounding the four islands where the Soviet Union had seized many Japanese fishing vessels.[27] For the Soviet Union, the Northern Territories problem was an issue that had already been resolved.

It was in 1987 that the Soviet Union changed her attitude and recognized the Northern Territories problem as a yet unresolved issue, carrying an interview in *Moscow News* with the newly appointed Japanese Ambassador in Moscow.[28] The following year the Soviet Union clearly showed a positive attitude. Yevgeni Primakov, Gorbachev's close aide and director of Moscow's Institute of World Economy and International Relations, who was working to shape a new Soviet–Japanese foreign policy, stressed in an interview with *Yomiuri Shinbun* the need for flexibility on both sides to solve the boundary disputes.[29]

Though Japan had not gained anything concrete from the Japan–Soviet high-level meeting in Moscow on 20–23 July 1988, the leaders discussed squarely and openly the Northern Territories problem. With this meeting the way the Soviets and Japanese interact diplomatically was changed. This drastic change of attitude in Soviet diplomacy towards Japan was no doubt closely linked to the domestic changes: *perestroika* and *glasnost* based on the 'New Thinking' brought forward by Gorbachev in 1986.[30]

On Gorbachev's visit to Japan on 18 April 1991, a Soviet–Japanese Joint Communiqué was released in which it was stated that the officials of Japan and the Soviet Union, taking into consideration the standpoints of both states in relation to Habomai, Shikotan, Kunashiri and Etorofu, had talked exhaustively on the matters relevant to a settlement of territory. This was the first time that the Soviet Union had explicitly recognized the four islands as a long-pending question between the two states, offering a faint hope to the Japanese that the islands would be returned to Japan in the not-so-distant future.[31]

President Yeltsin linked the return of the Northern Territories to Japanese financial aid to Russia. In 1991, he suggested that financial support from Japan could lead to a settlement of the territorial dispute and said that relations between Russia and the rest of the world should not suffer from the political adventurism of the former leaders of his country. However, Yeltsin twice suddenly cancelled his planned visit to Japan, which made the Japanese distrustful. Yeltsin finally realized his visit to Japan in October 1993, but it seems that he could not gain the confidence of his hosts, although he admitted the existence of the issue as well as the need to resolve it and apologized for the inhuman treatment of the Japanese prisoners of war in World War II. The islands question continues to be a delicate subject of domestic debates in Russia.[32]

Japan's formal policy towards the Northern Territories consisted of the following three principles, which were formed at different stages.

The first is the 'Principle of the Reversion of the Four Northern Islands'. This principle was firmly established, in 1956, under the third Russo-Japanese negotiations aimed at concluding a peace treaty. Japan dropped her claim on the southern part of Sakhalin and concentrated on claiming the Four Northern Islands. To justify this principle, Japan has been adducing reasons based on facts and international law.

The second is the 'Principle of Politico-Economic Non-Separation'. This principle means that Japan should not make economic cooperation with the Soviet Union/Russia a primary consideration, unless the Northern Territories issue goes well. The principle came about in the 1960s as a countermeasure, when the Soviet Union hardened her attitude and refused the return of Habomai and Shikotan by linking the territorial transfer issue with abrogation of the US–Japan Security Treaty.

The third is the 'Principle of an Expanded Equilibrium', developed from the politico-economic non-separation principle. This principle signifies Japan's measures to expand all Russo-Japanese relations maintaining an equilibrium, in order to solve the territorial issue and to conclude a peace treaty. The principle was presented in 1989, replying to Gorbachev's conciliation with the West. The 'Principle of Expanded Equilibrium' is used to improve Russo-Japanese relations in practical affairs including economic matters, while observing the 'Principle of Politico-Economic Non-Separation'.

In October 1991 the Japanese government announced that it was prepared to provide financial aid of US\$ 2.5 billion to Russia if the territorial dispute should be solved to its satisfaction. Till now only modest aid has been provided to Russia. The reason is that Japan doubts the effectiveness of the aid to Russia and the fact that Russia has not yet made enough effort to help herself.[33]

Quite recently, in April 1993, the Japanese government decided not to apply the 'Principle of Politico-Economic Non-Separation' any more, because this principle is a by-product of the era of the Cold War when the Soviet Union did not even admit the existence of the yet-unresolved territorial problems remaining since World War II, and because this principle has become ill-matched to the present world situation where the West as a whole spares no effort to support Russia.[34] Even after the making of this decision Russia seems to continue to see Japanese acts in a less positive light. This is expressed in Yeltsin's statement of 13 October 1993 in which he suggested that no change had occurred in Japanese policy and that Japan would continue to link politics to aid.[35]

5. THE LOCAL ATTITUDE

The attitudes of the present residents towards the Northern Territories have changed considerably since the collapse of the Soviet Union. A poll taken in Kunashiri and Shikotan in March 1991, i.e. before the fall of the Soviet Union, showed that around 22 per cent of the residents were for, and around 69 per cent were against the transfer of the islands to Japan.[36]

A poll late in 1992 said that 22 per cent of voters in Far-Eastern Russia answered affirmatively to the return of the Northern Territories to Japan, provided Japan gives financial support, in contrast with only 3 per cent of some years ago.[37] The poll also said that 45 per cent of voters said yes to the idea of putting the four islands for the time being under the common administration of both states. A poll carried out in April 1992 in Shikotan showed that 83 per cent of 1,098 voters were in favour of the transfer of Habomai and Shikotan to Japan, in contrast with only 30 per cent the previous year.[38]

It is not so easy to obtain definite information about the actual life of the residents and their own original thoughts on Moscow's policy towards the Northern Territories. According to reliable reports and accounts of travellers depicting how things stand for the residents in the Northern Territories, many of the inhabitants seem to feel uncertain about their future as islanders and to feel somewhat neglected by Moscow, being left behind in economic development. Some residents feel Japan is psychologically closer to them.[39] In fact, geographically, the distance from Kunashiri to Hokkaido is 16 kilometres, and Habomai is only 3.7 kilometres from Hokkaido.

According to a Russian poll in October 1993, 43 per cent of the permanent inhabitants of Kunashiri, Shikotan and Etorofu (there are no permanent residents on Habomai) were for the transfer of the four islands to Japan, and 21 per cent were against.[40] According to uncertain information the inhabitants on Sakhalin are against the transfer of the Northern Territories to Japan. Sakhalin Governor Valentin Fedorov has been one of the fiercest opponents of the transfer of the islands. We do not know, though, how these attitudes affect opinion-making of the islanders.

Today, some 75 per cent of the former inhabitants of the Northern Territories live in Hokkaido. They have formed organizations aimed at realizing the return of the Northern Territories. In 1958 these organizations united in one organization called the Chishima Federation.

Besides this federation, there are more than one hundred grassroots organizations and associations to promote the return of the four islands. Of these the central organization is the Northern Territories Issue Association. They give publicity and information about the Northern Territories to citizens. The number of signatures they collected totalled sixty million. We do not know exactly how many former residents want to move back to the islands. According to an opinion poll conducted by the Japan

Broadcasting Corporation (NHK) Kushiro Branch in October 1991, 20 per cent of 849 former residents said they would like to move.[41] Some people working for the Chishima Federation suggested a rather higher percentage. It is worth noting that the second generation of former residents have considerable interest in the Northern Islands.[42]

In 1981 Japan declared, by Cabinet decision, 7 February as the Day of the Northern Territories, the very same day of the conclusion of the Treaty of Friendship, Commerce and Navigation of 1855. Mutual visits without a passport or visa by the former and present residents of the Northern Territories started in 1992 between Hokkaido and the Northern Territories in accordance with the agreement of both states. By this grassroots exchange, 232 Russians visited Japan and 268 Japanese visited the Northern Territories last year. This exchange system, accelerated through the intermediary assistance of the many organizations working for the return of the Northern Territories to Japan, has been welcomed by the residents concerned. For the year 1993 the total number of mutual visitors has been estimated to be about 600 people.[43]

6. THE FUTURE PROSPECTS

There are many uncertain elements in understanding the internal affairs of the Russian Federation, as well as her position in international society. This uncertainty affects the disposition of the Northern Territories. Concerning the future of the Northern Territories, the following five scenarios and their consequences are conceivable, theoretically or practically, judging from the existing conditions:

1. The transfer of the Northern Territories to Japan. This coincides with the formal claim of the Japanese government. So it goes without saying that this settlement would gratify Japan.

2. The transfer of Habomai and Shikotan to Japan. The transfer of these two islands to Japan was promised in the Russo-Japanese Joint Declaration of October 1956. There are opinions that to claim all four islands is rather unrealistic and that the return of half of the Northern Territories would be beneficial for the Japanese fishing industry, as the vast fishing zone around these islands is very productive. However, the total area of the two islands is 356 square

kilometres, i.e. only 8 per cent of the Northern Islands, and not 50 per cent. This solution does not accord with Japanese national sentiment.

3. The transfer of Habomai and Shikotan to Japan, and later negotiations on the settlement of Kunashiri and Etorofu. This way of settlement is commonly called the Two Islands Plus Alpha Process, and is certainly better than the previous scenario. The weak point of this settlement is in leaving the settlement of Kunashiri and Etorofu unresolved for the indefinite future, without obtaining a guarantee of the transfer of these islands to Japan.

4. The referral of the Northern Territories case to the International Court of Justice. The referral can be made either unilaterally by a signatory party (in this case Japan) in accordance with Article 22 of the Peace Treaty of 8 September 1951, asking for the interpretation of the Court with regard to the scope of the term, the Kuriles, which Japan renounced by the treaty, or with both states' (Japan and the non-signatory Russia) agreement on the jurisdiction of the court over the territorial issue, asking for the settlement of the disputed territories. The possibility of this kind of settlement, however, is very remote.

5. The transfer of Habomai and Shikotan to Japan, combined with the full recognition by Russia of Japan's territorial sovereignty over Kunashiri and Etorofu and with her peaceful use of these latter two islands. According to this scenario, Russia would transfer Habomai and Shikotan to Japan in accordance with the Russo-Japanese Joint Declaration of October 1956. Japan would have free use of these islands. On the other hand, Kunashiri and Etorofu would be demilitarized and utilized to develop the economies of citizens of both countries.

For the present, the Japanese government has not formed any definite plan, concerning the return of the Northern Territories. It is now time to show a concrete plan to Russia from Japan, which will be useful to both states. Personally, I consider the fifth scenario to be the best way for resolving the Northern Territories issue. However, one modification will be necessary, i.e. all the four islands would be demilitarized. A possible model for this plan might be the case of Svalbard (Spitsbergen).

Japan and Russia should take into consideration the following matters:
1. Japanese law and order would be valid on the islands. No discrimina-

tory measures would be permitted. 2. A guarantee of the right of residence for the present Russian inhabitants on the four islands. Russians could remain on the islands without Japanese citizenship or Japanese nationality. Perhaps a special certificate for islanders would be necessary for the residents of both countries. 3. Financial support from Japan for revitalizing the economies of the four islands would be paid. The amount would be calculated in cooperation with Russia. 4. Positive and peaceful utilization of resources would be realized.

At the time of Yeltsin's visit to Japan in October 1993, the Tokyo Declaration on Japanese–Russian Relations was released. The declaration lists the names of all four islands as the source of conflict between Japan and Russia. And Yeltsin promised that Russia would respect all treaties signed by the former Soviet Union and try to resolve the issue on the principle of 'law and justice'.[44] Negotiations continue.

NOTES

1. The term 'Kurile' comes from the Ainu word 'kur', which means 'man'. The most detailed etymological study is in Shichiro Murakami, *Kurirushoto no Bunkengakuteki Kenkyu* (Tokyo: Sanichi Shobo 1987), pp. 25–42. A full geographical depiction of the Kuriles is in John J. Stephan, *The Kurile Islands* (London: Oxford University Press 1974).
2. *Warera no Hoppo Ryodo* (Tokyo: The Ministry of Foreign Affairs 1989), p. 3.
3. Habomai, Shikotan, Kunashiri and Etorofu are sometimes called Minami Chishima, the Southern Kuriles.
4. *Warera* (1989), p. 4.
5. *Hopporyodo no Aramashi* (Hokkaido: Hokkaido Prefecture 1976), pp. 7–8.
6. The Shogun's rule was exercised through the authority of the feudal clan of Matsumae of the then Ezo, now Hokkaido.
7. The international legal term 'condominium' or 'coimperium' can also be used to designate this situation.
8. The Kurile–Sakhalin Exchange Treaty was drawn up in French. So, 'the group of the Kurile Islands which it possesses at present' is in French 'le groupe des îles Kouriles qu'elle possède actuellement'.
9. Shojiro Arai, *Tsuranuke Hoppo Ryodo* (Tokyo: Nihon Kogyoshinbunsha 1984), p. 47 and *Hopporyodo* (1976), p. 34.
10. David Rees, *The Soviet Seizure of the Kuriles* (New York: Praeger Publishers 1985), p. 85.
11. Keishiro Irie, *Ryodo Kichi* (Tokyo: Sanichi Shobo, 1959), pp. 14–15.
12. Rees (1985), p. 86.
13. Kimitada Miwa, 'Japan's "Northern Territories": A Predicament to Be Turned into a Point of Departure for the Building of a Nuclear Free Regional Security System in the Pacific', *Research Papers*, series A, no. 57, 1991 (Tokyo: Institute of International Relations of Sophia University 1991).
14. This was the first time in their two centuries-long history that there were no Japanese residents in the Northern Territories.
15. *Hokkaido Shinbun*, 1 January 1992 and *Asahi Shinbun*, 6 September 1992. Recently, many residents have left the islands because of worsening economic and social conditions and

shrinking employment opportunities. See *Supplement to the RFE/RL Research Report* vol. 3, no 32, 1994, p.5.

16. As regards the economic activities of the islands under the control of Japan, see *Hopporyodo* (1976), pp. 20–32.

17. *Hokkaido Shinbun*, 1 January 1992.

18. Rodger Swearington, *The Soviet Union and Postwar Japan* (Stanford: Hoover Institution Press 1978), pp. 182–4.

19. *White Paper of the Defence of Japan* 1992, pp. 58–9.

20. Russo-Japanese Joint Declaration of 18 April 1991, *Materials on the History of Russo-Japanese Territories Issue*. These material are made jointly by the Foreign Ministry of Japan and the Foreign Ministry of the Russian Republic (Tokyo: 1993), pp. 42–3.

21. *White Paper* (1992), p. 58.

22. Swearington (1978), pp. 77–9.

23. This does not mean that the Russo-Japanese Joint Declaration has less importance. This declaration has the same effect as an ordinary treaty and also has the character of a sort of peace treaty. See Keishiro (1959), p. 16.

24. Rajendra Kumar Jain, *The USSR and Japan 1945–1980* (Brighton: The Harvester Press 1981), pp. 51–3 and Shojiro Arai (1984), pp. 91–118.

25. This reasoning is full of contradictions: if these treaties lost their effect, the Treaty of Shimoda would be deprived of its legal effect, then the whole issue would be returned to the situation prior to the Treaty of Shimoda.

26. Gilbert Rozman, *Japan's Response to the Gorbachev Era, 1985–1991* (Princeton: Princeton University Press 1992), p. 118.

27. Rees (1985), p. 129.

28. *Moscow News*, 23 December 1987.

29. *Yomiuri Shinbun*, 1 February 1988.

30. Rozman (1992), pp. 119–20.

31. Russo-Japanese (1993), pp. 42–3. Recently, for example Gennadi Burbulis has stated that the seizure of the Kurile Islands was an aggression by Stalin and that Russia would eventually have to come to terms with the returning the islands. See *Supplement to the RFE/RL Research Report* vol. 3, no. 16, 1994, p. 4.

32. Stephen Foye, 'The Struggle over Russia's Kurile Islands Policy', *RFE/RL Research Report* vol. 1, no. 36, 1992, pp. 34–40 and Foye, 'Russo-Japanese Relations: Still Traveling a Rocky Road', *RFE/RL Research Report* vol. 2, no. 44, 1993, pp. 27–34.

33. Hiroshi Kimura, 'Doubts About Aid to Russia', *The Japan Times*, 30 March 1993.

34. *Asahi Shinbun*, 28 April 1993.

35. The Japanese Minister of Finance rejected this statement, claiming that Japan had already uncoupled economic aid from the territorial issue.

36. Magoruku Ide, *Hoppo Yonto Kiko* (Tokyo: Krirhara Shoten 1993) p. 155.

37. *Mainichi Shinbun*, 1 January 1993.

38. *Yomiuri Shinbun*, 27 April 1993.

39. Ide (1993), p. 116.

40. *Yomiuri Shinbun*, 11 October 1993.

41. Kunio Nishimura, 'A Matter of Justice', *Look Japan*, February 1992.

42. The information offered by the Chishima Federation and Northern Territories Issue Association.

43. *Asahi Shinbun*, 13 March 1993.

44. *Japan Times*, 14 October 1993.

PART IV

Conclusions

14. Comparison of the Annexed Territories

Tuomas Forsberg

The chapters in this book have examined eight cases of territories that had been annexed by the Soviet Union as a result of World War II. The study was designed in the hope that a comparison of the cases might reveal more than if the cases were scrutinized individually. Now it is time to discuss what the comparison might tell us about the territories and related disputes.

According to the classic principles of the comparative method, cases are compared in order to find either differences or similarities or both. The eight territories which have been discussed in this book share a similar historical background but their current status is dissimilar. They were all annexed by the Soviet Union as a result of World War II but after the Soviet dissolution Russia is directly involved in five of the cases, the Ukraine in three and Belarus in one. In any case, it is a matter of relativity and specific aims of the research whether one should stress similarities or differences when comparing cases. In this context, it is perhaps wiser to stress differences because similarities are more easily presumed and observed when processes of annexation and territorial disputes in general have been discussed. Yet, differences might be greater than is often suspected. That is to say that the territories not only differ in their general characteristics, such as size and population, but the cases are very different when it comes comes to the reasons for annexation, the present nature of the dispute and future prospects.

In line with the research themes set out in the introduction, three aspects will be discussed more closely from the comparative perspective in the following conclusion. These aspects deal with 1) Soviet and Russian policies towards annexed border areas; 2) regional politics; and 3) the saliency of the historical border dispute. In other words, we will first discuss the relations between the territory and the centre from the point of view of the centre, then from the point of view of the territory and finally from the point of view of the former possessor states.

1. SOVIET POLICY OF ANNEXATION AND INCORPORATION

Even if the eight territories share the fact that they were annexed by the Soviet Union as a result of World War II, the dissimilarities in the characteristics of the territories and declared motivations suggest that Stalin had no systematic basis for these annexations. No single type of motivation dominated; rather the reasons for and circumstances of the annexation differed from case to case. Some of the territories were annexed mainly for strategic reasons (Karelia, Kaliningrad [Königsberg], Transcarpathia [Carpatho-Ukraine], the Kurile Islands [the Northern Territories]) but some of the territories had no significant strategic value (Bessarabia [Moldova], Eastern Poland). None of the annexations were obviously motivated by ethnic concerns, but in some cases the annexation clearly seems to have depended on ethnic factors (Ivangorod [Jaanilinn] and Pechory [Petseri], Pytalovo [Abrene], and in part Transcarpathia and Eastern Poland). In some cases, in turn, ethnic principles were not involved at all (Karelia, Kaliningrad, the Kuriles). Earlier historical ownership was an important explanatory factor in some cases (Bessarabia, and in part Karelia and Eastern Poland) whereas in other cases history provided no direct reason for the annexation (Kaliningrad, the Kuriles, Transcarpathia, Northern Bukovina). Instead, the idea of rectifying historical sufferings motivated Stalin to incorporate territories from both Germany and Japan. Economic interests seemed to have less of a role in the annexations, although in some cases (Northern Bukovina) they had some importance. In sum, strategic reasons do not explain all the annexations and the mere wish to expand communist ideology is an inadequate motive, since it leaves unexplained why merely these territories were annexed.

The process of annexation took a somewhat similar course in most of the cases. In time of war they were simply seized by force or ceded on the basis of an ultimatum backed by force (Moldova). In one case (Transcarpathia) the territory was ceded to the Soviet Union as a result of an agreement of a former possessor country (Czechoslovakia), but in this case, too, the territory was occupied by the Soviet military forces. In all the cases, the Soviet Union sought to justify the annexation and legalize the transfer of territory internationally by referring to various historical and political arguments. Most of the annexations occurred with the consent of the Western powers.

The main difference in the treatment of the annexed territories was the fate of the original residents. In three cases (the Kuriles, Karelia, Kaliningrad) the original population was expelled and a new, mainly Russian population was settled. In all these three cases, the original population moved to other parts of their home country, and they were not able to visit their former home districts for a long time. In one case (Eastern Poland) a large number of original residents left the area but in the rest of the cases (Ivangorod and Pechory, Pytalovo, Transcarpathia, Moldova) the original residents for the most part remained in the territory, although many of those who belonged to the ethnic majority of the former possessor state moved or were expelled from there, so that the historical continuity of the local society was disrupted. Soviet policy with regard to the original residents seemed to depend on ethnic and strategic factors. Where the majority of the population in the territory was ethnically related, it was allowed to stay; where the territory was annexed for strategic reasons, the potentially disloyal ethnic population was expelled.

In all the annexed territories the seizure was followed by a process of Sovietization and Russification. Administrative and economic structures were changed to fit the Soviet model. Towns, streets and other places were renamed and Soviet symbols were established in the region. Rewriting the history of the annexed territory and silence on the annexation as such similarly belonged to the methods of incorporation. In all the annexed territories the composition of the population changed: where the original residents had left the area Russians and other Soviet citizens moved into the territory. Where the original residents remained, as in Moldova, territories with a Russian or East-Slavic majority were connected to the same administrative unit.

Today, the official Russian view of the eight annexed territories does not vary much. Even if the annexation of the territories is admitted as being part of Stalin's aggressive policy; the injustice, in the Russian view, cannot be undone by returning them. Territorial questions are regarded as sensitive issues in Russian domestic politics and there is a fairly clear consensus that Russia will not cede parts of her territory to other states.

Concessions in territorial questions would certainly give a powerful weapon to conservatives in the domestic political struggles of Russia. Only one out of the five territories (the Kuriles) that now belong to Russia seems to be considered as open by the Russian side as far as Yeltsin's policy is concerned, but in this case the adopted stand is very controversial because of the domestic politics of Russia. In any case, according to many Russians the Kurile Islands issue differs from other historical border questions, because it can be regarded as legally open. The other four cases where Russia is now directly involved are considered to be already resolved and not open to any discussion on the course of the border and in some cases extraordinary measures have been executed in order to strengthen their belonging to Russia. The Russian border policy has up to now consistently relied on the principle of inviolability of borders in these as in other border questions. The governments of the Ukraine and Belarus have also adopted a similar view *vis-à-vis* their boundaries.

Despite the clearly reluctant view regarding the possibility of border changes, the former Soviet and present Russian authorities now see many of the annexed border territories from a cooperative perspective. Instead of border changes, Russia sees the possibility of opening the border and making it as transparent as possible. For example, the idea of a special economic zone has been raised in three of the border territories that were annexed as a result of World War II (Kaliningrad, Karelia, the Kuriles). Although the economic basis of these areas was otherwise not very promising, it was hoped that the geographical proximity and the historical affiliation would draw foreign economic investments, especially from the respective Western countries, Germany, Japan and Finland. However, so far the borders have remained relatively closed and the plans for special economic zones have been ineffective. These plans have failed partly because their content has been unclear, partly because the economic and political situation in Russia has remained unstable, and partly because measures that would favour certain areas and not others have not been acceptable to all in Russia.

2. REGIONAL IDENTITIES AND POLITICS

The local identity and political mood in the annexed territories have varied considerably. Under the Soviet regime, it was especially important that border areas remained loyal to the centre, and therefore regional identities could not develop freely. After the collapse of the Soviet Union, regional activity has in many cases replaced the former passivity. Some of the border territories have been striving for self-determination but in some other areas there are hardly any specific signs of a separate regional identity or political efforts based on such an identity.

The wish for self-determination has been most clearly manifest in Moldova as the region was a Soviet republic and after the breakup of the Soviet state it has become an independent state. The self-determination that has been achieved, however, led to a violent conflict between the government and Transdnestria which is inhabited by a Russian majority. Mainly because of ethnic tensions the population of the region was divided into distinct camps. The conflict between the Moldovan government and the Transdnestrian area indicates the strength of ethnic boundaries, but on the other hand, the Moldovan unwillingness to join Romania shows also that the quest for self-determination can at least in the short term exceed the wish for reunification with the former possessor state, in spite of ethnic and historical ties.

The Kaliningrad area, Karelia and the Kurile Islands in their current situation share many similar features. In all these regions some people, and in particular the younger generations, see many opportunities in developing ties with the former possessor states, or to the outside world in general, because they are economically more advanced. Others, especially older people, are often strongly opposed to any changes in the status of the region that might undermine the identity and strategic value connected with the area. Both material and mental changes have in these regions been more striking and sudden than in most other parts of the former Soviet Union. In all these areas a new kind of tourist business has grown around the nostalgic trips home of former residents and their descendants. In many towns, old monuments are being rebuilt and restored, and the history of the region before the Soviet annexation is being revived in the public consciousness at the same time as symbols of the Soviet era are being pulled down. Although major economic plans have mostly failed, the growth in tourism has revitalized the local mood. In recent years, various markets, festivals and seminars based on the old identity of the area have been organized both by the local people and by the former possessors. Although tourism has become a remarkable source of income for the region, the visitors and the tourist business in general irritate many local inhabitants, not because they awake fears of a new conquest, but because prices have gone up as a consequence of the increased purchasing power.

For these reasons, these three regions have faced a trend of political polarization. In the Kaliningrad area there is a strong liberal movement urging more autonomy, but the conservative forces are also considerable with their emphasis on the strategic importance of the area and its inseparability from Russia. Although German financial and technological assistance for reconstruction is widely sought after, unification with Germany is not the aim of the local inhabitants. The same problem of a growing gap between reformers and conservatives also describes the situation of the Kurile Islands, where many of the local inhabitants favour the transfer of the islands to Japan, but at the same time the province of Sakhalin has been one of the major opponents of such ideas. The Karelian case shares similar traits to a lesser extent. A considerable, though a minority, part of the population has been supporting the idea of unification with Finland, but the local support for border transfer is more hesitant in those parts of Karelia which belonged to Finland before the war than in some parts of the Republic of Karelia which never belonged to Finland.

In Transcarpathia the local identity is both historically and ethnically more diverse than in other territories. The quest for self-determination has been raised in terms of both minority rights and regional autonomy. The historical background of the area is a significant part of the local identity formation, but it is connected more to the time of the former Austrian Empire than to the inter-war period. Although the Hungarian minority has been a central political force in the region, it has not defined its goals in terms of unification with Hungary.

In three other areas the history of the regions seems to be of less interest and politically less tempting. In the former Eastern Poland and in the Baltic cases no specific local identity emphasizing the historical background of the areas has been developed. The history of the territory, in the sense of having been part of another country, does not seem to play any central role in local politics and it is not a mobilizing force for ideas for the future.

Roughly speaking, it seems that historical ties, especially to the more prosperous areas rather than to ethnic relatives, feed ideas of self-determination or autonomy in the border territories. Even if economic affiliation is not the only basis for identification, in the shorter term it seems to explain the divergent trends in political orientation. Kaliningrad, the Kurile Islands and Karelia are more eager than other areas to enhance local and regional rights and special contacts with the former possessor countries, and the lack of economic benefits was also one of the main reasons why Moldovan unification with Romania has not taken place. In all areas the issue of how to approach the former possessor state is controversial, and part of the population still sees the former possessor as a threat, which leads them to tighten the links with the centre.

3. THE SALIENCY OF HISTORICAL BORDER DISPUTES

As historical border disputes the cases have differed in their degree of saliency. During the Cold War only the dispute over the Kurile Islands was internationally recognized. In the other cases the annexation of the territory had become a taboo issue. Today, three out of the eight annexed territories are openly contested (the Kuriles, Pytalovo, Ivangorod and Pechory), two are not open at the interstate level but public sympathy is widely in favour of the return of the territory (Karelia, Moldova) and in three of the cases border changes are supported only by some ultranationalist groups or organizations of the expelled population (Kaliningrad, Transcarpathia, former Eastern Poland). Because the reactions vary, the interesting question to be addressed is, what factors most clearly explain the re-emergence of a historical dispute in the cases discussed?

First of all, the variation in the saliency of the territorial dispute is hard to explain by domestic political factors or by individual belief systems. Although territorial disputes are always somehow linked to domestic politics, in none of the cases does the saliency of the border question depend decisively on the domestic political coalitions or individual decision-makers. Also, neither the changes of the governing party, nor of the leading politicians affect clearly the saliency of the dispute. True, more rightist and thus nationalistic governments are usually more eager to stress such questions, but these territorial questions do not divide domestic political actors clearly into competing parties: in most cases the policy towards the lost territory is not contested among major parties or major established interest groups. The main interest groups that have supported border changes are mainly non-party political issue-based movements composed of former residents, such as the Karelian Association in Finland, the *Petserimaa* movement in Estonia and the expelled organizations in Germany. Otherwise, the territorial claim is either widely accepted nationally or marginalized into some ultranationalist groups. Likewise it can be noted that the degree of democracy does not determine the saliency of the dispute. On the contrary, in some cases more democracy might mean more territorial claims, if democracy is understood simply as the impact of public pressure upon leaders. It seemed that political leaders at least in Germany, Finland and Romania showed more reluctance to open the dispute than did the public.

Secondly, changing power relations at the end of the Cold War have obviously catalysed those territorial disputes which are based on historical changes of territory. A comparison of the cases nevertheless shows that favourable power relations are neither a necessary nor a sufficient reason for a dispute to emerge. In two out of the eight cases (Pytalovo, Pechory and Ivangorod) territorial disputes began as a consequence of changing power relations and in two other cases (Moldova, Karelia) public opinion significantly reflected the change. Yet, in three other cases (Kaliningrad, Eastern Poland, Transcarpathia) no territorial claim has been made and no significant change in public opinion has occurred in spite of the changes in power relations, and in one case (the Kuriles) the territorial dispute existed before any clear change in power relations had occurred. Moreover, at least some of the territorial disputes might have emerged not because of the decreasing power position of the Soviet Union/Russia, but because of her change into a democracy, which awoke expectations that Russia might take a different view of the territories that the Soviet Union had annexed.

Third, the significance of the territory did not greatly affect the saliency of the dispute. Among the eight cases none was richly endowed in terms of raw materials or other economic benefits and the three officially contested territories (the Kuriles, Pytalovo, Ivangorod and Pechory) in particular were small in size and of no great economic value. Strategically, the contested territories might have some value, but they are hardly more important than the territories that were not disputed. Even if the significance of the territory is understood as a question of national identity or ethnic unity, as is often preferable, no clear connection on the basis of these eight cases emerged. A national identity dimension in a historical and symbolic sense has some relevance in all of the cases, but also in many that are not contested (Kaliningrad, Moldova, Karelia) and not particularly in those that are disputed. Ethnic relations played no role in the three open cases whereas in the two cases with a significant ethnic dimension (Transcarpathia, Moldova) the territorial dispute was not so salient. Thus, although the value of a territory in question is naturally very difficult to estimate, it can be argued that in most cases the return of the contested territory would offer no clear rational advantage to the claimant state in terms of traditional national interests.

A fourth category which can be used in the explanation of territorial disputes is norms. On the basis of the comparison it seems to be the case that contrary to the dominant realist theory in international politics norms are far more clearly connected to the salience of a historical territorial dispute than power relations. All the disputed cases seemed to be contested in terms of international law. In other words, if the rules of international law do not clearly determine the case, it is much easier to raise the issue. There are significant thresholds to breaking treaties, because the position of the state in the eyes of the international community might be endangered. On the basis of the comparison, it seems that political commitments, too, particularly those of the OSCE, clearly prevent states from raising territorial questions. Although states have a need to maintain a norm-obeying image independently of their power position, in many cases the significance of obeying the norms seemed to be connected to their need to signal stability and reliability to the outside world in general and to the European Union in particular.

Norms were important also as subjectively understood conceptions of justice, which played a major role as a motive for the dispute. The comparison suggests that a legitimacy that depends on subjectively-held norms and moral principles affects the degree of salience of historical border disputes. That is to say that international law and other commitments of states do not cover the whole meaning of norms but that subjective moral considerations, even outside the current provisions of international law and politics, are important policy-guiding factors as well. It seemed that a strong feeling of injustice motivated the disputes in Japan, Estonia and Latvia as well as in Finland and Romania more than any strict 'rational' interest. Of course, some sense of injustice motivates almost all disputes. If the source of the injustice in these territorial disputes is to be identified, it appeared to be strongly connected to the unlawfulness of the historical loss of the disputed territory even if it has been confirmed afterwards by a peace treaty. In those cases where a certain compensation was made (Eastern Poland), a feeling of a deserved punishment could be more widely adopted (Kaliningrad), and where the circumstances by which the territory was achieved were shady and the historical possession only of a short duration (Transcarpathia), historical claims were less likely to emerge. Although it appears to be the case, as Machiavelli suggested, that the deportation of peoples makes the revindication of territory more difficult than if the original inhabitants had stayed in their territory, the deportation of people does not prevent historical disputes from arising since a historical injustice associated with a territorial question can itself be a cause for disputes.

To sum up, among domestic politics, power politics, importance-related and norm-based explanations, the latter seemed to be the most promising for explaining the saliency of historical border disputes concisely. Neither the power political hypothesis nor the idea of the importance of the territory is entirely false: territorial disputes, as other social phenomena, are multicausal. As far as the eight cases of territorial changes examined here are concerned, power politics seemed the most plausible explanation of *when* the territory becomes openly contested, and rational interests explain *why* one of perhaps several disputed areas in a state is selected for such a contest; norms and subjective conceptions of justice appeared to offer the most convincing explanations of *whether*, *why*, and *how* a piece of territory which was transferred some fifty years earlier is still an object of contention.

4. FUTURE OF THE ANNEXED BORDERLANDS

The future of the territories that were annexed by the Soviet Union as a result of World War II remains open – far more open than the future of the former Soviet Union itself. Some of the authors of this book have put forward ideas and visions for the future. They argue that in some cases territorial changes might be possible (the Kuriles, Moldova) but in most cases it seems to be less likely (Karelia, Kaliningrad), although only a few regard their cases as being fully settled territorial issues (former Eastern Poland). Although such visions cannot predict the future, they may sometimes be more than merely good guesses.

Anyway, it is fairly clear that in none of the cases will the future resemble the past. Moreover, when discussing the future of the annexed territories, it is important that the territorial disputes are not discussed as simple questions of 'mine' or 'yours'. Rather, the crucial question is how open territorial disputes can be resolved or best managed without a destructive conflict. Discussion of the historical background of the issue should not be banned, since changes offer not only a basis for conflict but also for increased and novel cross-border cooperation.

In most cases, the future of the contested territory depends surely on the general trends of Russian politics. It is plausible that a democratic Russia will be much more able to deal with historical territorial problems constructively than an authoritarian one, and that cooperative rather than confrontational approaches would dominate, but it is not necessarily so. Democracies are perhaps not likely to expand in the same way as authoritarian states but democracy does not indicate a readiness to cede territories or, as is the case with some of Russia's neighbours, to bury historical territorial disputes. In other words, the mere form of domestic regime hardly determines the stand towards territorial issues in Russia. Rather the question is about more fundamental societal and cultural developments that concern the value of territory, interpretations of and commitment to Soviet history, conceptions of Russian identity and the general expectations of the significance and content of justice in international relations. Territorial questions are still extremely sensitive and unlikely to be treated as normal political issues in the near future. Among all the challenges that face Russia, those that threaten her territorial sovereignty are still difficult to deal with other than by unilateral means owing to the central symbolic value of territory. Paradoxically, a strong Russia might be more willing to discuss territorial issues, even in terms of cession, than a weak Russia.

Answering the questions put by historical territorial disputes in the former Soviet Union remains a huge task for politicians and researchers alike. This study does not suggest any immediate solution to these problems, since it has to be left to the parties involved, but it may give some important insights on the subject. Yet, because there are certain risks that unduly harsh conclusions will be made on the basis of studies such as this, the limits of the analysis should be recognized. But in short, if moral principles have a bearing upon the future salience of historical border disputes they should be given more weight than power relations in the design of international border regimes and in the resolution of particular border questions. If territorial changes have a sufficiently legitimate base, they will not be a cause for future conflicts. In other words, the fear that territorial changes necessarily provoke further disputes over territory may prevent us from seeing possibilities for resolving these issues. Yet, moral issues that arise from history should be compromised with present realities. It is not possible simply to turn the clock back fifty years and imagine that there never was an annexation and history resulting from it as a part of the Soviet Union. Rather, the aim might be that, through compromise, the parties succeed in cultivating those aspects of the situation that they regard as important today, for example by sharing sovereignty. In any case, historical territorial disputes are not only about territory as such but also, and perhaps to a greater extent, about historical interpretations and related conceptions of justice. In this respect, both Russia and her neighbours need a better understanding of their common history, since historical territorial disputes are often only the tip of an iceberg of unresolved historical items, but in many cases sharp enough to prevent a truly normal neighbourly relationship from developing.

Although the future of Russia and the former Soviet Union in general will remain a riddle that cannot be solved by scientific methods, the border territories that have a historically contested background nevertheless play a major role as indicators of the possible course of events in the years to come. They reflect the changes in Russia's historical, geographical and cultural identity and the contest between peripheral regions and centres in the former Soviet Union, as well as the changing relations between Russia and her neighbours. At best the once annexed territories can grow into bridgeheads of cooperation and openness and at worst they can be causes for renewed antagonism, conflicts and suppression. We naturally hope for the former alternative.

Index

DATE DUE